Weight Watchers™

COACH APPROACH

How to Motivate the "Thin" You

Macmillan • USA

MACMILLAN

A Simon & Schuster Macmillan Company

1633 Broadway

New York, NY 10019

Weight Watchers Publishing Group

Editorial Director: Nancy Gagliardi

Senior Editor: Martha Schueneman

Food and Nutrition Editor: Regina Ragone, M.S., R.D.

Editorial Assistant: Christine Senft, M.S.

Text: Stacey Colino, Joyce Hendley, Deborah Kotz, Beryl Meyer

Nutrition Consultant: Mindy Hermann, M.B.A., R.D.

Photographer: Rita Maas

Food Stylist: Mariann Sauvion

Prop Stylist: Cathy Cook

Book Design and Illustrations: Rachael McBrearty

Weight Watchers coach approach: how to motivate the "thin" you

      p.   cm.

  ISBN 0-02-862218-9

  1. Weight loss—Psychological aspects.   I. Weight Watchers International.

RM222.2.W3155   1998

613.2'5—dc21   97-36752

                          CIP

Manufactured in the United States of America

10 9 8 7 6 5 4 3

contents

A Word About

WEIGHT WATCHERS

Since 1963, Weight Watchers has grown from a handful of people to millions of enrollees annually. Today, Weight Watchers is recognized as the leading name in safe and sensible weight control. Weight Watchers members form a diverse group, from youths to senior citizens, attending meetings virtually around the globe.

Weight-loss and weight-management results vary by individual, but we recommend that you attend Weight Watchers meetings, follow the Weight Watchers food plan and participate in regular physical activity. For the Weight Watchers meeting nearest you, call 1-800-651-6000.

foreword

more than at any other time in our nation's history, Americans are concerned with achieving and maintaining a healthy weight. Yet obesity in the population is at an all time high, even though people know that it can lead to a number of health ailments, including diabetes and heart disease.

Weight Watchers is recognized around the globe as a trusted name in weight loss information. Since 1963, when it was founded, millions of women and men have lost weight following the Weight Watchers program. They have learned that sound nutrition and physical activity are crucial and that the route to success is modifying and changing unhealthy behaviors.

Weight Watchers Coach Approach: How to Motivate the "Thin" You provides a thorough, yet personalized approach to losing weight and maintaining that weight loss. It includes current information about nutrition and physical activity that provides a safe and sensible path to weight control. *Coach Approach* also provides the psychological insight that is necessary for changing behaviors so as to achieve health and wellness.

Weight Watchers Coach Approach is an excellent reference for anyone interested in maintaining a healthy weight. It provides readers with information that will allow them to be successful not only in losing weight, but in keeping it off.

Whatever your goal—to lose weight, to keep it off, to exercise regularly, or simply to better understand your lifestyle so you can change it for the better—you will find *Coach Approach* an excellent starting point.

Xavier Pi-Sunyer, M.D.
Director, Van Itallie Center for Weight Loss and Maintenance
Chief, Division of Endocrinology, Diabetes, and Nutrition
St. Luke's-Roosevelt Hospital Center
Professor of Medicine
Columbia University College of Physicians and Surgeons
New York, New York

introduction

Perhaps you've just seen photographs of yourself from the last wedding you attended. Or perhaps you've experienced discrimination that you suspect was linked to your size. Or maybe you're simply tired of the hurtful comments from well-meaning friends and family members concerning your health habits.

What sparks the epiphany people experience when they know it's time to take control of their health? The answer to that question is as individual as a person's genes, but the fact remains that losing weight and getting in shape can reduce your risk for a host of ailments and chronic diseases, including diabetes, heart disease, high blood pressure, osteoarthritis and even some forms of cancer.

Weight Watchers has long been recognized as *the* trusted name in weight loss information. *Coach Approach* provides a personalized plan to help you lose weight. It includes the most up-to-the-minute, safe information about nutrition, health and exercise, as well as the psychological information necessary for exploring the whys and hows of good health. It's almost like having your own personal trainer.

Yet before you go any further, you should consider a critical question: Are you truly ready to change your ways and get in shape?

When Are You Ready?

Researchers who specialize in behavior modification, or the science of changing habits, have pinpointed five stages of "readiness": Precontemplation, Contemplation, Preparation, Action and Maintenance.

In the **Precontemplation** stage, there's little awareness of the problem. You might be comfortable with your weight and your health might be fine. In the

Contemplation stage, you're aware of the problem, but still not ready to take action. In the **Preparation** stage, you're priming yourself for action: At this point, you're reading articles, paying attention to advertisements and collecting the information necessary to act (you can spend months in Contemplation and Preparation stages). In the **Action** stage, you begin utilizing the tools you've collected in the last few months. But be aware that if you're forced into the Action stage, say by a doctor who tells you to lose weight, you're less likely to be successful. In the **Maintenance** stage, the new behaviors you've learned and attitudes you've developed become second nature, a part of your life.

Why Is Good Health So Hard?

With the proliferation of fat-free foods, light menus and exercise machines touting dramatic results, you'd think that shedding unwanted pounds and maintaining a healthy weight would be within anyone's reach. Why, then, are so many Americans overweight?

Despite all we know about good nutrition and exercise, the average American's diet is still too high in fats and refined carbohydrates and woefully low in nutrient-rich fruits and vegetables. Even if you eat the most nutritious diet in the world, your idea of portion size may be a problem: In a world of 64-ounce sodas and 16-ounce steaks, knowing what constitutes a healthy portion is not always easy.

As hard as learning new eating habits can be, few would argue that exercising regularly is *the* most difficult habit to learn and the easiest one to break. There also are emotional and psychological reasons why losing weight can be difficult, especially if you've lost and tried to maintain that loss in the past. With every pound that's crept back on, you've probably berated yourself for your lack of willpower. What's more, if your expectations are unrealistically high, you may be setting yourself up for another cycle of success, then failure.

Two things must happen in order to be successful long-term: First, you need to decide to lose weight for *yourself*—not your partner, kids, doctor or mother—and second, you need to make permanent changes to your behavior. There also is a critical "attitude shift" that must take place during your weight loss efforts: After several months, you might find yourself reaching for an apple even though you want chips. Or you may splurge on a pecan roll for breakfast—confident in the knowledge that lunch and dinner will be the healthy low-fat meals you had planned.

Where Does Weight Watchers Stand in the Readiness Equation?

At Weight Watchers, we teach people that the core of weight loss is good nutrition and sensible habits. If you eat fewer calories, you'll lose weight; if you eat fewer calories and you exercise, you'll enhance weight loss results.

Yet the difference between losing weight on your own and following the Weight Watchers program comes into play with the program's educational and emotional components. At weekly meetings, you're given sound health information and surrounded by people who have experienced the same struggles you have; they become role models and compatriots with whom you can share your challenges and celebrate your successes. Weight Watchers also teaches you how to rethink your attitudes toward food and fitness and how to set attainable goals. Once you've lost weight, you'll also discover the key to maintaining weight loss over the long term: ongoing contact with those who aided you during the weight-loss phase.

Where Does *Coach Approach* Fit In?

If you're a Weight Watchers member, this book will supplement the information and materials you get from your weekly meetings. If you're not, it will be an invaluable resource or tool to help you get in shape.

Coach Approach will help you determine how ready you are to lose weight; you'll learn how to evaluate your goals and transform the temporary weight-loss mindset into the long-term weight-management mentality—in other words, you'll learn how to think and act like a healthy, fit person. *Coach Approach* will also show you alternative ways to measure fitness and how to keep going when you hit a weight-loss plateau.

With this book you'll learn a flexible, realistic approach to healthy eating. *Coach Approach* also provides you with strategies for navigating a supermarket, converting your kitchen to a low-fat chef's dream without spending big bucks and avoiding mindless eating while cooking. You'll learn why "dieting" doesn't work for most people and that preparing tasty, nutritious meals doesn't cost more or take much more time than preparing high-fat meals.

Coach Approach has the same attitude toward exercise. We focus on 10 activities that practically any person can try and provide instruction on how to get started without looking like a klutz. You'll learn easy ways to get more movement in your life and to increase your flexibility while you're improving your muscle tone and cardiovascular system.

The information in *Coach Approach* is easy to incorporate into your daily life. It's sane, it's safe and there's nothing complicated involved. Best of all, you'll learn how to take this information and put your own spin on it, because at Weight Watchers, we know that when you personalize a program, your chances for success improve dramatically.

The bottom line is that there is no magic pill that melts off pounds, improves your cardiovascular system or strengthens muscles. Losing and maintaining weight requires learning a new way to live. But it can be done, and by helping you to determine your needs and the most effective way for you to meet them, Weight Watchers *Coach Approach* will help show you the way to success.

part 1

ARE YOU REALLY READY TO LOSE WEIGHT?

CHAPTER one

READY TO LIVE A HEALTHY LIFE?

Watch your portion sizes. Eat low-fat. Exercise. You've heard it all before. You know these are the rules to staying healthy and slim, and to reaching and maintaining a healthy weight. But the thought of revamping your lifestyle can be daunting.

Whether you're just a few pounds overweight or have an unwanted 30 pounds to shed, know that you are not alone. Despite the nation's obsession with health and the hundreds of fat-free products streaming into supermarkets, the percentage of overweight Americans has sharply increased from 25 percent in 1980 to a remarkable 33 percent today.

Consider these facts:

- Forty-eight million Americans (nearly 20 percent of the population) are on some form of weight-loss program at any given time.

- Most people trying to lose weight are women—as many as 50 percent of whom diet two or more times each year with little

or no long-term success at reaching or maintaining their desired weight.

- Only 10 percent of people who lose 25 pounds or more are able to sustain their target weight beyond two years.

The good news is that researchers are beginning to learn what distinguishes the successful individuals from those who regain lost pounds. Before we look at the success stories, let's examine the 90 percent of us who don't fare as well the first time around.

The Dangers of Yo-Yo Dieting

For most of us, the hardest part about weight loss may not be losing the weight but keeping the pounds off. Some of us throw in the towel after one failed diet, but most of us keep striving toward an ideal weight. If you've seen your weight plunge, then creep up, you know how yo-yo dieting can leave you feeling out of control and sap your motivation for implementing healthy habits.

While there is plenty of anecdotal evidence on the psychological downside to yo-yo dieting, the weight loss experts are not in agreement on whether it takes a toll on your physical health. A scant few studies found that rats who were put on yo-yo diets had a harder time losing weight on the next go-round. Other research has found a link between yo-yo dieting and heart disease, although many have criticized and doubted the possibility of such a link.

The most current thinking on yo-yo dieting is that it does not harm your health. A 1994 review of studies analyzed by National Institutes of Health researchers found that yo-yo dieting does not carry any health risks and does not imperil the success of future weight loss efforts. The researchers concluded that the health benefits of losing weight permanently outweigh the questionable risks of repeatedly gaining and losing weight. In other words, you should not allow your concerns about yo-yo dieting to keep you from shedding excess pounds.

Habits of Success

So what is it that separates the yo-yoers from those who are successful at weight loss? The answer is simple: They keep doing whatever is was that got them to lose weight in the first place. To see what qualities dieters need to possess to maintain a weight loss, researchers from the University of Colorado and the University of Pittsburgh started the National Weight Control Registry, which enrolled 784 men and women who lost at least 30 pounds and kept the weight off for at least a year.

At a 1996 meeting of the North American Association for the Study of Obesity, the researchers presented their data showing that 88 percent of successful weight losers continued to both diet and exercise. All but 7 percent restricted their food intake in some way, and many said they watched their portions, counted calories and avoided fat. They also ate fast food less than once a week. The average reported daily caloric intake for women was 1,297 and for men, 1,725.

Exercise was also a staple in maintaining weight loss. The average woman in the registry reported burning over 2,000 calories a week on exercise, and the average man burned over 3,000 calories. Walking was, by far, the most common exercise, followed by aerobics and competitive sports.

The successful dieters seemed to be motivated by several factors. One-third attributed their weight loss to a desire to improve their health, while another third said they were motivated by an emotional setback, such as a failed relationship. One in 10 of the women said they wanted to improve the image of themselves they saw in the mirror or in photographs.

Virtually all the participants in the registry were pleased with their efforts. At least 90 percent reported they had a higher quality of life and enjoyed more mobility, better moods and greater self-confidence.

Weighing Your Options

What does it take to lose weight for good? Many experts contend a lifelong plan to maintain a healthy weight after you reach your goal is crucial. In its report evaluating weight management programs in the United States called "Weighing the Options," a National Academy of Sciences panel of experts recommended that you outline your own individualized plan for losing weight, which can be altered and reworked as your needs change.

The first thing you need to realize is that no single weight loss plan is right for every individual. You may want to join a commercial weight loss program; you may want to rely on the support of family and friends; you may want to seek out a physician's or nutritionist's guidance. Whatever you decide, you should have a complete physical and consultation with your doctor before beginning any weight loss plan.

How do you know what's right for you? You need to consider your health status (such as whether you have high cholesterol, hypertension or diabetes) as well as how much weight you want to lose. You also need to consider whether you are losing weight mainly for health reasons or to enhance your appearance. For instance, if you have heart disease you should undergo a weight loss program only under your doctor's supervision. If you are trying to lose the extra 25 pounds from your last pregnancy, you might look to loved ones, a support group or a guide to weight loss and maintenance, such as this one, for advice.

Once you've set your weight loss goals, consider your personal preferences and what has, or has not, worked in the past: Do you prefer a formal plan with a day-to-day diet outlined for you, or would you rather experiment with low-fat cookbooks? Are you better in a one-on-one situation with a nutritionist, or do you prefer to deal with the emotional side of eating with the support of a group? You can choose any or all of these options depending on what works best for you.

How "Ready" Are You?

Before you actually make the necessary lifestyle changes for losing weight, you should evaluate your mindset: Are you really ready to make long-term changes? What are your strengths that will help you along the way? What are your weaknesses that could hinder your efforts?

Before you begin a weight loss plan, ask yourself the following questions. If you answer yes to any, you may need to seek out professional help from a counselor.

Do you frequently binge uncontrollably on huge amounts of food?

Do you ever use laxatives or diuretics or induce vomiting to get rid of some of the food you've eaten?

Do you think you're fat even though your doctor has told you your weight is in the healthy range?

To help you assess your attitudes before embarking on a weight-loss program, answer the questions in the self-evaluation below. For each question, circle the answer that best describes your perspective. As you complete each of the four sections, add the numbers of your answers and compare them with the scoring guide at the end of the section.

SECTION 1:
Your attitude about weight loss

1. If you've tried to lose weight before, how certain are you this time that you will lose weight for good?

    1. Not at all certain

    2. Somewhat certain

    3. Quite certain

    4. Extremely certain

2. Consider the current challenges in your life (the stress of being a working mother, a family sickness, a new job, etc.). In light of these challenges, to what extent can you commit to major lifestyle changes?

    1. Cannot commit

    2. Uncertain

    3. Can commit somewhat

    4. Can commit fully

3. Think about why you want to lose weight (for health reasons, to make your family happy, to look good for a class reunion, etc.). How certain are you that this motivation will keep the weight off for the rest of your life?

    1. Not at all certain

    2. Somewhat certain

    3. Very certain

4. How much do you want to change your behaviors of overeating and under-exercising?

    1. Not at all

    2. A little

    3. A good deal

    4. Very much

5. If making healthy lifestyle changes is sometimes difficult or uncomfortable, how willing are you to stick with the changes?

    1. Not at all willing

    2. Somewhat willing

    3. Very willing

    4. Extremely willing

Add up answers and total score _____

If you scored:

5 to 12: Rethink whether this is really the best time to begin a weight-loss regime. If you lack commitment or have unrealistic expectations, you may be setting yourself up for failure. Consider altering your goals and how you plan to fulfill them, then reassess your attitudes in a few months.

13 to 16: You are on the brink of being mentally ready to make some permanent lifestyle changes. Consider how you can dispel the last of your doubts before you embark on a plan.

17 to 19: You have a healthy mindset. The time to implement changes is now.

SECTION 2:
Your hunger and eating patterns

6. How often do you eat when you're not hungry?

1. Throughout the day

2. Once a day

3. A few times a week

4. On rare occasions

7. If an opportunity arises to eat something delicious (you smell fresh bread as you pass a bakery, or your coworker brings in cookies), how likely are you to act on it?

1. Very likely

2. Somewhat likely

3. Somewhat unlikely

4. Very unlikely

8. If your favorite fattening foods are in the house, how careful are you to control your portions?

1. Not careful at all

2. Somewhat careful

3. Very careful

4. Extremely careful

9. You had planned to eat just a salad for lunch to make up for last night's dinner splurge. Your coworker invites you out to lunch at your favorite restaurant. How likely are you to stick to your salad plan?

1. Not at all likely

2. Somewhat likely

3. Very likely

4. Extremely likely

Add up answers and total score _____

If you scored:

4 to 9: You respond strongly to tempting foods around you. You may need to avoid having your favorite foods in the house, or buy only serving-size portions. Try not to place yourself in situations where you may be tempted to go off your eating plan. Bag your lunch instead of eating out, and make sure your walking route circumvents the bakery.

10 to 13: You may have a moderate tendency to eat just because food is available. Dieting may be easier for you if you try to tune into your physical hunger and tune out external cues.

14 to 16: You may occasionally eat more than you would like, but it does not appear to be a response to environmental cues. Controlling your attitudes and emotions about food might be helpful.

SECTION 3:
Your emotional eating patterns

10. If you're anxious, depressed or lonely, do you toss your good eating habits to the wind?

   1. Always

   2. Frequently

   3. Occasionally

   4. Rarely

   5. Never

11. Do you react to hearing good news by eating?

   1. Always

   2. Frequently

   3. Occasionally

   4. Rarely

   5. Never

12. If you've just had a quintessential "bad day," do you eat more than you'd like?

   1. Always

   2. Frequently

   3. Occasionally

   4. Rarely

   5. Never

Add up answers and total score _____

If you scored:

3 to 8: You respond to emotional highs and lows by eating. You need to find other outlets to give yourself a boost or a pat on the back when needed. Take a bubble bath or schedule a massage to unwind after a long week. Reward yourself with a pedicure or a new outfit to celebrate your promotion.

9 to 11: On some occasions, you respond to your emotions by eating. Learn to clue in to this behavior and substitute another pleasurable activity for food.

12 to 15: Emotions don't seem to play a large role in your eating habits.

SECTION 4:
Your exercise attitudes and medical readiness

13. How often do you do some form of physical activity?

   1. Never

   2. Once or twice a month

   3. Once or twice a week

   4. Three or more times a week

14. How sure are you that you can commit to a regular exercise program?

   1. Not at all sure

   2. Somewhat sure

   3. Highly sure

   4. Completely sure

15. When you picture yourself exercising, do you have positive or negative feelings?

   1. Completely negative

   2. Somewhat negative

   3. Neutral

   4. Somewhat positive

   5. Completely positive

16. Do you feel confident you will find time in your day to exercise?

    1. Not at all confident

    2. Somewhat confident

    3. Pretty confident

    4. Extremely confident

Add up answers and total score _____

If you scored:

4 to 9: Your negative feelings about exercise leave you stalled at the starting gate. Remember, exercise doesn't have to be regimented. Start small by filling your quota through short bursts of activity throughout the day: 10 minutes of raking leaves, 15 minutes of scrubbing the floor and a stroll around the block all count as exercise.

10 to 14: You need to develop a more positive attitude about exercising so you can do it more often. Determine what it is that you don't like about exercising. Is it the group classes, or the monotony of walking nowhere on a treadmill? Find an activity that you enjoy and look forward to doing, whether it's Rollerblading or starting a walking group with your friends.

15 to 17: You've got the right attitude. Now think of ways to stay firmly committed to your activity plan.

After tallying your score in each section of the readiness test, you should have identified some of your dieting strengths and weaknesses. Understanding the attitudes and behaviors that influence your eating and exercise habits is the first step toward making the vital changes.

REALITY CHECK

Healthy Truths

1. No one has ever become obese or fat from eating too much steamed broccoli.

2. Eating any food described as "overstuffed" or "oversized" will probably make you feel the same way.

3. Experiences last longer than flavors.

4. Think positive. Thoughts like "I'm strong and like to exercise" often become self-fulfilling prophecies.

5. Any time you don't feel good about yourself, you can remedy the situation by doing something good.

6. Nobody's perfect.

7. You are in control. No one but you puts food in your mouth.

8. Any product that promises to "effortlessly melt pounds" will merely melt money.

9. Little calories that don't count have a way of adding up.

10. The law of inertia: A body in motion tends to stay in motion; a body at rest remains at rest.

The "I Can't" Roadblocks
You Need to Overcome

Apprehensive about embarking on yet another weight loss plan? Fear of failure often can become a self-fulfilling prophecy. Here's how to clear those mental hurdles.

I can't lose weight because I'm genetically programmed to be fat.

True, genes play some role in whether you will be fat or thin. But that doesn't mean you can't do anything about your weight. For example, if you think you're predisposed to having a slower metabolism, regular exercise can boost it. Moreover, genetics doesn't tell the whole story. Obesity researchers point out the number of obese Americans has jumped sharply over the past two decades even though our genes haven't changed at all. The general consensus is that lifestyle habits are the foremost cause of obesity, with genes playing a secondary role.

I can't lose weight because my spouse and kids hate low-fat meals.

Most Americans now realize that it's a misconception that low-fat means low-taste. You can save on fat by preparing your family's meals with subtle differences. For example, some simple ideas that will ease the family into a low-fat eating style include using meat as a seasoning instead of as a main course (spaghetti with meat sauce instead of meatballs). Or you can make your own pizzas by keeping pizza crust in the freezer and adding healthy toppings (heavy on the veggies, light on the cheese). Also, try making low-fat dairy substitutions to your favorite meals or look for ways to skim the dairy fat. For instance, instead of thickening soup with cream, add a pureed potato to the mixture; use nonfat yogurt or buttermilk instead of sour cream in dressings and baked goods; and opt for skim or 1-percent low-fat milk instead of cream. A final thought: There's no need to make a family announcement concerning your new cooking style; simply prepare the dishes and serve—and see if anyone notices.

I can't lose weight because I don't have the time to change my lifestyle.

While embarking on a weight loss plan does require planning, it need not turn your life upside down. It's those little changes that can make the biggest difference. For example, drive to work, park a few blocks away and walk. (A brisk 15-minute walk to and from work each day is an ideal way to fit in daily exercise.) Take the stairs whenever you can. At home, make several trips up and down for small items rather than stockpiling and bringing them all up at once. At work, use the stairs instead of the elevator. Also, eat from your own kitchen whenever possible: Restaurant meals with huge portions and hidden amounts of fat can sabotage your weight loss efforts. Bring a lunch from home or grab a fresh salad with a plain roll or bagel from a take-out deli or supermarket.

I can't lose weight because no one will support my efforts.

Ultimately, you need to lose weight for yourself—not for your spouse, family or friends. However, it helps to have emotional support along the way, especially when you're trying to maintain the loss (often the most difficult part). If your family and friends are not meeting your support needs, look elsewhere. Perhaps you can link up with co-workers or friends who are also trying to lose weight. Another option is to join an organized support group like Weight Watchers.

I'm afraid that if I lose weight, I'll just gain it back.

Your fears are justified, particularly if you've been on the yo-yo roller coaster before. You need to evaluate your reasons for losing weight. If it's for a high school reunion or the summer swimsuit season, chances are you'll be tempted to take a permanent vacation from your healthful eating habits once the event passes. If your goal is to improve your health and pump up your energy for a more active lifestyle, then your chances for success are vastly improved.

READY TO EXERCISE?

Before you begin an exercise program, answer the following questions. As always, it's best to check with your physician for advice before getting started. If you've been sedentary, your physician may want to perform a complete physical before giving you the go ahead.

1. Has your physician ever said you have a heart problem or suspected a cardiac condition of any type?

_____

2. Do you have or have you ever had:

- pressure, pain or tightness in the chest brought on by exertion?

- bouts of irregular or uneven heartbeats?

- fainting spells or severe dizziness?

- diabetes or high blood sugar?

- high cholesterol, triglycerides or high lipids (or fats) in your blood?

3. Is your blood pressure high enough to require medication, or has it been in the past?

_____

4. Has any close blood relative (parent, sibling, child) had a heart attack or stroke under the age of 50?

_____

5. Do you smoke more than a pack of cigarettes a day?

_____

6. Are you a smoker (more than 15 cigarettes daily) who also takes birth control pills?

_____

7. Are you more than 50 pounds overweight?

_____

8. Do you have any bone, joint, muscular or vein problems (such as arthritis, rheumatism, gout, back pain or varicose veins)?

_____

9. Are you over 65 and not accustomed to vigorous exercise?

_____

10. Are you pregnant?

_____

11. Are you short of breath after climbing one flight of stairs?

_____

12. Is there a good physical reason not mentioned here why you should not follow an activity program?

_____

_____

_____

_____

_____

_____

_____

_____

What Is Your
Eating Personality?

Before you begin a weight loss journey, you must identify your Achilles heel—that time of day when you're most likely to venture off your healthful eating course. It isn't essential that you break these habits, but you should rework them.

The Breakfast Skipper: Breakfast is often the most nutrition-packed (and lowest-fat and -calorie) meal of the day. Since breakfast foods, such as cereal, tend to be low in fat, they can help with weight control. Skipping breakfast could lead you to a doughnut as a mid-morning snack or to a high-fat binge at lunch. What's more, preliminary research shows that breakfast skippers have metabolic rates that are 4 to 5 percent below normal, which can result in a weight gain of as much as eight extra pounds a year. Even if you're an avowed breakfast skipper, try working in a mini morning meal, even if it's the bare minimum. Try juice and toast or fruit and cereal; then boost your nutrition by having a piece of fruit or container of no-fat yogurt at mid-morning.

The Grazer: You have no defined meal times, but grab five or six "snacks" throughout the day. Researchers haven't found any weight loss benefit to grazing over eating three square meals. Nevertheless, grazing can work if you're nutrition wise. In other words, make sure several of these snacks are based on healthy produce. For instance, schedule a daily fruit snack: a slice of melon topped with low-fat cottage cheese, or a banana with a glass of orange juice. Also, schedule a regular vegetable snack: crudités or mixed greens topped with plain tuna drizzled with lemon juice and pepper.

The Late Afternoon or Late Night Snacker: You have one time of day that is your downfall. Usually, it's before dinner or before bed. Of course, there's nothing wrong with a small snack—say, a

serving of pretzels or frozen yogurt during the day. But eating straight from a box of cookies or crackers is an invitation to overeat. To keep your snack attacks under control, buy only serving-size portions of your favorite snacks, or save the after-dinner dessert until later in the evening.

The Weekender: You carefully follow your eating plan during the week but need the weekends off to overindulge. This approach need not hinder your weight loss efforts if you plan accordingly. For example, if you're planning a big night out at your favorite restaurant, eat lighter the rest of the day: skip the snacks and make sure your breakfast and lunch are low-fat. If you're scheduled for a Sunday brunch, a light dinner that evening should suffice.

Take a look at your dieting "history," outlining the crazy crash diets you embarked on over the years. How did those diets make you feel? How did you feel once you regained the lost weight?

. . . .

. . . .

. . . .

. . . .

. . . .

. . . .

. . . .

. . . .

. . . .

. . . .

. . . .

. . . .

. . . .

CHAPTER two

KNOWING YOUR BODY

efore getting started on a weight loss plan, you need to clue in to your body's health cues. Nowadays, this entails going beyond jumping on the scale. You need to know where your body fat is distributed, whether your weight puts you at a health risk and how hard your heart is working. Health factors such as these all can be measured, and this chapter will tell you how. You may also want to consider having certain screening tests, such as a blood pressure, cholesterol and triglyceride checks, at your doctor's office.

Health checks will not only tell you what shape you're in now, but can provide you with a way to monitor your improving health as the pounds are shed. For instance, if your scale doesn't budge for a week even though you've remained faithful to your weight loss plan, you can feel good about the fact that you're improving your heart if your waist is a little smaller and your biceps are a little larger.

The Body Basics

Most weight loss experts now believe that simply weighing yourself periodically will not provide the whole picture on your health progress; health conditions such as heart disease and diabetes can be improved as you shed pounds. Adding mild activity (such as a 15-minute stroll each day) to your weight loss plan will boost your weight loss efforts, as well as strengthen your bones and heart.

Before you do the self-assessments below, it's important to understand some basic facts about weight loss. First of all, be aware that the scale can be deceiving. Every pound you lose contains a combination of water, muscle and fat. (In reverse, adding muscle mass through exercise can result in an initial weight gain of a few pounds.) Eventually, each of these components dwindles at its own rate, so you don't lose weight in a steady decline. During the first few days of dieting, you'll lose weight more rapidly, largely through water loss. After that, the pounds will come off more slowly from fat burning—which is what really counts. You could also lose some muscle mass through dieting, but exercise, especially light to moderate resistance training, can prevent this.

As the weeks pass, you may find your weight loss drags to a halt. Some researchers believe a plateau is your body's message that you have dropped below a comfortable weight zone and its attempts to get back to its preferred weight, or set point. This phenomenon was explained in a study published in *The New England Journal of Medicine* that found after losing weight, your body's rate of calorie burning slows down and after gaining weight, its rate of calorie burning speeds up. The researchers discovered that the body adjusts its internal calorie-burning systems to maintain its preferred weight. So even if you are eating a consistent amount of calories every day during weight loss, your body learns to function efficiently by burning fewer of them. Fortunately, your body will readjust to a new set point within about six months, but keeping the weight off during those six months can be a challenge. Doing moderate exercise, such as biking and walking, combined with weight training will give your metabolism a boost while your body adjusts to its new weight.

Another point on plateaus: If you're a petite woman, your stalled weight loss may be traced to the simple yet often overlooked fact that a smaller body requires fewer calories—regardless of set point. So a minor readjustment in your daily food intake may be all that's needed to retrigger the weight loss.

Hormones also may be a reason your weight loss has stumbled to a halt. The hormonal surges related to the menstrual cycle, for instance, cause the kidneys to retain salt and water. Some experts contend that over the course of a month, water weight can lead to anywhere from a one- to six-pound gain. In addition, as a woman enters her thirties and forties, the incidence of bloating may increase due to changes in hormonal patterns. The key to conquering a hormonal-triggered gain or plateau? Be patient. Within a week of your period, you should see the excess weight vanish. Also, watching your intake of salty foods and increasing vigorous aerobic exercise may help. The latter causes you to perspire, reducing bloating and releasing endorphins, those mood-enhancing chemicals.

Assess Your Weight Risks

While a scale can help you monitor weight loss and maintenance, the experts agree it should not act as your sole gauge. Here are two important tests you should do to see if your weight puts you at higher risk for disease. You should also take these tests periodically while losing and maintaining your weight to monitor your progress.

According to government health officials, a good way to assess your weight and disease risks is the Body Mass Index (BMI). BMI is a calculated value of weight and height, and while it is correlated with body fat, it isn't directly connected (a change in a BMI unit translates into 5 pounds for the average woman and 7 pounds for the average man). The higher your BMI, the greater your risk of developing heart disease and other weight-related medical conditions, such as hypertension, aggravation of arthritis and diabetes, to name a few. Your BMI won't change if your weight shifts by a pound or two, which could be due to water retention or fluid loss, not a change in body fat.

I. To calculate your BMI:

1. Weight (in lbs.): ___ × 0.45 = ___ (a)

2. Height (in inches):___ × 0.025 = ___ (b)

3. Multiply (b) × (b) = ___ (c)

4. Divide (a) ___ ÷ (c) ___ = ___ (BMI)

Depending on your overall health picture, a BMI from 20 to 25 is in the healthy range for most adults; from 25 to 27 means an increased risk of some diseases in some people—especially those who have a high waist–hip ratio (see below); 27 to 30 means an increased risk of diabetes and heart disease; 30 or more puts you at even greater risk.

Another telling indicator of disease risk: the waist–hip ratio test. Research has found that the larger your waist in comparison to your hips, the greater your risk of dying from heart disease, cancer and diabetes.

II. To calculate your waist–hip ratio:

1. Measure your waist with a fabric tape measure:___ (a)

2. Measure the fullest part of your buttocks/hips:___ (b)

3. Divide (a) ___ ÷ (b) ___ = ___ (waist–hip ratio)

For women, a number greater than 0.8 indicates a higher-than-average risk; for men, it's 0.95.

REALITY CHECK

A Good Night's Sleep

1. Take an early-morning walk for at least 30 minutes. Exposure to bright light helps your body "rest" its internal clock so you will be awake when the sun is up and asleep when it has set.

2. Limit activities in the bedroom to sleep and sex.

3. Don't nap.

4. Don't exercise within three hours of bedtime.

5. Avoid eating within two hours of bedtime.

6. Make your bedroom a sanctuary. If you live in a noisy neighborhood, buy a fan or a white noise machine to help mask external sounds. Paint your walls a soothing color such as pale peach or ivory, and consider lining your drapes to block out unwanted light and muffle street noise.

What's Your Fitness Level?

Today, experts acknowledge no plan for improving health is complete unless it includes a fitness component. Consistent exercise is crucial to weight loss, as well as to promoting good heart health, strengthening your bones, toning muscles and boosting your mood. While a little exercise is better than none at all, if you're looking to reap the biggest health benefits (and the most calorie burning) you need to exercise moderately and regularly.

Taking your pulse can provide valuable information on how hard your heart is working. When your heart is well conditioned, it is more efficient at pumping blood and doesn't need to beat as often at rest and for the same level of exercise. To check your pulse, grab a watch with a second hand and follow these steps:

1. Place the first two fingers of the hand on the underside of the opposite wrist. (If you're wearing a watch, take your pulse on the other wrist.) Put the pad of your fingertips on the area nearest your thumb, just below the wrist bone. Never use your thumb to take your pulse; unlike your other fingers, you can feel your thumb's pulse.

2. Press down and feel for a pulse. Try different pressures, if necessary, until you can easily discern the beats.

3. Count the number of beats in 15 seconds and multiply the result by 4 to get your heart rate in beats per minute.

When you exercise, aim for a heart rate in your target zone. (To get the lower end of your zone, subtract your age from 220 and divide the result in half, or by 0.5. To get the upper end, multiply the 220-minus-age result by 0.8.) If you're not physically fit, shoot for the lower number and gradually work toward the higher one. To monitor your progress, take your resting pulse regularly. As you become more fit, this number should drop.

How Much of You Is Fat?

Studies are finding that women who pack more than 30 percent body fat (and men, more than 20 percent) are at increased risk for heart disease, high blood pressure and diabetes. Some body fat tests, however, are more reliable than others. The following is a listing of the most popular tests available. *Be forewarned that while a few can provide you with an approximate body-fat count, most are extremely unreliable.*

■ **Skin-Fold Calipers:** This device has tongs that pinch the fat beneath your skin in several places and a gauge that measures the hunks of fat. It's a quick and simple test, but results can be skewed if you had the test done after a workout or on a hot, humid day (because skin may swell). Results can also be affected if your tester fails to pinch all of your fat, pinches muscle as well as fat, or pinches the wrong places. **Where to get tested:** Many health clubs and weight loss centers offer this test free to members.

Do-it-yourself calipers sold in health catalogs will give you only a rough estimate.

- **Underwater Weighing:** This is the gold standard of body fat tests. After exhaling all the air from your lungs, you're submerged underwater for 5 seconds while your underwater weight registers on a scale. It's the most accurate, but it's also an uncomfortable method of testing since you have to hold your breath with only minimal air in your lungs. **Where to get tested:** Only a few research labs and sports medicine clinics have the necessary apparatus. They charge $50 to $100.

- **Bioelectrical Impedance:** This test is fast and painless (a machine sends electrical signals that determine how much muscle you have), but can overestimate your body fat if you're dehydrated. You can't eat or exercise within three hours of the test, and you can't have any caffeine or alcohol within 24 hours of the test. **Where to get tested:** Many health clubs and hospitals offer the test for about $50.

- **The Bod Pod:** The newest way to measure body fat, this combines the simplicity of the skin fold calipers with the accuracy of underwater testing by measuring your body volume by the amount of air you displace. It's very expensive and is available in only a handful of research clinics and fitness centers. **Where to get tested:** Sometimes the machine is trucked to health fairs and gyms, where the service is offered for $50. To see if there's one in your area, call the manufacturer at (510) 676-6002.

- **Near-Infrared Interactance:** A light wand, which emits a low energy beam of near-infrared light, is passed over your arm and a detector measures the amount of light that bounces back from your fat, muscles and bones. The greater the intensity of light emitted from your body, the more body fat you have. This safe, easy-to-use, painless test is also perhaps the least accurate body fat test. It tends to underestimate body fat in overweight people while overestimating it in thin people. Near-infrared interactance works best in those who are of average build and weight. **Where to get tested:** The test is offered in health clubs, hospitals and weight loss centers for about $50.

Tests You Should Get from Your Doctor

Before beginning a weight loss or overall fitness plan, it's wise to have a general physical—especially if you haven't had one in the last few years. Your doctor may suggest you have certain screening tests, such as those described below, to further assess your state of health. Keep in mind that once you start a weight loss or exercise program, your doctor also must taken into account any medications you are taking for conditions such as diabetes. In addition, be aware your dosage of medication may need to be changed as you lose weight.

- **Cholesterol & Lipid Profile:** All healthy adults should have their cholesterol levels tested every five years. You may need to be tested more frequently, depending on your total and HDL (the "good cholesterol") levels and other risk factors. The general guidelines for total cholesterol: under 200 is desirable; 200 to 239 is borderline high; and 240 or more is considered high. An HDL level of 35 or below is considered unhealthy.

According to the National Cholesterol Education Program Guidelines, a lipoprotein analysis is required for those whose cholesterol is greater than 240 mg/dL. (The initial screening test measures only total cholesterol and HDL.) The fasting test includes a measure of total cholesterol, total triglyceride and HDL. LDL is calculated from these numbers.

Levels of LDL cholesterol of 160 mg/dL or greater are considered high-risk; those 130 to 159 are considered borderline high risk; and those less than 130 are considered desirable levels.

- **Blood Pressure:** You should have a blood pressure check during every physical. An elevated blood pressure means your heart is working harder than normal, which puts both your heart and arteries under greater strain. The top number (called systolic pressure) should be no greater than 120. The bottom number (called diastolic) should be no greater than 80.

- **Thyroid Screening:** Since weight gain can sometimes result from an underactive thyroid, you may want to have your levels of thyroid hormone checked via a simple blood test. Other signs of an underactive thyroid include constipation, intolerance to the cold, lethargy, brittle nails and hair, dry skin and low sex drive.

The Weight Stages of a Woman's Life

As most women know, there are certain stages of life or ages when hormones can wreak havoc on weight. Consider the following:

The Pregnancy Years

Whether you want to have one baby or ten, going through a pregnancy can be a weighty challenge—even for the slimmest of women. Here's how to handle the before, during and after to minimize the pounds that remain after baby comes into the world.

Planning for pregnancy. Thinking of abandoning your weight loss plans because you may be pregnant in the coming months? Don't, say experts. More and more research is finding that mothers who are obese increase their baby's risk of health problems. Two studies that appeared in the *Journal of the American Medical Association* found that obesity doubles your risk of having a baby with neural tube defects such as spina bifida. Other data from the Nurses' Health Study found that babies weighing more than 10 pounds at birth (often born to mothers who are obese) are more likely to be obese when they grow up.

Achieving a healthy weight and fitness level before becoming pregnant will also benefit your own health. You'll have a little leeway in gaining during the pregnancy and find it easier to lose weight after giving birth. Women who are more than 20 percent above their ideal weight range are also more likely to have trouble conceiving and may experience more lower back pain, gestational diabetes and constipation than leaner women.

If you're planning to become pregnant, one of the most important nutrients you need for reducing your baby's risk of birth defects is folic acid. Since many women don't get enough folic acid in their diets, the U.S. government has required food manufacturers to add it to most enriched breads, flours, cornmeals, pastas, rice and other grain products. The Public Health Service recommends that all women of childbearing age consume 0.4 milligrams of folic acid daily to reduce their babies' risk of neural tube defects, which occur in the first few weeks of pregnancy. For example, a $1/2$-cup serving of cooked spinach, a $1/2$-cup serving of beans and two glasses of orange juice meet the daily requirement.

In the thick of it. Once you're pregnant, don't diet. However, you can help limit excessive weight gain by following a two-step plan: wise nutrition habits and moderate exercise. To nourish your fetus, you need to consume only 300 additional calories per day (which is nearly met just by drinking the extra two glasses of skim milk that's recommended during pregnancy). Minimizing your fat and sugar intake while maximizing your fruits and veggies will help keep your weight in check. As far as exercise, the American College of Obstetricians and Gynecologists' guidelines suggest that pregnant women can derive health benefits from mild to moderate exercise performed at least three times a week in a cool environment. (You and your doctor should decide what's safe and appropriate for you depending on your fitness level before pregnancy.)

Bringing up baby. After a woman gives birth, she's likely to retain 10 pounds or more for years after her pregnancy, according to a study from the University of Alabama at Birmingham. Once you give birth, give yourself a little time to get accustomed to your new lifestyle, such as the fact you can no longer go to the gym on a whim. Start by taking short strolls with the baby in the first few weeks following birth. If you didn't have a Caesarian section, you can also do some abdominal strengtheners like crunches. After the first six weeks, your gynecologist will probably give you the green light to resume your normal exercise activities.

In terms of your eating habits, you shouldn't cut back on calories if you're nursing: Theoretically, the body needs an additional 1,000 calories per day to produce enough high-quality breast milk. For most women, this means you should eat about 500 extra calories a day to maintain your supply. (The other 500 calories come from your pregnancy fat store accumulated for this very purpose.) Current research recommends that weight loss while breast feeding should be limited to an average of a pound a week.

If you go straight to bottle feeding or after you have stopped nursing, you can step up efforts to lose weight. The earlier the better. Stick to the tried and true method: Lose weight slowly and steadily—up to two pounds per week. Don't be tempted to go on a fad diet for a fast fix.

The Menopause Years

First, the bad news: Large weight increases are typical for women in their 40s and 50s. A University of Pittsburgh study looked at 485 women ages 42 to 50 and found that during a three-year period, the average woman gained five pounds. Twenty percent of the participants gained 10 pounds or more.

Now the good news: Hormone replacement therapy (HRT) to ease menopausal symptoms and provide protection against such illnesses as heart disease and osteoporosis does not appear to cause weight gain. Results of a three-year study at the National Heart, Lung and Blood Institute found that women on a placebo actually gained slightly more weight than those on HRT. Other research also found no connection between weight gain and HRT use when women were on hormones for 15 years.

So what's the reason for the boost in body fat? Aging changes cause a drop in your body's metabolism. Also, you may become more sedentary as you grow older. To give your metabolism a jump start, initiate a regular activity program that includes muscle-building exercises. (The more muscle you have, the higher your body's metabolic rate.) Some of the best exercises to build your muscle mass are circuit weight training (using machines such as Nautilus equipment at the gym) and cross training (alternating walking, swimming and biking).

30 Minutes Burns

Activity	Calories Burned*	Food You Can Eat
Basketball (vigorous/full court)	364	2 cups cooked fettucine (352 calories)
Bicycling (13 mph)	266	McDonald's regular French fries (220 calories)
Cross-country skiing (8 mph)	390	Dairy Queen regular sundae (300 calories)
Golf (twosome)	169	3 Keebler chocolate-chip cookies (160 calories)
Jogging (5 mph)	225	1 packet of M&M's (229 calories)
Rowing (vigorous)	364	2.5 ounces of barbecue-flavored potato chips (340 calories)
Running (8 mph)	390	2 burritos with beans and cheese (377 calories)
Swimming (55 yd/min)	330	2 burritos with beans and cheese (377 calories)
Tennis (beginner)	120	12-oz. bottle of light beer (90 calories) plus one cup air-popped popcorn (31 calories)
Walking (4.5 mph)	180	$1/_2$ cup rich vanilla ice cream (178 calories)

*For a 125-pound woman.

What were the highs and lows in your weight history? What was your life like when you were heavier? Thinner?

CHAPTER three

OVERWEIGHT IN THE '90s

Will there one day be a cure for being overweight? If genes are responsible for making some individuals overweight, can doctors somehow alter those genes to make the same people thin? Will there someday be a pill that will enable you to stick to a healthy lifestyle forever? Does the future hold a drug that will take away cravings for chocolate—or one that will allow you to eat as much chocolate as you want without gaining a pound?

Some tantalizing findings have been emerging from the labs of obesity researchers. For now, scientists are focusing their efforts on learning what causes one person to be overweight and another to be thin. Yes, fat and calories are still culprits, but why are some people predisposed to eat more than others? Do our genes program us to crave certain foods? Is obesity hereditary?

Over the past few years, scientific evidence has been filling in the pieces of the obesity puzzle, and the picture that is emerging is much more complex than researchers once believed. It seems there are at least 20 genes that could predispose you toward obesity by controlling your metabolism, food cravings and even propensity toward a sedentary lifestyle. In addition, a spate of new medications could help compensate for poor genes—although they won't let you off the hook for following good eating habits.

Fortunately, genetic makeup does not necessarily predetermine whether you will be obese. The key to overcoming extra pounds lies in taking charge of controllable weight factors. What follows are some cutting-edge discoveries and ways to use these advances to maintain your weight and maximize your weight loss goals.

Of Genes and Hormones

Scientists are gathering more and more evidence that genes somehow play a role in whether you will be fat or thin. Some genes may control your preference for sweets; others boost your appetite and tell you when you're full; still others may alter your rate of calorie burning.

Many of these genes are still mysteries. Several years ago, researchers from Rockefeller University in New York made a landmark discovery when they found a gene in mice that has come to be called the obesity or Ob-gene. The gene controls a hormone called leptin, which tells the brain how much fat is stored away. In the study, mice who had this gene (and lower amounts of leptin in their blood) were given injections of leptin and lost 30 percent of their weight within two weeks. The research has strengthened the idea that the body's rate of fat metabolism is partially determined by genes and has triggered a rush to produce drugs that can compensate for inheriting obesity genes.

But the genetic picture is more complex in humans. Researchers believe many genes may play a role in obesity. For instance, while some obese people may fail to produce enough leptin, research is finding that many others have adequate or even high amounts of the hormone. Scientists theorize that overweight people with high leptin levels have faulty receptors in their brain cells that don't get leptin's "stop eating" message.

As the researchers continue to explore and fine tune their theories, what can you do in the meantime? Take charge of those weight factors you can control:

- **Boost your activity levels:** Adding moderate physical activity to your lifestyle can mimic the effects of leptin by reducing your appetite and thus the amount of food eaten. Do any form of exercise that is rhythmic (involving a repetitive, continuous motion), can be sustained for 30 to 40 minutes (start with less and work up) and works the large muscles in the legs and upper body. Try hiking, vigorously raking leaves, cross-country skiing or walking on a treadmill.

- **Lose a little weight:** A modest weight loss, on the order of 5 to 10 percent, may make cells more responsive to leptin—in a manner similar to the way diabetics become more responsive to insulin as they lose weight.

- **Be honest about the reasons behind those extra pounds:** Obesity researchers estimate that about 30 percent of overweight cases can be attributed to genes and the remaining 70 percent to lifestyle factors. Eating more and exercising less plays a much bigger role in weight gain than genes.

- **Keep a written record:** Write down for two weeks everything you eat and all your exercising activities to assess whether your excess weight is due more to nature or nurture.

The Health Benefits of a Little Weight Loss

Soon after the discovery of the Ob-gene, the National Academy of Sciences' Institute of Medicine issued a landmark report in 1995. The report concluded that obesity is a chronic disease, which can be adequately managed with moderate weight loss. Reaching a healthy weight doesn't always require huge weight losses, according to the report's expert panel. Losing as little as 10 pounds and maintaining the weight loss is often enough to alleviate certain health conditions and improve your risk outlook.

As you may well know, obesity increases a person's risk for heart disease (by increasing your blood pressure and cholesterol levels), strokes, diabetes, arthritis and some cancers, including, breast, colon and skin cancer. Moderate weight loss can reverse these risks. The following strategies will help you reach and maintain a healthy weight:

- **Consider the six-month plan:** Set a weight loss goal of no more than 5 to 10 percent of your current body weight. Maintain the weight loss for at least six months before you set a new goal.

- **Rethink your food choices:** For many people, the difference between losing weight and maintaining their current weight is only a few hundred calories a day. Assess your overall habits and identify two or three things that contribute to your extra weight. If you drink two or three glasses of sugar-sweetened sodas each day, switching to calorie-free beverages could reduce your calorie intake enough to make a difference. If diet sodas turn you off, add a shot of cranberry or orange juice to plain seltzer,

or try water flavored with lemon and lime slices.

- **Stop seeing the way you eat as "dieting":** Although diets can be a useful tool to get you started on weight loss, depriving yourself of all your favorite foods isn't a plan you can maintain. Make changes you can live with permanently. For instance, instead of eliminating all the fat from your diet, eliminate one or two fattening foods at a time (e.g., switch from creamy salad dressings to a low-fat vinaigrette and from stick margarine to low-fat tub magarine). Once you've adjusted, add in other small changes: Use smaller portions of meat when you cook, and add two extra servings of vegetables to your meal plan each day. If you start to feel deprived, eliminate one or two of the changes that seem the hardest to follow and reassess your eating plan once you feel ready to make additional changes.

- **Slip in some moves:** Even light exercises, like strolling or swimming slowly, are effective calorie burners. Try to work at least one activity into each day: Push your baby in the stroller to the store; go Rollerblading for 20 minutes in the park; climb up and down the stairs in your house while listening to your favorite music. Once you reach your weight goal, you can actually eat a little more and maintain your weight loss if you keep up the exercise.

Fad Diets: **The Same Old, Same Old**

As study after study confirms that exercising and eating a low-fat diet packed with fruits, veggies and whole-grains is the safest way to lose weight, it seems hard to believe that anyone places faith in fad diets. Truth is, you still may be seeking a quick and simple way to lose weight. But as fast as the pounds fly off, they fly back on the minute you go back to your regular eating habits. Below is a closer look at several get-thin-quick schemes:

■ *The Empty Plate Club*: Everyone knows that unsupervised fasting is not a safe way to slim down. What's more, it can slow down your metabolism and cause you to lose lots of muscle. Still, fasting diets, promoted as a way to "detoxify" the body of impurities and toxins (based on the misconception that the body produces toxins), are still popular. Nutritionists warn that fasting can lead to headaches, dizziness and fatigue. Prolonged fasting can cause health problems such as kidney failure and gallstones—and may even result in death. Except in a supervised hospital setting (reserved for extreme health-threatening

obesity), fasting as a dieting technique should be avoided. Instead, you should opt for a diverse diet that will prevent nutrient deficiencies and maintain muscle mass. This will keep your metabolism boosted and will actually help you lose weight.

■ *The Meat Diet*: Many people have the idea that carbohydrates (fruits, vegetables, refined sugars) make you fat and protein (meat, eggs and fish) makes you thin. This erroneous concept is the sum and substance of several popular new weight loss books. These diets date back to the 1970s high-protein diet gurus Tarnower (the

"Scarsdale Diet") and Atkins. The bottom line: The diets didn't work for long-term weight loss then, and they don't work now.

Research has shown that overweight individuals following low-calorie diets lose comparable amounts of fat regardless of whether the calories come from high-carbohydrate or low-carbohydrate diets. The real culprit in weight gain is eating more calories than are burned off. Lean proteins like chicken, fish, peas, beans, grains, nuts and certain lean cuts of meat (rib eye and select ground beef) should compose 12 to 15 percent of your caloric intake. Choosing high-fat protein sources like T-bone steaks and fast-food burgers will not only widen your waistline, but will clog your arteries. They should be eaten in moderation.

- *The One-Note Diet:* The grapefruit diet from years past is making the rounds again. You may also have heard about the cabbage soup diet. While it's true that centering your diet around one food will probably lead to weight loss, you'll also be depriving your body of much-needed nutrients. You're also setting yourself up for an eating binge once you go off the diet and start sampling your favorite foods.

- *Food Combining:* This diet is based on the concept that eating certain foods at certain times of the day will help you lose weight and gain energy. It stresses eating five daily servings or more of fresh fruits and vegetables, which is nutritionally sound. However, its rules are rigid and difficult to follow. You're supposed to have one meal a day composed solely of fruits and vegetables, eat protein and a salad for lunch, and eat pasta and other complex carbs only at dinnertime. What's more, you are not allowed to mix proteins and starches. This means no pizza, meatballs and spaghetti, or hamburgers on a bun.

- **Focus on a shift from losing to maintenance:** Although you'll probably eat less while losing and eat more while maintaining your loss, you need to be careful not to return to your old habits. Establish an eating philosophy, and stick with it. For instance, you can decide to shoot for meals containing unprocessed foods that are high in fiber and low in fat. Or you may decide to minimize snacking between meals.

- **Indulge, but spend calories wisely:** You won't damage your waistline if you splurge on a box of chocolate on Valentine's Day or on a five-course meal on your anniversary—just don't find things to celebrate with food on a regular basis. You can also fit small portions of your favorite foods into your everyday eating plan provided you make some tradeoffs. If you have a hot fudge sundae topped with whipped cream, skip the steak you planned for dinner and opt for a large salad. Make sure you fully enjoy what you're indulging in. Don't waste calories snacking on stale potato chips or leftovers in the fridge.

Diet Drugs: Boom or Bust?

In recent years, diet drugs have been grabbing headlines and making news. The use of these medications have been nothing if not controversial: One day portrayed as a magic bullet, the next as a death sentence, Americans are understandably confused when the topic turns to drugs and weight. Who should take them and when? Are they safe? What's the real story behind these pills? And, the most important question in the minds of countless overweight individuals is in light of recent controversy, what does the future hold?

The newest chapter in the diet drug story dates to 1992, when a physician and researcher made a fascinating discovery when he combined two, nonaddictive appetite suppressants that were individually approved as diet aids in the 1970s: People who took both drugs—fenfluramine and phentermine, which quickly became known as fen/phen—lost significantly more weight than when they ingested either drug on its own.

Despite the fact that some individuals experienced side effects (including dry mouth and digestive disturbances), and the fact that the Food and Drug Administration (FDA) never approved this drug combination for the treatment of obesity, countless physicians began prescribing fen/phen. (It should be noted that this is a not uncommon practice in medicine which is frequently referred to as "off label" use of a drug. For example, some physicians are suggesting that Prozac, a drug used in the treatment of depression, might also be prescribed to treat some cases of obesity since it was noted that some individuals who took Prozac for depression also lost weight.)

As prescriptions of fen/phen were written, another weight loss medication was introduced: Dexfenfluramine (sold under the name Redux) was approved by the FDA in the spring of 1996, giving the distinction of being the first new appetite suppressant introduced in the U.S. in over 20 years.

As national statistics on obesity grew, so did interest in fen/phen and Redux. The media highlighted countless "success stories" of obese individuals who claimed these drugs were their last hope in their battle of the bulge. As public interest heightened, so did the number of physicians (many not adequately trained in the nuances of these drugs) prescribing them. Several commercial weight loss companies even incorporated a "drug" component into their programs.

The diet-drug binge went bust in the fall of 1997. It began with a report published in the *New England Journal of Medicine* that found people who took Redux for more than three months may have up to 23 times greater risk of developing a rare but life-threatening condition called primary pulmonary hypertension. Next, physicians reported an apparent increase in instances of severe damage to the heart valves of their patients who took these drugs.

Based on these finding, the FDA requested that those drugs that appeared to be linked with heart damage—fenfluramine, one half of fen/phen duo, and dexfenfluramine, or Redux—be removed from the market immediately.

Yet the concept of developing drugs that can be used as safe and effective tools in the treatment of medical obesity continues. While some traits of the older drugs will remain for the new breed (for instance, diet drugs are not for slightly

Future Fat-Fighting Drugs

Despite the popularity of Redux, several powerhouse drugs, currently awaiting FDA approval or being tested in clinical trials, may prove to be more effective at fighting fat. Researchers are aiming to readjust the body's method for burning fat. The new generation of drugs will directly target the complicated pathway that causes the body to retain (rather than burn) fat. As more and more medications become available, doctors may begin prescribing the pills in different combinations to custom-tailor treatments to achieve maximum weight loss and minimal side effects.

■ *Sibutramine:* This drug will be marketed under the trade name Meridia by Knoll Pharmaceutical. As this book was going to press, it was expected to be approved by the FDA in 1998. It works as an appetite suppressant by boosting levels of serotonin in the brain. Studies so far show that patients lost an average of 5 to 10 percent of their body weight and maintained the loss over the course of a year. Possible side effects include dry mouth, insomnia, constipation and headaches.

■ *Orlistat:* This will be marketed under the name Xenical by Roche Laboratories and, at the time that this book went to press, it was expected to be approved by the FDA in 1998. It works on the intestines instead of the brain by blocking the absorption of one-third of all dietary fat that people consume. The drug may cause moderate side effects such as diarrhea and cramps.

■ *Leptin:* Manufactured by Amgen, this drug is still being tested in clinical trials. A hormone secreted by fat cells, it tells the brain to decrease hunger signals and increase calorie burning.

■ *Neuropeptide-Y blockers:* Several companies are testing these in early clinical trials. They block the brain receptors for neuropeptide-Y, a hormone associated with overeating.

■ *BTA-243:* Manufactured by American Home Products, BTA-243 enhances activity of fat cells' "Beta$_3$ andrenergic receptors" to stimulate the burning of fat. It is currently being tested in clinical trials.

overweight people, or those interested in losing a fast 10 pounds), it appears that future drugs will probably target the complicated pathway that causes the body to retain, rather than burn, fat (see box).

For the record, Weight Watchers has never participated in the pill binge that characterized the mid–1990's. Weight Watchers always maintained that these medications, when used appropriately, may be an effective component of comprehensive weight management program whose core centers on a lifestyle modification program. Moreover, Weight Watchers stresses that the use of medication is a medical decision that is best made between a patient and his or her qualified physician.

Binge R$_X$

1. Analyze what happened. Were you stressed? Did you get too hungry because your meals were too far apart? Were you feeling sorry for yourself? As painful as some of these questions are, answering may help you avoid future mishaps.

2. Put it behind you. After you're satisfied that you know what caused the binge, give yourself a fresh start. There's no use crying over spilt milk or dwelling on your mistakes.

3. Get right back on track. Eat exactly what you had planned for the next meal. Right now getting back in the saddle is of primary importance.

4. Don't skip your next meal. If you deprive yourself, you'll only get hungry and resentful—a perfect setup for another binge.

5. Give yourself a treat for every day. If planning for one big treat at week's end doesn't work, consider having one small indulgence each day. Knowing that there is a small splurge waiting may take away the temptation to binge.

Something to Think About

Complete the sentence: When I look in the mirror, I see . . .

. . . .

. . . .

. . . .

. . . .

. . . .

. . . .

. . . .

. . . .

. . . .

. . . .

. . . .

. . . .

. . . .

. . . .

part 2

THE WEIGHT LOSS EQUATION

CHAPTER four

NUTRITIONAL BASICS

how often have you heard the advice to "eat low-fat, but don't overindulge" in fat-free treats? Or to cut back on cooking with oil—unless it's olive? Or to go for a high-carbohydrate diet, but make sure the carbs you choose are high in fiber? Or to choose margarine over butter—or maybe butter over margarine?

At best, the tenets of good nutrition can be confusing; at worst, they can be maddeningly baffling. With the newest health information seeming to change from day to day, you may have received mixed messages concerning what's good for your health and what isn't. For instance, if you've heard that eating too much fat is bad, you assume consuming foods that are touted as non-fat is the ideal. But, as you already may have learned the hard way, fat-free goodies and snacks are not the answer. In fact, surveys show that although many people have reduced the percentage of fat in their diets, they're eating so many more calories that the actual amount of fat consumed is the same as it always has been.

In terms of weight, however, your body's main concern is calories, not whether the calories are from fat, protein or carbohydrates. From the moment you put a morsel in your mouth, your body activates its tracking system to determine where the food is needed most: Does it need to be burned for energy or to keep your organs functioning? Or should it be ferried over to your muscles for energy or your fat cells for storage?

Contrary to what you might think, your body can convert *any* kind of food into fat—regardless of whether it's a protein, carbohydrate or fat. So if you eat enough slices of bread (which contains little fat), you will still pack on pounds. All in all, your fat cells swell when you consistently take in more calories than you need for energy. (Swollen fat cells cause the spongy cellulite bumps on your thighs and cushy love handles on your waist.)

Working from this starting point, the next nutrition basic makes things a bit more complex: Calorie-wise, fats, carbs and proteins are not created equal. Gram for gram, carbohydrates and proteins have less than half the calories of fat. What's more, your body burns a meager 2.5 calories to convert 100 calories of dietary fat into body fat; it expends nearly 25 calories converting carbohydrates or protein into fat.

Nutrition Made Simple?

In recent years, nutrition researchers have been honing in on the nutrients you need to maintain a healthy weight and ward off disease. In this process, they've discarded some of the old models of nutrition; for instance, the meat-and-potatoes meal of the 1950s isn't considered healthful by today's standards.

Several years ago, the U.S. government attempted to make it easier to understand nutrition by creating the Food Guide Pyramid. The Pyramid's message is that fruits, vegetables and grains are the foundation for a nutritious diet. It also illustrates how many servings you should have each day from each of the five food groups. The tip of the Pyramid advises people to consume fats, oils and sweets sparingly.

Grain products are contained in the Pyramid's wide base, and the government recommends eating six to 11 daily servings (one slice of bread; $^1/_2$ bun, bagel, or English muffin; 1 ounce of cereal; and $^1/_2$ cup cooked oatmeal, rice or pasta each count as a serving). Directly over the base rest the vegetables and fruits. The government recommends eating three or more servings of various vegetables (one cup of raw leafy greens and $^1/_2$ cup of cut-up vegetables) and two or more servings of fruit (one medium apple, orange or banana; $^1/_2$ cup of small or diced fruit; $^3/_4$ cup of juice). Dairy products, meats, poultry, fish and other proteins are found higher up, with two to three servings recommended from each group. For milk, one cup of milk or yogurt or about 1.5 ounces of cheese count as a serving. For meat, poultry, fish, dry beans, nuts and eggs, a daily total of 6 ounces fulfill the number of recommended servings (one egg, $^1/_2$ cup of cooked dried peas or beans, 2 tablespoons of peanut butter and $^1/_3$ cup of nuts are each considered the equivalent of 1 ounce of meat).

The emphasis on grains, fruits and vegetables makes nutritional sense. After all, they are naturally low in fat and high in fiber. Yet only 10 percent of Americans consume the recommended five to nine servings of fruits and vegetables per day, according to the American Council on Science and Health. Using meat as a side dish, rather than the main course, is also sound advice. Moreover, the Food Guide Pyramid allows vegetarians to fulfill all the food groups by including beans and nuts in the meat group.

Unfortunately, the Pyramid also has its weaknesses. For example, it offers no explicit advice on how to reduce fat and oils in the diet. It also doesn't distinguish between high-fat and low-fat foods or high-fiber foods from low-fiber ones (for instance, high-fiber whole-grain products are lumped into the same category as high-fat, low-fiber crackers and biscuits). Cheddar cheese gets the same nutritional value as low-fat yogurt.

What's more, the Pyramid recommends using olive and other monounsaturated oils (which are heart healthy) as sparingly as butter and other saturated fats (which are heart damaging).

What to do? Working with the premise that the science of nutrition can be complex for the average person, a wise rule of thumb to follow is if it sounds too good to be true, it is. Cheesecake isn't healthful even if it falls into the dairy category of the Food Guide Pyramid. And you don't have the green light to eat fat-free chips in limitless portions. Of course, you are allowed to bend the rules occasionally and can work your favorite treats into your eating plan. Rather than berating yourself for an indulgence, focus on what you can prepare for dinner that will get you back on track. Good nutritional habits shouldn't be a battle between do's and don'ts. Instead, work on adapting your eating mindset to find foods that you enjoy eating and are good for you as well.

Also, be aware that nutrition news flashes that grab headlines can be misleading. Although the science of nutrition is a slowly evolving one, the media often make it appear as if new diet dictums are being released at breakneck speed. Again, common sense should prevail. To help you make informed decisions concerning your health and eating habits, review the following points when it comes to assessing whether a headline warrants a second look:

- **Consider the source.** A single study from one obscure university should not prompt you to rework your lifestyle. Ask your doctor or a nutritionist for several names of reputable sources (such as the American Dietetic Association or the American College of Obstetricians and Gynecologists).

- **Size can matter.** Studies that are based on a large population of diverse people, say 2,000, may be more telling than a study focusing on 20 individuals.

- **Of women, not mice.** The findings of animal studies don't necessarily translate for humans; ditto for research on men that may not apply to women.

- **Look at the mix.** If a large study utilized a diverse population (a variety of races, ages and sexes), the results would have a greater likelihood to apply to you.

- **Watch for the backup.** A study that confirms finding of previous research warrants your interest in probing further into the topic.

The Power of Produce

The message from nutritionists is abundantly clear: Eat nutritious foods that fuel, protect and energize your body and you will lose weight, as well as boost your health. True, many of us are taking supplements, but researchers are finding that fruits and vegetables offer more than vitamins: They contain compounds called phytochemicals and carotenoids that can help ward off disease. For

(continued on page 42)

Test Your
Nutrition Knowledge

1. Which makes a better breakfast when you're in a rush?

a. A large bran muffin

b. A bagel smeared with a tablespoon of cream cheese

2. Which two habits are most likely to lower your risk of breast cancer?

a. Drinking little or no alcohol

b. Avoiding weight gain after menopause

c. Eating more fruits and vegetables

d. Exercising regularly

3. Which restaurant dinner has the lowest amount of fat?

a. Hamburger with fries

b. Sirloin steak with a baked potato topped with a tablespoon of sour cream

c. Chicken Caesar salad with dressing

d. Grilled chicken with a baked potato topped with cheese sauce

4. When selecting a snack at a vending machine, your best choice is:

a. A 2-ounce package of trail mix

b. A 2-ounce package of pretzels

5. The best low-fat snack to share at the movies is:

a. A small box of plain M&Ms

b. A small tub of unbuttered popcorn

c. A package of licorice

6. Which of the following is least likely to keep your blood pressure from rising?

a. Eating fruits and vegetables

b. Exercising regularly

c. Avoiding alcohol

d. Drinking skim milk

e. Losing excess weight

7. When scanning the cookie aisle at the supermarket, which is the better choice?

a. Fig bars

b. Fat-free sandwich cookies

8. Which food is most likely to protect your heart?

a. Tuna sandwich

b. Broiled salmon

c. Baked filet of sole

9. Which has less fat?

a. A 3.5-ounce serving of roasted chicken thigh without skin

b. A 3.5-ounce serving of roasted pork tenderloin

10. A package of 75% lean ground beef is low in artery-clogging fat.

TRUE or FALSE

Answers

1.b. A bagel with cream cheese contains 300 calories and 11 grams of fat, compared to a 6-ounce bran muffin, which packs 600 calories and 22 grams of fat.

2. a and b. The evidence for exercise and fruits and vegetables is preliminary, though it may be proven in future studies. One study published in the *Journal of the National Cancer Institute* found that premenopausal women who exercised one to three hours per week cut their risk of breast cancer by 30 percent; those active for four hours per week cut their risk by 60 percent. Fruits and vegetables contain cancer-fighting phyto-chemicals; they also can help you control your weight, which research suggests can help reduce your risk of breast cancer.

3. b. The grilled chicken (8 grams of fat) has less fat than the steak (20 grams), but the loaded baked potato (31 grams) is much fattier than a plain baked potato with sour cream (3 grams). The chicken Caesar salad has 46 fat grams, while the burger and fries weigh in at 67 grams.

4. b. The 2-ounce serving of pretzels has 220 calories and 2 grams of fat. The trail mix has 260 calories and a whopping 16 grams of fat.

5. c. Licorice is virtually fat-free, and half a 4-ounce pack will set you back only 190 calories. A half serving of the smallest-size, pre-packaged popcorn will set you back only 200 calories but contains 14 grams of fat (although it also has some nutrients and fiber). Half of a 2.6-ounce box of plain M&M's will cost you 180 calories and 8 grams of fat.

6. d. Cutting back on salt, losing as few as ten pounds and limiting your alcohol can all keep blood pressure from rising. So can brisk walking, cycling and swimming. Eating fruits and vegetables can also help.

7. a. Fig bars are naturally low in fat and are on a par with fat-free cookies in terms of fat and calories. However, fig bars are more healthful because of their nutritional and fiber content.

8. b. The omega-3 fats in salmon and other dark-fleshed fish may cut the risk of sudden cardiac death. The salmon has less saturated fat than the tuna mixed with mayonnaise. Baked sole is a good nutritional choice, although it is not as rich in omega-3 fats.

9. b. A 3.5-ounce serving of chicken thigh supplies 11 grams of fat. A serving of lean pork tenderloin has only 5 grams of fat.

10. False. Beef labeled "75% lean" actually packs four times as much saturated fat as does "93% lean."

example, the phytochemical sulforaphane in broccoli may neutralize cancer-causing substances in the liver, and the beta carotene in dark leafy vegetables may help protect your retina, thus offsetting macular degeneration (a disease that can eventually result in blindness).

What's more, scientists are also uncovering the potent effects of produce on longevity. Although a good deal of the research on anti-aging is still in its preliminary stages, scientists are uncovering some fascinating information on specific foods. For example, tea—particularly green and black teas—contains polyphenols, antioxidant compounds that may slow down the aging process by protecting cells from structural damage. Antioxidants work by acting as bodyguards that capture "free radicals," which may harm cells and contribute to the development of certain cancers.

When the subject turns to memory—a hot topic as you age—the talk always turns to the B vitamins, particularly B_{12}, B_6 and folic acid. Researchers have found that a lack of these crucial vitamins may disrupt your body's manufacture of neurotransmitters (or the chemicals that regulate alertness, memory and mood), which speed nerve signals to the brain.

The key is to include a variety of fruits and vegetables in your diet. Preparing them in certain ways can also help maximize your body's absorption of nutrients.

■ **Follow a rainbow diet.** Aim to eat fruits and vegetables from all the colors of the rainbow— from red tomatoes to yellow squash to purple plums. This will give you a wide variety of vitamins, including the disease-fighting antioxidants. For beta carotene, eat cantaloupes, carrots, sweet potatoes, red and yellow peppers and green leafy vegetables; for vitamin C, cabbage, citrus fruits and tomatoes; for vitamin E, almonds, sweet potatoes, mangoes, avocados and wheat germ; for folic acid, spinach, collard greens, kale and beans; and for the B vitamins, try bananas, sweet potatoes and prunes.

■ **Lightly steam your veggies.** From a nutritional perspective, you get the most nutrients from certain vegetables by minimally cooking them in the microwave or steamer. Eating veggies raw makes it harder for your body to absorb the nutrients. Carrots, broccoli, cauliflower and other high-fiber vegetables have vitamin C and other nutrients locked into the fiber, which your body doesn't digest. Cooking them lightly releases the nutrients from the fiber. Steam or microwave vegetables until they are fairly tender but still retain a bit of the crunch (overcooking destroys nutrients).

■ **Work in the five to nine daily servings wherever you can.** You don't need to eat a large piece of fruit or an entire salad to get a serving of vegetables. Slice a banana on your cereal and wash it down with a glass of orange juice. Cut some strawberries into your cottage cheese at lunch. Munch on some celery sticks as a snack. Spread a few leaves of spinach on your tuna sandwich. Sprinkle some grated zucchini in your lasagna. The toppings, fillings and flavorings added to your everyday meals will help you get your daily quota of fruits and veggies.

The Take-Out and Restaurant Conundrum

For most of us, eating healthy is a goal sandwiched between tending to our home, work, family and friends. In light of this, you are probably always on the lookout for the easiest and speediest ways for preparing meals. But when dining or ordering out, you could unknowingly veer off your weight loss plan.

For instance, restaurant and take-out fare is loaded with hidden fat and calories, according to the Center for Science in the Public Interest (CSPI), a nonprofit consumer health group in Washington, DC. The CSPI analyzed popular dishes at restaurants and delis throughout the country to find out just how many calories and fat grams the meals contain. What CSPI found would make you shudder: A typical serving of the popular Chinese dish kung pao chicken had almost as much fat as four McDonald's Quarter Pounders. A side order of Buffalo wings, the latest trend served at happy-hour havens, weighs in at 1,000 calories and 80 grams of fat. Even a measly tuna sandwich from a typical take-out deli has 716 calories and 43 grams of fat, more than half the fat you should have in an entire day.

Food as the Fountain of Youth

- If you're a coffee drinker, replace one of your daily cups with a strong cup of green or black **tea** (steep for at least two minutes to produce a good, strong brew). Also, have the cup of tea with a meal; it may neutralize some of the cancer-causing compounds you consume with other foods.

- If you're experiencing some of the symptoms of menopause (such as hot flashes), use **soy** products. Research shows that soy contains high amounts of phytoestrogens, plant hormones that act like estrogen in the body. Try soy milk in your cereal, make a soy and vegetable stir-fry or broil burgers made from soy.

- If you crave foods with flavor, use **garlic** liberally. A study at Pennsylvania State University found that regularly ingesting garlic may cut cholesterol levels. Other research has demonstrated that garlic can help combat mild high blood pressure and prevent dangerous blood clots that can lead to heart attacks. Bypass the salt shaker and sprinkle on fresh, chopped garlic for a **shot of flavor.**

All in all, the food detectives found that no type of cuisine is immune from menus packed with fattening appetizers, entrées and desserts. The good news is they also uncovered some simple ways to navigate your way healthfully through your maze of favorite restaurants.

- **Mind the munchies.** Before you even decide what to order, you're confronted with pre-dinner freebies such as tortilla chips, Chinese noodles and the bread basket stocked with butter. You can eat an entire meal's worth of calories and fat by mindlessly munching these foods while you wait for your meal to arrive. Take a small serving and then pass the basket to the other end of the table or ask the waiter to remove it.

- **Watch out for side dishes.** French fries, potato salad, onion rings and creamed spinach can weigh down an already fattening main course. Try to substitute more healthful side dishes such as an ear of corn, mixed vegetables, rice or couscous.

- **Use condiments wisely.** You can improve the nutritional profile of your meals by choosing low-fat condiments (ketchup, mustard, preserves, or salsa) instead of high-fat mayonnaise, sour cream or butter.

- **Ask for it on the side.** Request that salad dressings, sauces and spreads be served on the side so you can determine how much goes on your food. The same goes for cheese and bacon toppings. Chances are the amount you sprinkle on will be less than the fistful thrown on in the restaurant kitchen.

- **Have the cooking customized.** Restaurants can be quite accommodating when it comes to preparing a meal to your specifications. Chinese restaurants can steam instead of stir-fry; many French restaurants will broil instead of sauté. Mexican restaurants can replace refried beans with plain black or pinto beans and substitute salsa for guacamole. And almost any restaurant will honor a request for a plain broiled piece of chicken or fish. If you're ordering a sandwich, ask them to pile on the veggies and leave off some of the meat or cheese.

- **Do it family style.** Split an entrée with your dining partner and mix it with a side order of plain pasta, rice or bread or baked potato. (If you're eating alone, ask your waiter to wrap half your entrée for takeout before it is brought to the table.) The strategy is to weight your plate with low-fat starches, paring down the fat content of your meal without leaving you hungry.

- **Sidestep the sinful.** Certain dishes served in restaurants should be reserved for very special occasions. For instance, CSPI found a plate of fettucine Alfredo served in Italian restaurants had a whopping 1,498 calories and 97 grams of fat. Look out for any entrée that is obviously high in fat or calories. This includes any dish that is deep fried, is covered in pastry-shell crust, contains mostly cheese or is bathed in a creamy sauce such as hollandaise, béchamel or Alfredo.

REALITY CHECK

Choosing Vitamins

1. Steer clear of stores, catalogues or individual distributors that offer a single brand or seem to be pushing a house "favorite."

2. Keep an eye on the price. Quality vitamins aren't cheap, but they shouldn't break the bank. Be wary of catalogues touting "super-potent" supplements—they're overpriced and overhyped.

3. Don't fall for magic diet pills. Many health food stores have shelves lined with purportedly fat-burning, metabolism-upping, appetite-suppressing wonders. Though most are harmless, several are dangerous. Bottom line: save your money.

4. Make vitamins a daily habit. Many people mistakenly stop taking vitamins because they don't feel any healthier. Keep in mind: vitamins generally don't have an immediate impact on your health; they're designed to protect over the long term.

5. Follow directions. For maximum effectiveness and safety, don't take a bigger or smaller dose than the label specifies.

6. Get your medical advice from appropriate sources. The helpful cashier in the vitamin store is not a physician. If you have a medical question, see your doctor.

Where Does Salt Fit In?

The rule of sodium in the diet—and its effect on your health—has been a complex issue. Several new studies have shown that the amount of salt in your diet may not have the deleterious effect on your blood pressure or heart attack risk as was once believed. One study, from the Albert Einstein School of Medicine in New York City, looked at 1,900 men and found that those who consumed a low-salt diet actually had a higher rate of heart attacks than those who ate twice as much salt. A second study found that switching to a low-sodium diet does not seem to lower normal blood pressure. However, a third report published in the *British Medical Journal* reviewed data from more than 10,000 people and found that the more salt a person consumes, the higher his or her blood pressure is.

What should you do? For one thing, you shouldn't add more salt to your diet. Most Americans eat 10 grams of sodium per day—much more than the 2.4 grams per day that is recommended by most major health organizations. If you have hypertension, you still may be able to lower your blood pressure via reducing your sodium intake—as well as via exercise and medications. (A certain percentage of people are salt sensitive and can reduce their blood pressure and possibly lower their heart disease risk by lowering salt intake.)

Even if you don't have high blood pressure, too much salt in your diet can lead to other health woes:

■ **Sodium can rob your bones of calcium, increasing your risk of osteoporosis.** You lose around 23 milligrams of calcium for every teaspoon of salt you consume. It's recommended that you eat 800 milligrams of calcium per day, but you would need to eat around 1,500 milligrams to offset the amount of salt in a typical American's diet. Too much salt can also wreak havoc on potassium and magnesium levels.

■ **Excess salt may increase your risk of stomach cancer.** Sodium irritates the stomach lining, causing cells to reproduce more often, which might make it easier for cancerous cells to arise. (This may explain why stomach cancer rates are higher in Latin Americans, African Americans and Asian Americans, whose diets are high in salt.)

To reduce the salt in your diet, throwing out the shaker may not do the trick. The majority of the sodium consumed comes from processed foods such as tomato sauces, cookies, salad dressings and dried soups. Processed meats and cheeses and canned foods are also among the worst offenders. The best tack is to check food labels and watch your intake of processed food. Until more research is complete, aim to follow the American Heart Association recommendation and keep your sodium intake below 2,400 milligrams a day. And focus on eating plenty of potassium-rich foods, such as oranges, bananas and grapefruit, and magnesium-rich foods, such as milk, grains and legumes.

Something to Think About

The last time you tried to lose weight, what were your biggest obstacles to sticking with a plan? How might you overcome those obstacles?

. . . .

. . . .

. . . .

. . . .

. . . .

. . . .

. . . .

. . . .

. . . .

. . . .

. . . .

. . . .

. . . .

. . . .

CHAPTER five

A USER'S GUIDE TO CARBOHYDRATES

he low-fat craze of the nineties fueled our love affair with carbohydrates. Pasta, bread and fat-free cookies became politically correct foods, and we consumed them eagerly without a trace of guilt. But as the decade unfolded, the unthinkable occurred: as a nation, we did not slim down; in fact, we actually gained weight over the past few years. In the past decade, the average American adult has put on eight pounds.

Where did we go wrong? The problem may lie in ballooning portion sizes. Bagels, muffins and restaurant portion sizes have increased tremendously since the eighties. What's more, popular weight loss books gave us permission to eat more calories, as long as we drastically reduced the fat in our diets and, of course, increased the carbs.

Carbohydrates do contain calories, and enough of those calories can make you fat. That said, the carbohydrate equation becomes a bit more complicated. A whole host of foods fall into the category called "carbs": fruits, vegetables and sugar are the simple carbs, and pasta, bread and other starches are complex carbs. Simple or complex, your body breaks down all carbohydrates into a single sugar called glucose, which is used for fuel. But that's where the similarities between carbs end.

All carbohydrates aren't the same nutritionally. The high-fiber, low-sugar carbs (say, an apple) are a lot less calorie-dense than the low-fiber, high-sugar carbs (such as an apple strudel). Simple carbs don't require quite as much digestion, which is why you reap a quick energy boost after eating a sweetened cereal or drinking juice. Complex carbs generally take longer to break down into glucose, which means some are digested and absorbed rapidly, thus providing your body with a steadier stream of energy while helping you feel sated.

Carbohydrates, especially the unrefined complex varieties, also are a source of that all-important nutrient, fiber, an undigestible form of carbohydrate found only in plants. On average, Americans consume a mere 11 grams of fiber, or about half the recommended amount, per day. Fiber rich foods have been linked to a feeling of comfortable fullness, lower cholesterol and provide the bulk necessary for normal gastrointestinal function. What's more, the higher the dietary fiber in a food, the less fat and calories it contains, and the more slowly it is absorbed by the body.

Another reason carbohydrates may have become the nutritional darling of the nineties revolves around the oft-cited fact that carbohydrates contain four calories per gram or about half the calories of a gram of fat (or about 9 calories). Carbs and fat are stored differently in the body: Most fats head straight for adipose, or fat, tissue while carbs are stored, with a little help from insulin, in muscles and the liver as ready-to-use glycogen (the stored form of glucose), which supplies muscles with fuel for exercising. However, once you've hoarded enough glycogen, the body does store the remaining carb calories as fat. Because of this biological process, you can get fat by eating excess calories in the form of carbohydrates.

The Insulin Resistance Connection

In recent years, some diet gurus have adopted an opposite approach, promoting low-carbohydrate, high-protein (and thus high-fat) diets with the notion that carbs (such as pasta) are addictive and eating pasta will trigger a weight gain. This carbs-as-the-enemy premise can be traced to a condition known as insulin resistance—a precursor to diabetes that may affect an estimated 60 million Americans. According to proponents of the insulin resistance theory, a high-carbohydrate diet—or one that focuses on low-fiber, starchy carbs like potatoes and white bread and rice—creates a vicious nutritional cycle in certain individuals that ultimately leads to high blood insulin levels, carb cravings and weight gain. In order to break this cycle, the researchers contend people need to drastically cut back on their carbohydrate intake.

This carb-and-insulin theory of dieting has its roots in a study of over 65,000 women who were followed over six years. The women who ate a low-fiber, starchy diet (as well as high-sugar soft drinks) had over twice the rate of diabetes than those who ate a diet consisting primarily of high-fiber carbohydrates (including whole-grain cereals, fruits and vegetables). The researchers of the study surmised the diabetes link may be traced to the digestion rates of the carbs: Low-fiber, processed carbs are absorbed into the bloodstream more quickly than high-fiber carbs (fiber dulls the carb breakdown), triggering a surge in blood glucose and, in turn, insulin. Regularly eating a sugary, low-fiber high-carbohydrate diet may lead to a condition in which the body is less sensitive and more resistant to insulin.

Yet many nutrition experts contend that the link between carbohydrates, obesity and insulin resistance is not well established and, in many instances, obesity usually *causes* insulin resistance—not the other way around. In addition, most would agree that to reduce your risk for obesity and diabetes, a diet focusing on slowly absorbed, unrefined carbs (such as brown rice and whole-grain pastas and breads), in addition to regular exercise, has a potent and positive effect on weight and the body's sensitivity to insulin.

Can You Eat More and Truly Weigh Less?

Our love affair with carbohydrates was sparked by the popular theory that cutting fat to less than 10 percent of your total calories will allow you to lose weight without measuring portion sizes. Bread and pasta diets became popular in the early 1990s until people realized that they weren't losing weight. Weight loss experts who advocate drastically cutting fat also warn against gorging on processed starches like pasta and fat-free cookies and crackers. In other words, you have the green light to eat as many asparagus spears, carrot sticks and bowls of brown rice as you want—exactly what you've always known all along.

Unless you enjoy a Spartan lifestyle, you'll probably find the all-carb plan difficult to follow. (You're allowed only one nonfat dairy product each day and just a smidgen of mayonnaise, oil, butter or margarine.) Fortunately, you can still make carbs count toward your weight loss by making an effort to replace high-fat foods with high-fiber ones. Consider following these tips:

- **Use carbs as the main course.** Divide your plate into quarters. Fill three of the quarters with pasta, rice, vegetables or other low-fat carbs and allow your meat, chicken or fish "main" course to fill the other

quarter. Another option is to fill your entire plate with carbohydrates and use the protein as a seasoning: grilled chicken strips mixed with fresh veggies served over brown rice or meat sauce—instead of meatballs—to top whole-grain pasta.

- **Halve your normal portion of cheese or meat and replace with a carb filling.** Making a lasagna? Reduce by half the amount of ricotta cheese you would normally use and mix in chopped spinach or broccoli. For pizza, sprinkle on half your normal amount of mozzarella cheese and add sliced eggplant, tomato, mushrooms or your other favorite vegetables. Halve the amount of meat in your meatloaf and mix in rice, bulgur or crumbled pieces of day-old bread for a filling.

- **Use high-fiber foods as snacks.** When you have the afternoon or midnight munchies, think fiber. High-fiber foods (more than 3 grams per serving) add bulk that will fill you up for a few hours in between meals. If you're in the mood for something salty, shake a little salt on a celery stalk. Need something sweet? Peel the top off an apple and top with cinnamon, nutmeg and a teaspoon of sugar. Add two tablespoons of water, and microwave on high for four to eight minutes until tender. For something a little more substantial, top a piece of raisin bread toast with a spoonful of low-fat cottage cheese and a handful of raspberries.

- Keep portions in mind. You still can't go overboard on portions if you want to lose or maintain your weight. Estimate your portion sizes. One cup of cereal, spaghetti or vegetables is the size of your closed fist. One ounce of snack food is one handful of small foods like granola, or two handfuls of larger foods like pretzels.

Carbs as Energy

Besides the weight loss benefits, a big plus to increasing the carbs in your diet is that you'll feel better. High-fat meals take longer to digest, which can leave you feeling sluggish. Low-fat meals, on the other hand, work differently in the body.

Researchers from the Massachusetts Institute of Technology have shown that carbohydrates have serotonin-like effects on the brain. Serotonin is a feel-good protein that can relax you when you're feeling stressed. The right combination of protein and carbohydrates can leave you energized the entire day.

- Have a breakfast combo. Breakfast is essential to give you that morning boost, but eating a plain bagel or dry cereal is not the most efficient way to get it. Consider eating a combination of protein and carbs. Carbohydrates will smooth out the rough edges or stressed-out feelings you may have in the morning. Protein will help sustain blood sugar levels throughout the morning, keeping you energized. Smear low-fat cream cheese on your bagel, douse your cereal with skim milk or mix some fresh fruit with cottage cheese.

- Don't overdo lunch. Mid-afternoon is the time when you're most likely to feel a power shortage, and eating a high-calorie, high-fat lunch can compound your drowsiness. Aim for a light lunch that, like breakfast, contains a protein-carb combo: a grilled chicken breast on a multi-grain roll with a small side salad, or a piece of fruit sliced into low-fat yogurt and a cheese sandwich.

- Divvy up your meals. If you're plagued by many energy lags, try eating five to eight small meals, rather than three large meals, throughout the day. This approach also may offset episodes of ravenous hunger that can lead to a binge. Don't go more than four hours without eating. Supplement three small meals with energy-boosting snacks such as salt-free saltines topped with fruit spread, carrot sticks dipped in salsa or air-popped popcorn sprinkled with a teaspoon of Parmesan cheese.

- Make dinner a downtime. If you usually have a meal laden with chicken or beef, start reassessing your dinner. A protein-packed meal will rev you up when you need to be winding down. Increasing your servings of carbs (pasta, bread, whole grains) will make you feel calmer and help you sleep.

The Fiber **Count**

Check out this list of fiber-rich foods, and you'll see that upping your fiber is a snap.

20 Foods for a Fiber Fix	Total Fiber
8 ounces pear nectar	1.6 g
$1/2$ cup cooked broccoli spears	2.0 g
1 ounce dry-roasted peanuts	2.2 g
1 ounce banana chips	2.2 g
$3/4$ cup cooked instant oatmeal	2.8 g
$1/2$ cup boiled corn	3.0 g
1 cup cooked carrots	3.0 g
$1/2$ cup oat bran cereal	3.0 g
1 apple	3.0 g
2 slices whole wheat bread	3.2 g
$1/2$ cup blackberries	3.3 g
1 cup cooked long-grain brown rice	3.3 g
1 medium baked sweet potato, with skin	3.4 g
$1/2$ cup boiled brussel sprouts	3.4 g
$3^1/2$ cups air-popped popcorn	4.3 g
1 pear	4.3 g
1 cup black bean soup	4.9 g
$2/3$ cup raisins	5.3 g
1 cup baked beans	7.0 g
1 cup boiled lentils	7.9 g

* *Source: Bowes and Church's* Food Values of Portions Commonly Used, *16th edition.*

The Carbo-Loading Theory

Carbohydrate loading, eating a carb-rich meal at least 24 hours before a particularly strenuous workout, is a strategy that has been used by athletes such as marathon runners who require plenty of endurance. While nutritionists clearly approve of this strategy for professional athletes, the average exerciser need not take such a drastic approach. For a regular exerciser, a diet based on 55 to 60 percent of calories from carbohydrates will supply muscles with sufficient fuel. Also, during a moderate workout, muscles reap about half their energy from glycogen and the other half from fat.

If you're a regular exerciser, experts have outlined some general recommendations. First, about four hours before a workout, have a hearty sandwich, with a protein such as lean turkey, with a piece of fruit and a glass of milk. If you're eating two hours before a workout, snack on a bagel or crackers with low-fat yogurt or cheese. If you're grabbing something an hour or so before a workout, drink a glass of juice for quick energy.

High-Fiber Feasting

The key hidden asset found in many carbohydrates is fiber. Dietary fiber generally refers to the parts of fruits, vegetables, grains and legumes that can't be digested by your body. The two basic types of fiber are soluble and insoluble. Most high-fiber foods contain both, but one type is usually found in greater amounts and determines whether the food will be tough and chewy (as from insoluble fiber found in foods like popcorn and wheat bran) or gummy and mushy (from soluble fiber found in foods like oatmeal and kidney beans).

The Fullness Factor

It may not be as mouth-watering as a croissant, but a baked potato will stave off hunger longer than the fatty French roll. This is according to the Satiety Index devised by scientists at the University of Sydney in Australia. They based their finding on an experiment in which volunteers rated their hunger two hours after eating 240 calories worth of foods. The researchers determined that high-fiber foods, such as grains and vegetables, were significantly more filling than high-fat processed carbs like chips and cookies. The following list will give you a way to make food choices that will keep you feeling full for longer:

- Eat two slices of whole-grain bread instead of a croissant.
- Eat a handful of low-fat crackers instead of a bowl of corn flakes.
- Eat a baked potato instead of French fries.

Scientists have shown that soluble fiber can improve your cholesterol levels, whereas insoluble fiber can lower your risk of colon cancer and reduce the likelihood of constipation. A recent study found that the more fiber you consume, the lower your risk of suffering a heart attack. Every 10-gram increase in fiber results in a 20 percent decrease in risk. Most Americans consume only about 11 grams of fiber a day. The National Cancer Institute recommends eating 20 to 35 grams a day.

Following are some tips for increasing the amount of fiber in your diet.

■ **Tip #1:** Gradually increase the amount of high-fiber foods you eat. You may experience gas or bloating if you add fiber to your diet too quickly. Add 5 grams on the first day, give your body a day or two to adjust, and then add another 5 grams. If you experience gas, cut back a little and slowly add a few more servings. Also, try a variety of fiber-rich foods until you find some that do not cause problems. If you're having trouble tolerating high-fiber foods, liquid or tablet food enzyme dietary supplements can help—but don't make using them a habit. Taking the supplements makes the fiber easier to digest, but since insoluble fiber should be indigestible to produce health benefits, taking the supplements defeats the purpose of eating extra fiber.

■ **Tip #2:** Try to eat the same amount of fiber every day. Wide fluctuations in your day-to-day fiber intake can contribute to feelings of discomfort. Also, spread your high-fiber foods throughout the day, having, say, a bran cereal in the morning, some dried fruit for a snack and some vegetable soup for dinner.

■ **Tip #3:** Cook vegetables—it helps break down some of their gas-producing components. Just steam them lightly; overcooking them can destroy nutrients.

The PMS Connection

One of the biggest hurdles many women face on the road to weight loss may occur regularly each month, or that time when hormones are surging and you snap at coworkers, feel bloated and blue, and only want to eat chocolate.

The next time the premenstrual munchies strike, take heart in the fact that you burn 5 to 7 percent more calories between ovulation and menstruation than at other times of the month, according to research from the U.S. Department of Agriculture. This translates into about 100 extra calories per day and may explain why some women crave extra calories in the two weeks before their period.

Try these tips to alleviate PMS symptoms.

■ Blue Moods: Eating smaller, more frequent meals during the days before your period can help prevent mood swings. Eating carbohydrates, which boost your brain's level of serotonin, can ease blue moods once they strike, according to research conducted by

Massachusetts Institute of Technology scientists. Try a handful of animal crackers or low-sodium pretzels.

Other studies suggest that the endorphins released during exercise are also a great cure for the blahs. To get the hormone high, you need to work out intensely for at least 30 minutes. Try circuit weight training at your gym or jumping rope in front of the TV.

■ **Bloating:** To rid your body of excess water, build up a sweat. Do any activity that gets you vigorously moving. Rake some leaves; scrub your bathtub; play tag with your kids. Swimming a few laps is especially good at reducing bloating. Also, avoid high-sodium foods like tomato sauce, canned vegetables and soup mixes. Drinking six to eight glasses of water daily can ease swelling, too.

■ **Cramps:** Take an over-the-counter pain reliever containing ibuprofen (make sure you're not allergic), which seems to be more effective at inhibiting hormones that can cause cramps. Some experts think that calcium (found in low-fat and skim milk) can help ease cramping and mood swings.

■ **Anxiety:** Thirty minutes of fast walking, stair climbing or biking can help ease anxious feelings. Yoga may also be a good way to relieve PMS-induced stress. Try a technique called Bellow's Breath: Exhale for 10 short breaths. Take one final deep breath and then breathe comfortably, focusing on your breathing.

REALITY CHECK

Job De-stress

1. If you suddenly feel the urge to eat when you're busy, stop and ask yourself whether you're really hungry. Some people find that they snack just to give themselves a break.

2. If you've been sitting at your desk for more than a half hour, get up and walk around the office. Stroll by the fax or make photocopies.

3. If you've had a tense confrontation with a colleague, you may feel the need to swallow your anger—along with a lot of food. But a recent study found that the most effective way for women to dispel anger is to commiserate with a friend. Call a good listener on your lunch hour and vent.

4. Break up difficult projects with a few less challenging tasks. If you've been working for three hours on a presentation, push the project aside and open mail for half an hour. You'll feel less pressured and return to the project with a clearer head.

5. Give yourself a reasonable to-do list. Lists not only organize your time, they also help you keep track of your progress. Most people find it very satisfying to cross off tasks as they accomplish them.

6. Feel free to leave your office building for a breath of fresh air. If you feel guilty, remember that disappearing for a few minutes each day to gather your thoughts hardly qualifies as slacking off.

Sneaky Calorie Burning

1. *Do laundry.* Carrying load after load up and down stairs exercises your arm and thigh muscles. If you hang your wash out to dry, you'll get in some more arm strengthening.

2. *Walk the dog.* A brisk (12-to-15-minute-mile) half-hour walk or jog burns approximately 120 to 210 calories. If you're ready for more challenge, raise the intensity by going uphill.

3. *Green up your lawn.* Ditch that gas-guzzling, ear-split-ting power mower for an eco-friendly, old-fashioned push mower. Not only will you get a great cardiovascular workout, you'll preserve the peace and tranquillity.

4. *Make a clean sweep.* Sweeping stairs burns 50 to 70 calories per half hour.

5. *Go to the playground.* Climbing on the jungle gym is a great upper-body strengthener. You also can use other playground equipment like health club machines (provided there are no youngsters waiting): Use a see-saw as a tilt board for sit-ups or a ride on the swing to stretch your calves.

6. *Wash the car.* It doesn't sound strenuous, but toting buckets of water and vigorously polishing the car builds up biceps, as well as shine.

Something to Think About

What are your carb trigger foods? When do you tend to binge on them and why?

. . . .

. . . .

. . . .

. . . .

. . . .

. . . .

. . . .

. . . .

. . . .

. . . .

. . . .

. . . .

. . . .

CHAPTER SIX

THE FACTS ON FAT

t puts the smoothness in chocolate, the juiciness in a burger, the creaminess in cheese. Yet fat, alas, is a forbidden food, a pleasure we must resist. We've learned that we need to avoid it at all costs. We know that high-fat foods are a concentrated source of calories and can lead to obesity. We also know that too much fat can raise our risk for heart disease and certain cancers.

In light of this knowledge, zero fat has become a misconceived virtue. Evidence of our demand for no fat can been seen on supermarket shelves bulging with fat-free cookies, chips, dips, ice cream and cheese. There even is a fake fat called olestra. Available in certain brands of snack foods, olestra gives them flavor and texture similar to their fat-filled versions (albeit with some unsavory side effects—see box on page 61).

Still, we crave the real thing. Witness the demise of botched marketing products ranging from carob bars to McDonald's low-fat McLean burger, the burger that was sacked because people prefer Big Macs. Even more discouraging is the news that those who eat the most reduced-fat and nonfat foods actually consume more calories than those who don't use such products at all, according to a 1996 report based on five U.S. Department of Agriculture (USDA) food surveys.

Should you bother with low-fat? A small, but growing, anti-dieting movement is urging America to reclaim the pleasure principle, with pleasing the palate a first priority. A best-selling book by a respected Cornell University professor touts the virtues of fat, further fueling the backlash against fat-free foods.

What does this fat paradox mean for the average person who simply wants to create a healthier lifestyle? The key is to understand that just because a low-fat diet is good for you doesn't mean a no-fat diet is better. Also, you must learn to distinguish between the types of fat you eat and to eat fat in moderation.

A Word on the Basics

The types and amounts of fat vary from food to food, as do the health implications of consuming these different fats. By far the worst offenders, saturated fats (found in meat, poultry, dairy products, butter, eggs and tropical oils like coconut and palm) can clog your arteries by raising your LDL, or "bad," cholesterol levels. Hailed as the heroic fats, monounsaturated fats (in olive, peanut and canola oils, most nuts and avocados) tend to leave the "good" HDL cholesterol while lowering the "bad" LDL.

The polyunsaturated fats (sunflower, safflower, corn and soybean oils, found in some nuts and seeds, margarine and seafood) are somewhat of a mixed bag. These fats lower both LDL and HDL levels. The USDA finds that margarine is the leading source of polyunsaturated fat in our diets. The problem is that margarine contains varying amounts of trans fatty acids, a byproduct of the hydrogenation process (it makes liquid oils spreadable). Research suggests that trans fatty acids raise your LDL cholesterol levels about the same as saturated fat does. Unlike saturated fat, however, hydrogenated oils also may decrease your levels of HDL cholesterol.

One type of polyunsaturated fats that you should make an effort to include in your diet is essential fatty acids, found in Omega-3 and Omega-6 fatty acids. Researchers at Boston University Medical Center have found that a diet lacking these fatty acids can increase your risk of heart disease. Foods rich in Omega-3 include fish, walnuts, spinach, soybeans and canola oil. Vegetable oils (corn, safflower, etc.) are rich in Omega-6 fatty acids.

You should get no more than 30 percent of total calories from fat, according to the USDA's 1995 Dietary Guidelines for Americans. According to these guidelines, no more than 10 percent of your total calories should come from saturated fat, and no more than 10 percent should come from polyunsaturated fat. Nutrition experts have been debating the wisdom of this advice. Many feel that you should actually aim to get no more than 20 to 25 percent of your calories from fat. Other experts contend that if your diet is high in monounsaturated fats, you don't have to worry about going above the 30 percent mark.

Living the High (Fat) Life Healthfully

On a remote chain of islands 400 miles southwest of mainland Japan lives the world's healthiest people. On the archipelago called Okinawa, women live to an average age of 84-plus years (in contrast, American women live to an average age of 79). What's more, Okinawans manage to postpone for decades, or avoid altogether, osteoporosis, prostate and breast cancer, diabetes, heart disease and stroke, the illnesses that tend to drain an older individual's quality of life.

Surprisingly, the Okinawans do not subsist on a fat-free diet. Their fat intake is about 30 percent of their daily calories. What makes their diet different are the daily staples: seafood, tofu and a variety of fresh vegetables. Researchers believe the high amount of Omega-3 fatty acids in the seafood helps ward off heart disease. Tofu and other soybean products contain monounsaturated fats

(continued on page 62)

Fake Fat:
Does Taste Outweigh Risk?

After years of flavorless fat-free potato chips, dieters were hungry for a guilt-free chip that tastes like the real thing. Then, along came olestra (brand name Olean™), a fat substitute added to potato chips, tortilla chips and crackers. Studies at Pennsylvania State University found that volunteers couldn't tell the difference between regular potato chips and those made with olestra. Even better, the fake fat has no calories: A 1-ounce package of potato chips made with olestra contains no fat and 70 calories, compared to 10 grams of fat and 150 calories for regular potato chips.

Proponents of olestra claim it is superior to other fat substitutes because it can be used to fry foods, is indigestible and supplies the "mouth feel" of fat. Those who oppose olestra say this dieter's dream is really a nightmare. The Center for Science in the Public Interest, a nutrition health advocacy group based in Washington, DC, has warned that olestra robs the body of carotenoids, which reduce the risk of cancer and heart disease. Olestra also has been shown to cause some nasty gastrointestinal problems including gas, cramping and diarrhea. Furthermore, olestra can hamper absorption of fat-soluble vitamins in the body, although the product's manufacturer has enriched foods made with olestra with these vitamins.

Before olestra makes its way into dozens of snack foods, a new fake fat may be on the market. Biochemist George Inglett, at the U.S. Department of Agriculture, has created an imitation fat without olestra's unsavory side effects. Grinding up insoluble fiber from oats and corn, Inglett created a powder that when mixed with water becomes a creamy gel that can be mixed in hamburgers, cheese and baked goods such as brownies. Unlike olestra, however, the fake fat, called Z-Trim, can't be fried.

Z-Trim is still being tested in trials, and so far no one has reported any side effects. Since it is made from natural fiber that people normally eat, nutritionists don't expect to see any ill effects crop up in further studies. Products with Z-Trim should be introduced in grocery stores during this year.

and are particularly rich in isoflavonoids, estrogen-like compounds that may help deter osteoporosis by aiding in calcium absorption. Pork is also a part of the Okinawan's diet, but portions are a lot smaller than those typically consumed by Americans; it is generally used as a flavoring rather than as the main course.

On the other side of the world are the Mediterraneans. They consume about as much fat as we do, yet they also have a much lower rate of heart disease. Walter Willet, M.D., a professor of epidemiology and nutrition at the Harvard School of Public Health, has been on a mission to extol the virtues of the Mediterranean diet. He is striking out against the simplistic message that all fat is bad and no fat is good. Most of the fat in the Mediterranean diet comes from olive oil (rich in monounsaturated fats), whereas our diets tend to be richer in saturated fats and partially hydrogenated oils. Like the Asians, the Mediterraneans consume smaller portions of meat than Americans. They also dine on plenty of fresh vegetables, as well as fruits and whole grains (fat-free cookies and chips aren't features in their diets).

To incorporate ethnic diets into your eating plan, follow these tips:

- **Pile on the rice or pasta.** Starches are staples in the Asian and Mediterranean diets. For variety, try creamy risottos and orzos; mix grilled vegetables with fettucine and a little olive oil. Go for fragrant basmati, delicate jasmine or nutty brown rice to give new taste to your Asian cooking.

- **Shell out for the seafood.** It tends to be more expensive than meat or chicken, but it's hard to put a price tag on the omega-3 fatty acids that fish like salmon deliver to help keep your arteries clear.

- **Try cooking with tofu.** Dice it into stir-fries. Crumble it into soups. Mix it into lasagnas. It's adaptable to many dishes, and the soy compounds seem to fend off breast cancer and osteoporosis.

- **Use meat as a condiment.** Try linguine with tomato sauce and a handful of diced pancetta. Do a veggie stir-fry with a few small strips of beef for a seasoning. The key, however, is to keep meat portions small.

- **Vary your vegetables.** Asians and Mediterraneans owe their longevity in part to their taste for fresh, brightly colored vegetables. Most supermarkets now carry mustard greens and Chinese cabbage (bok choy), and artichokes, red peppers, eggplants, zucchini and leeks are always around through the seasons.

- **Reach for the spices.** The antioxidants in hot peppers and phytochemicals in garlic and ginger help neutralize and reverse some of the cell damage that can turn healthy cells into malignant ones. Several studies have also shown that eating two cloves of garlic a day can lower cholesterol levels by 10 percent. Health benefits aside, spices can add a kick to any dish.

How's Your Appetite?

If your primary concern is weight loss, you must be aware of the effect fat has on your health and your appetite. Fats are more calorically dense than carbohydrates (fats have about 9 calories per gram, whereas carbohydrates have about 4 calories) and, once in excess of your body's energy needs, are shuttled by your body directly into fat cells. In addition, more and more studies have been weighing in with the verdict that high-fat foods can alter your appetite and lead to weight gain. Research performed by John Blundell, Ph.D., a psychobiologist at the University of Leeds in England, has suggested that eating high-fat foods suppresses your appetite control while you eat the food, for the rest of the day and possibly even the day after.

In a theory he calls the "fat paradox," Blundell believes that high-fat meals block the release of biochemical signals that cause you to feel full and stop eating. The signals don't reach your brain quickly enough when you eat fatty foods, so you may eat more at one sitting. In one of Blundell's studies, obese adults were offered dinners and told to eat until they were full. Those who ate a low-fat, high-carbohydrate meal consumed 680 calories, but those given a high-fat meal consumed twice as much—1,350 calories. What's more, researchers from the University of Michigan have conclucded that some individuals are born with a "fat tooth," which prompts them to crave and consume high-fat foods.

Fat doesn't just release the dietary brakes. Overeating high-fat foods may occur due to what the researchers call "mouth feel"—they taste good, smell good and feel good in your mouth. Moreover, fatty foods are energy-dense, which means a lot of fat calories are contained in small portions of food. For instance, a 3.5-ounce cooked hamburger patty supplies 219 calories, of which 102 come from 11.3 grams of fat. A 3.5-ounce banana supplies 85 calories and virtually no fat, yet the quantity of food is the same.

Blundell emphasizes that not everyone eating a high-fat diet becomes obese. Still, it may increase your chances. In his survey that questioned the eating habits of 3,000 people, those who ate high-fat diets were 20 times as likely to be obese.

Losing Your Fat Buds

In order to lose your taste for fat, you must be willing to make dietary changes and to reeducate your taste buds. You also have to give yourself time to adjust to low-fat foods.

A study from Monell Chemical Senses Center in Philadelphia aimed to see how long it would take for people to adjust to low-fat diets. Richard Mattes, Ph.D., a researcher at Monell, put 27 healthy adults on one of three diets for 12 weeks. The first group was placed on a low-fat diet that excluded even low-fat versions of fats such as salad dressings and mayonnaise. The second group was given the same low-fat diet but permitted to eat reduced-fat food products. Group three could eat anything they wanted.

After tracking the eating habits of the participants for three months, Mattes discovered that

Butter vs. Margarine:
And the Winner Is...

The butter-versus-margarine debate has been batted back and forth among nutritionists for years. A review of recent research has added fuel to the discussions. According to an analysis from Harvard University, the trans fatty acids found in margarine are responsible for 30,000 deaths from heart disease in the United States per year. (Trans fatty acids are formed when vegetable oils are hardened into margarine.) Many health professionals dismiss this estimate as being too high. Yet, they still can't agree on whether the heart hazards of butter's saturated fat content are worse than the heart hazards caused by margarine's trans fatty acids. The important piece of information, though, is that you should minimize your intake of *both* trans fatty acids and saturated fat. Here's how:

1. *Reduce overall fat consumption.* Eating less total fat will generally mean eating less trans fatty acids and less saturated fat.

2. *Cut back on your consumption of processed foods,* which tend to be made with hydrogenated or partially hydrogenated vegetable oils (the lower on the list of ingredients these are, the better), a sign they contain trans fatty acids. These products may also be high in saturated fat.

3. *Choose a margarine on whose package liquid vegetable oil is listed before hydrogenated oil.* Your best bet is to stick with tub margarine—a "diet" or "light" brand—which generally has less trans fatty acids than stick.

4. *Whenever possible, use olive or vegetable oils instead of butter, margarine or shortening.* Use unsweetened fruit butters, which don't contain butter at all, instead of butter or margarine. Apple is the most common fruit butter flavor.

5. *Beware of commercially prepared fried foods.* Many restaurants and fast food chains use partially hydrogenated vegetable oils for frying.

the first group had come to prefer low-fat foods, whereas the second group showed no change. Group 2 still had a mouth-feel for fat (i.e., they still preferred whole milk to skim milk). Group 1 got used to low-fat foods and learned to prefer skim milk to whole milk because of the taste. The researchers concluded that you can lose your taste for fat in about two to three months, but you have to be vigilant about eating foods naturally low in fat (such as whole grains and vegetables) rather than reduced-fat or fat-free products. Also, if you start eating high-fat foods again, you will train your palate to prefer fat again.

How to Get the Fat Out

Anyone can buy a bag of fat-free chips in an attempt to eat less fat, but can you cook low-fat? It's actually easier than you think. You just need to be creative: broaden your use of certain foods and try a few new cooking techniques.

■ **Be choosy about cuts of meat, chicken and pork.** Meat can fit into a low-fat diet if you choose the right cuts and keep the portions small. Buy servings in no more than 4-ounce portions. Have your butcher chop large cuts into cubes and split them into small portions that you can store in your freezer. That said, choose the low-fat cuts of meat. With beef, look for extra-lean select grade and trim off any remaining fat (if you cannot find them in your supermarket, ask the butcher): a 3.5-ounce serving of broiled eye of round trimmed of fat has 3.5 grams of fat; top round has 4.0 grams; top sirloin has 5.6 grams; round tip has 5.9 grams; tenderloin has 8.8 grams. A 3.5-ounce serving of trimmed pork tenderloin has 4.8 grams of fat; ham with the bone has 5.5 grams and a chop (top loin) has 7.2 grams.

With chicken, a 3.5-ounce skinless breast has 3.6 grams of fat; a drumstick without the skin has 5.7 grams. (A thigh without the skin has 10.9 grams of fat, and a wing with the skin has a whopping 19.5 grams!)

■ **Make your cheese count.** Choose strong flavors that deliver more taste per ounce. For a creamy, Alfredo-like sauce, blend $1/3$ cup of grated Parmesan with one cup of low-fat cottage cheese thinned with a teaspoon or two of warm water. Use feta to flavor a spinach or tuna casserole instead of a high-fat melter like cheddar.

■ **Think tomato.** Tomatoes are loaded with vitamin C and lycopene, another disease-fighting antioxidant. They're low in fat, flavorful and versatile. During the summer months, you can make your own tomato sauces and spreads. Chop up tomatoes and flavor with basil, garlic, a touch of olive oil and a dash of balsamic vinaigrette for a savory pasta sauce. Or mix chopped tomatoes with fresh squeezed lemon juice, chopped onion, garlic and jalapeño for a salsa. Keep canned tomatoes on hand in the winter.

- **Roast or grill your vegetables.** Roasting provides even more intense flavor than steaming, because it concentrates the natural sugars in vegetables. Cut the fast cookers (onions, peppers, eggplant and zucchini) into large wedges and cut the slow cookers (carrots and other root vegetables) into small strips. Put the slow cookers in a roasting pan and sprinkle with a little salt, olive oil and fresh or dried herbs. Bake at 400 degrees for 40 to 50 minutes; halfway through, add the fast cookers. During the summer months, put the vegetables on skewers and grill for about 20 minutes.

- **Don't shy away from canned or frozen goods.** Although canned fruits and vegetables have lost valuable vitamins and minerals, canned beans, roasted peppers and pickled chiles are as or almost as nutritious as their fresh counterparts. Frozen vegetables retain most of their nutrients—just make sure that you don't overcook them when you prepare them. It's often best to steam them in a few tablespoons of water in the microwave until vegetables are crisp, not rubbery.

- **Defat your dairy.** Think of the obvious. For sauces, use low-fat or skim milk instead of cream. Thicken soups with a pureed potato instead of cream. Use nonfat yogurt or buttermilk in place of sour cream (or use nonfat sour cream).

Fat Calculations

The U.S. government recommends keeping your fat intake below 30 percent of your total calories and your saturated fat intake below 10 percent of your total calories.

If you eat this number of calories per day:	Total fat per day: (grams)	Total saturated fat per day: (grams)
1,600	53 or less	18 or less
2,000	65 or less	20 or less
2,200	73 or less	24 or less
2,500	80 or less	25 or less

*All fats are a combination of saturated, polyunsaturated and monounsaturated fatty acids. Each of these types of fats contains 9 calories per gram.

■ Change your oil. Although all vegetable oils are pure fat, a little can go a long way if it has a full-bodied flavor. Extra-virgin olive oil can be a staple for salad dressings; regular olive oil can be used for cooking. Sesame oil can liven up a stir-fry, and nut oils can add taste to pasta salads.

The Cholesterol Connection

Although high-fat foods often are high in cholesterol, the two do not necessarily go hand in hand. Cholesterol is found only in animal foods such as dairy products, egg yolks, organ meats, chicken, beef and shellfish. Processed foods made with vegetable or tropical oils can be high in fat and low in cholesterol, but these high-fat foods will contribute to high cholesterol levels. Saturated fat—not cholesterol intake—is actually the biggest culprit in an elevated cholesterol level.

A product labeled "no cholesterol" or "cholesterol free" by law must have less than 2 milligrams of cholesterol and 2 grams of saturated fat. (The National Cholesterol Education Program recommends eating less than 300 milligrams of cholesterol daily.) Unlike most fats, cholesterol is manufactured by your liver, so you don't need to get any from your diet. Unfortunately, you can't burn off cholesterol the way you can burn off fat; it isn't metabolized by the body. Moderate exercise, however, can raise your HDL (good) levels, so get moving!

Something to Think About

List your 10 favorite high-fat foods; alongside this list write down 10 lower-fat substitutes.

CHAPTER seven

IN SEARCH OF THE QUICK FIX

You know that controlling your portions and boosting your activity level are the only tried and true ways to lose weight safely and for the long term. Yet even the most savvy consumer can be tempted by the promises of a quick, painless fix: herbal weight loss teas, diet supplements, appetite suppressants and thigh creams all are hot sellers. What's the harm in trying them to get a jump start on weight loss? More than you think.

Lax Laws, Little Protection

In 1994, Congress passed the Dietary Supplement and Health Education Act, which created a new category, distinct from food or drugs, that is immune to almost all regulations by the Food and Drug Administration (FDA). The category includes vitamins, minerals, herbs, amino acids and anything else that was labeled a "supplement" before the rule took effect in October 1994.

This ruling means that products—including the hundreds of weight loss aids available in drug and health food stores—can appear on the market without any testing for whether or not their claims are true. The burden of proof for safety now lies with the FDA: It is the responsibility of this governmental agency to verify that a product is *unsafe*, rather than requiring the manufacturer to prove that a product is safe. The manufacturer must provide "reasonable assurance" that no ingredient presents a "significant or unreasonable risk of illness or injury."

A manufacturer also is given latitude with the claims it makes on a product's label. In the past, labels were not allowed to contain medical or scientific claims if the product had not been approved by the FDA. Today, labels can describe how a supplement affects the body's structure or function as long as claims are "truthful and nonmisleading." The label must state that the claims have not been reviewed or approved by the FDA, but this caveat may be in small type. It should be noted, however, that the Federal Trade Commission (FTC) regulates all drug advertising.

Although the laws have drastically altered the way supplements are marketed, most of us are unaware that the changes have taken effect. The Congressional Research Service has commented that most consumers still believe that "any product that appears in pill form has been reviewed for safety by the FDA, which is not true for supplements." With this in mind, here is a brief rundown of some popular diet aids. If you opt to try one, know that you are taking a gamble with a product that has not been thoroughly reviewed for safety or efficacy.

The "Natural" Cure for Obesity

Natural doesn't mean safe. No one knows if herbal weight loss remedies are safe because, unlike prescription weight loss drugs, herbal products are not reviewed by the FDA for safety. Since no one systematically tracks reactions from these products, it often takes several months or even years for the FDA to assess a product's harm and yank it from the market shelves.

Take the case of ephedra (also called ma huang), an herb commonly used in weight loss teas and supplements. Touted as a diet aid and energy booster, the active ingredient in ma huang increases metabolism by stimulating the thyroid. Ephedra works like an amphetamine; it gives you a natural high, so you don't feel like eating.

To date, a total of 400 adverse reactions, including hypertension, heart palpitations, nerve damage, muscle injury, stroke and memory loss, and 15 deaths linked to ephedra have been reported to the FDA. Formulas that contain caffeine can augment the herb's side effects. Herbalists warn that ma huang can be especially dangerous to those who have high blood pressure, heart disease or diabetes or who are pregnant. The FDA has issued a warning about the use of ephedra. And several states have already restricted or are moving to restrict sales of ephedra and products with the active ingredient ephedrine.

Weight loss teas can also contain laxatives and cathartics, which can induce water loss and bowel movements. Some main ingredients include senna (a laxative), comfrey leaves (another laxative), fennel seeds (a diuretic) and nettle leaves (which promotes urination and sweating). Drinking a single cup of these teas probably won't hurt you, but drinking a cup or two a day for several weeks can cause dehydration and possible mineral imbalances.

The Dangers of Diet Supplements

If herbs aren't your cup of tea, perhaps you've considered the fat-burning pills stocked on the shelves of your neighborhood drugstore. Chromium picolinate has been widely marketed as a weight loss aid that will target fat, spare muscle and increase your strength. Chromium helps bind insulin to cell membranes and thus may play a role in the way the body uses carbohydrates. Not surprisingly, most of the research backing up chromium's claims that it increases fat burning and speeds weight loss has been done by the manufacturer and has not been published in peer-reviewed medical journals. Independent, unbiased studies haven't been able to support the claims.

An advertisement for one chromium supplement claims that it is "all natural . . . designed to stimulate weight loss safely and effectively." But research suggests otherwise: A study from Dartmouth College found that chromium picolinate causes cellular changes in animals that are associated with cancer. Proponents of chromium supplementation have criticized the study, claiming the doses given were excessive and not applicable to humans. However, the study's author calculated that daily ingestion of 600 micrograms of chromium for five years may lead to chromium accumulation in tissues that approaches the levels studied.

A sister supplement to chromium is lecithin; for years, this substance has been touted as a supposed fat burner. Lecithin is a phospholipid, a fatlike chemical made by the body to transport fat-soluble vitamins. Proponents claim that dietary lecithin breaks up fats and flushes them out of the body, but no well-designed study supports this claim. Moreover, the body manufactures all the lecithin it needs, so there is no such thing as a deficiency. Taking a short-term high dose (or as little as 2 grams), however, can cause excessive sweating, intestinal distress and drooling. Long-term use of high doses can cause depression and nervous system disorders.

OTC Diet Pills

While the FDA doesn't stringently regulate herbal products, it does keep a close eye on over-the-counter (OTC) diet drugs that were once sold only by prescription. Despite this, many of these

Self-Hypnosis 101

Although the idea of hypnosis conjures up images of swamis with bad mustaches and dangling pocket watches, some experts contend that the concept behind hypnosis, or completely relaxing your body and mind, can be a powerful tool if you're trying to lose weight, reduce stress or change your habits. Although there is no way to regulate those who claim to administer hypnosis, consider the following harmless, cost-free technique to get in tune with your body:

1. **Create an anchor.** The next time you feel full, press your fingernail into a specific fold of skin on a knuckle. (Remember which knuckle and which fold of skin.) When you need some willpower, take a deep breath, sigh loudly, and press the fingernail back into that fold of skin. You'll bring back the memory of the feeling of fullness and satisfaction.

2. **Rehearse for good health.** Imagine yourself as already fit, stress-free or at your weight goal, and create a detailed picture of your new self—everything from what you're wearing to how you're behaving. When the picture is very clear, step into it. Look out through the person's eyes so that you see what your future self is seeing, hear what your future self is hearing and feel what your future self is feeling.

3. **Practice relaxation.** Lie down. Starting with your feet, tense and relax each part of your body, working your way toward the top of your head. When you've completely relaxed your body, concentrate on your breathing. With each exhalation, feel the pounds leaving your body.

diet aids have come under fire for causing severe reactions in unsuspecting users. The pills contain the ingredient phenylpropanolamine (PPA), which is used in over 100 OTC and prescription cough and cold medicines and diet aids. The fine print on package labels says that PPA has been linked with such side effects as increased blood pressure, irregular heartbeat and, in rare cases, seizure and stroke. The label warns that anyone with high blood pressure, diabetes or a heart condition consult a doctor before taking such medication.

Diet aids usually contain 75 milligrams of PPA in time-released form, which has been found to increase blood pressure only slightly. Research suggests that blood pressure is substantially elevated by 150 milligrams of time-released PPA or 75 milligrams of immediate-released PPA. A study published in 1990 in *The Journal of American Medicine* documented 142 cases of side effects since 1965 that have been attributed to PPA. At least ten of the reactions were strokes, some resulting in death.

Pharmacologists say medications containing PPA are generally safe if used for short periods of time, such as a few days. However, people are often less careful when it comes to OTC products. They may take high doses or combine them with other drugs, including antidepressants and caffeine, which can worsen PPA's effects. If you decide to use drugs containing PPA, read the label carefully: It will tell you the amount of PPA in each dose, whether it's time- or immediate-released and what other drugs can cause dangerous interactions.

Herbs: How to Play It Safe

The Weight Watchers position on weight-loss drugs—OTC and prescription varieties—is clear. Taking these drugs is a personal decision you should make with the help of your primary care provider. If you are considering using herbs as a way to lose weight or boost your health, consider the following points.

1. **Try the proven first.** Before buying a supplement to lose weight, first consider making lifestyle changes: Eat more sensibly by cutting portions and fat, and increase your level of physical activity.

2. **Get the go-ahead from your doctor.** You may feel silly or embarrassed, but calling your doctor before you take a diet supplement will safeguard your health. Many ingredients in the supplements can interact dangerously with other medications or cause adverse effects if you have certain medical conditions. Other products, like ma huang, are so dangerous that no one should take them. Also, your doctor may recommend a conventional weight loss aid that you can try instead.

3. **Avoid herbal weight loss products altogether if you're pregnant or nursing.** Firstly, you shouldn't be trying to lose weight if you're pregnant. More importantly, no one knows the risks these unregulated products can have on a fetus or baby.

4. **Check the warnings.** Do you really want to take something that lists a potential danger

on the label if you know it is not regulated by the FDA? Read the indications carefully on the package and related material that may be in the pharmacy or health food store. Even if you feel the herb is safe, start with small doses. Also, realize that manufacturers are not required to put warnings on the label for most herbs and diet supplements.

5. **Look for the word "standardized."** When herb products claim to be standardized, the manufacturer is claiming to have the same potency of herbs in every dose. Although the manufacturer doesn't have to back up this claim, at least you have a fighting chance of not getting a toxic dose from one pill or tea bag.

6. **Stick with one-ingredient supplements.** Combinations can be more potent, and the combined actions of various ingredients can be difficult to sort out.

7. **Stop immediately if there's a problem.** Familiarize yourself with the potential side effects before you take a supplement. If you have any adverse reactions, stop immediately and call your doctor. For instance, if your heart begins beating rapidly, you may be having a reaction to the stimulants in the weight loss product. If you feel woozy or light-headed, you may be dehydrated from the diuretics. If you think a product has harmed you or made you ill, the FDA advises that you call your doctor, who should

then call the FDA's MedWatch hotline for professionals to report adverse effects.

Quitting Smoking and Weight Gain

The fear of gaining weight is a primary reason many smokers are wary to quit. While it's true that kicking the habit can lead to some weight gain, the health gains far outweigh the extra poundage. People would have to put on 100 pounds to offset the health benefits of quitting, and the average post-quit weight gain is between only four and 10 pounds.

The reason smokers tend to be thinner is because the nicotine in cigarettes speeds up metabolism. So smokers who quit the habit without changing food intake can expect to gain some weight. Another reason former smokers may gain weight is that they replace one bad habit (smoking) with another (overeating).

Studies have shown that most people who try to quit smoking and lose weight at the same time will not be successful in either endeavor. In other words, put off losing weight until you feel comfortable handling stressful situations as a nonsmoker. Even then, you should lose weight gradually—no more than a pound or two a week. If you are using nicotine replacement therapy and are concerned about weight gain, you may be better off with the gum than with the patch. People chewing the gum tend to gain less weight than those on the patch.

If you still aren't convinced that quitting smoking is worth the weight gain, remember that

Thinner Thighs **from a Jar?**

Rub a cream on your thighs and watch the spongy cellulite melt away—no dieting or exercise required! Who can resist? There are a slew of thigh creams on the market claiming to transform thick thighs into a svelte lower body, but most have no research to back up their claims.

There is, however, one cream that has been thinning thighs in clinical trials. Researchers at Harbor-UCLA Medical Center in Torrance, California, have been testing a substance containing the ingredient aminophylline, an asthma medication. Twelve women applied a teaspoon of the cream to one thigh and a placebo cream on the other five days a week for six weeks. The aminophylline-treated thighs lost an average of 1.5 centimeters, while the other thighs remained the same.

Although these results seem promising, there are still a host of unanswered concerns, say weight loss experts. If you stop using the cream, will the lost inches return? Is fat being lost, or it is some other substance, such as water? If fat is indeed released into your bloodstream, will it clog your arteries?

Weight researchers question the validity of the studies themselves, since they were performed on only a few women for a short period of time. What's more, the technique of measuring a woman's thigh with a tape measure can be subjective. The tape measure can be pulled tighter to yield a smaller measurement. Also troubling is that the studies have been conducted by only one group of researchers and haven't been confirmed by others.

For its part, the FDA is keeping watch over thigh creams containing aminophylline. If manufacturers decide they want to market the product as an over-the-counter drug, they will need to do more research on the potential health risks and obtain approval from the FDA. In the meantime, the cream is being marketed as a cosmetic, so its developers can sidestep the drug approval process.

smoking can cause brittle nails, yellow teeth and wrinkles—which are far less attractive than a few extra pounds!

Today, there are a number of options if you're ready to quit smoking: *Nicotine Replacement Therapy* (available via a patch, gum and nasal spray), which delivers small, controlled doses of nicotine and has anywhere from a 20 to 45 percent success rate; *scheduling,* a method outlined in the *Journal of Consulting and Clinical Psychology* that involves a five-week program designed to gradually wean you off cigarettes; and *cold turkey,* or immediate abstinence. The latter method, the number-one choice of most smokers, can be the most physically trying, since nicotine withdrawal symptoms—including headaches, fatigue and the jitters— surface immediately and can last an average of three weeks, approximately the time it takes the body to rid itself of most of its nicotine.

Once you pinpoint a method, consider the following helpful tips:

- **Rid the house of all smoking accoutrements.** Discard the lighters, ashtrays and any leftover packages or cartons of cigarettes.

- **Steer clear of smoky environments.** These include smoke-filled bars, restaurants and houses of friends or acquaintances who smoke.

- **Break your smoking habits.** If you tended to smoke while talking with your neighbor in the kitchen, move the conversation to the porch or living room. Changing a familiar smoking locale can help.

- **Find alternative hobbies.** Smoking can be tremendously time-consuming. Look for a healthy substitute, such as walking around the block, every time you crave a cigarette. Or learn or rediscover a hobby that can keep your hands busy, such as knitting, crocheting, writing or painting.

- **Reward yourself.** Smoking is an expensive habit. Place every dollar you don't spend on cigarettes in a jar. After a few months, add up your cash and treat yourself to something soothing, such as a day at a spa, a relaxation tape, a massage or a one-on-one yoga session.

Something to Think About

Take a health inventory. Call your physician and request the results of any recent medical tests (e.g., blood pressure tests, blood work, EEG, etc.). Ask him or her about starting a family medical tree to assess your risks for specific illnesses.

part 3

ONE BODY, ONE MIND

CHAPTER eight

BECOMING FIT

ooks, as you know, can be deceiving; after all, some slim people can't jog a mile. Nowadays, you probably know that being fit involves more than just body size, but you may not know what makes for a truly fit body. After all, fitness guidelines have evolved. For example, you've heard that your Body Mass Index (BMI) is a better measure of how healthy your weight is than the numbers reflected on the scale. Similarly, the current definition of a fit body has to do with more than simply having a sleek shape.

In truth, there are no one-size-fits-all standard measurements or form-fitting molds for a fit body: In real life, healthy bodies come in many shapes and sizes. But fit bodies do have these elements in common: cardiovascular/respiratory fitness, muscular strength and endurance and flexibility, as well as a relatively low percentage of weight from body fat.

When it comes to exercising for health, even lower levels of physical activity, such as moderate walking, have been shown to boost the function of your immune system, improve blood cholesterol readings and lower your risk of heart disease, among other health benefits. If you want to reap the maximum fitness rewards from exercise, however, the intensity, type and frequency of activity play a larger role. To achieve a truly fit body, according to the current definition, the exercise prescription involves cardio-respiratory (a.k.a. aerobic) training, strength training (also called resistance training) and flexibility exercises.

Truth be told, incorporating all three of these elements into your lifestyle isn't going to be a breeze. But it's not as tall an order as you might think, either. The latest guidelines from the American College of Sports Medicine suggest that healthy adults exercise aerobically three to five days per week for 20 to 60 minutes at a time and perform strength-training exercises at least twice a week. You can easily fit in flexibility exercises that stretch all the crucial spots before or after either type of workout. All it takes is a few extra minutes.

How Fit Are You Now?

Before starting on your fitness program, it's a good idea to assess where you stand on the fitness ladder so you will be able to formulate appropriate goals and see measurable progress along the way—both of which can keep you motivated. Then take some time to do the following fitness trials and log the results in an exercise journal. One point to keep in mind: quality, not quantity, is key; concentrate on maintaining proper form and positioning.

- **Aerobic capacity:** Mark off a mile—it could be four laps around a standard track or a mile on neighborhood streets—and clock how long it takes you to walk the distance briskly, but comfortably (you should be perspiring mildly and still able to carry on a conversation). Record the results, as well as how you feel afterward. Are you short of breath? Do your legs feel tired or achy?

- **Muscular strength:** See how many abdominal crunches you can perform maintaining the correct position before fatigue sets in (physical signs of fatigue include a burning sensation in your muscles and a difficulty in maintaining correct form). Record the results. Now see how many modified push-ups you can do correctly. Record those numbers.

- **Flexibility:** After you've warmed up properly (a five-minute jog in place should do), test your elasticity by sitting on the floor with your legs straight out in front of you, several inches apart. Place a yardstick between your legs, with the zero-end at knee level; put one hand on top of the other and slowly stretch forward (don't bounce!), sliding your fingertips along the yardstick, as far as you can. Record their resting spot to the nearest half-inch.

Once you know your starting points for these three components, you can map out appropriate fitness goals. The idea isn't to try to become an aerobics queen or a musclehead in a week or hit a specific number. Instead, you should plot out gradual goals that are realistic and attainable and designed to improve your overall fitness levels. For example, if it took you 20 minutes to walk a mile, try to shave one or two minutes off your time. If you can now perform five push-ups correctly, set your sights on working up to eight. By devising smaller goals, you'll be setting yourself up for success and minimizing the chances of injury or burnout. You may want to repeat these trials periodically, say, once a month, to gauge your improvements in each area.

You've probably read the recommendation to consult a physician before beginning any exercise program before. It's sound advice: Getting a check-up can unmask health conditions that can affect the safety or intensity of your exercise program. So get the green light from your doctor before getting started. If you're in good health, it won't have been a waste of time; you'll have peace of mind.

REALITY CHECK

Looking Good, Working Out

1. Tie a sweatshirt around your waist or shoulders to camouflage trouble zones (it also comes in handy if the temperature drops).

2. If your hair is long, try a half-up, half-down hairstyle. Pull hair from tip of ears and above to the back of head and fasten with a clip. Hair will be out of the face without a harsh, slicked-back look.

3. Choose trim socks instead of bulky ones. They keep feet cool and don't draw attention to your bottom half.

4. Ditch the sweatband. They look dated and can wreak havoc on your skin.

5. Stick with solids. Patterns such as stripes, dots and florals don't do anything for most figures. Subtle, solid colors in soft jersey are comfortable and flattering.

6. Don't wear makeup. Even waterproof makeup that won't end up a smeary, streaky mess looks out of place at the gym— remember, you're there to sweat, not pose.

How to Get Your Body Moving

Without question, aerobic exercise is the key form of exercise for losing weight. "Aerobic" simply means that oxygen is required for you to perform the exercises: Your heart pumps harder, delivering blood and oxygen throughout your body, burning body fat and calories for fuel. Not only does this condition the heart, lungs and blood vessels—which can lower your risk of heart disease and increase your life expectancy—but aerobic exercise also speeds up your metabolism while you're exercising and for a few hours afterwards which can help you shed pounds. Experts now recommend that you exercise aerobically three to five times per week for 20 to 60 minutes at a stretch. You can perform any activity that uses large muscle groups and requires oxygen— walking, hiking, jogging, bicycling, cross-country skiing, dancing, jumping rope, rowing, stair climbing, swimming, skating and so on— as long as you can sustain it for the recommended duration. (For details about these activities, see the next chapter.)

As far as intensity goes, you should be exercising at 50 to 80 percent of your maximum heart rate—what's often called your target zone— to obtain fitness and weight loss benefits. If you exercise at a lower intensity, you can still get the weight loss results but the fitness effects will be less. To calculate your maximum heart rate in beats per minute, subtract your age from 220. Now multiply this number by .5 to define your lower threshold for aerobic exercise; to gauge your upper limit, multiply your maximum heart rate by .8; this is the window of intensity you should aim for.

How can you tell when you've reached your target zone? The best way is to do a pulse-check on your wrist, counting the number of beats in 15 seconds; then multiply the result by four to get your heart rate in beats per minute. By taking an exercise break to do a pulse check every once in a while, you'll be able to gauge how hard your body is working (take your pulse rate immediately after you stop). Generally, when you are exercising in your target zone, you should be able to carry on a conversation, but it shouldn't be effortless.

Before exercising, be sure to spend five to ten minutes warming up, walking or biking at an easy pace, and perform some gentle stretches. Then exercise in your target zone for 20 to 60 minutes and end your workout with a five-minute cool-down period, in which you downshift into a slower, gentler pace to ease your body into a more relaxed mode. Afterward, spend a few more minutes stretching to prevent soreness.

Deciding when to exercise is a matter of personal choice. But some studies have found that people who exercise in the morning are more likely to stick with it, possibly because there are fewer distractions; later in the day the excuses can mount up. Another plus: If the mood-enhancing effects of exercise kick in first thing in the morning, you'll be on an even emotional keel to start your day—which can help you stay on track with your eating plan, as well.

On those days when you just don't have time for a full-fledged workout, remember that every bit of aerobic activity counts. There are plenty of easy ways to fit more movement into your life throughout the day. Take the stairs instead of the elevator at work. Walk or ride your bike to do errands. Play tag with your kids. Ride a stationary bike while watching TV. Walk your dog. All of these activities will burn extra calories and help you lose weight.

How to Muscle Up Without Bulking Up

Developing muscular fitness involves both strength and endurance. It's not enough to be able to bench press a certain amount of weight; how many times you can lift or how long you can hold that weight are also important considerations. If the idea of developing bulging muscles is deterring you from starting a strength-training program, don't let it: Most women will not develop large muscles through weight-lifting; it's simply not in their genetic makeup—or their hormones, to be more precise. Testosterone, of which men have much higher levels, is needed for muscles to become significantly larger. Adding lean muscle mass will, however, provide you with a variety of health benefits. Strength training can help prevent bone loss and protect against osteoporosis, improve your posture, boost your energy and help you perform everyday tasks more comfortably. It will also give your muscles greater definition.

What's more, adding muscle mass through resistance, or strength training (the terms are synonymous), can boost your metabolism. Not only will you burn extra calories while working out and afterward (experts call this the "afterburn" effect), but adding muscle will help you burn calories faster even at rest. In fact, maintaining muscle mass is one of the secrets to weight stability. Although many people who gain weight as they get

Gym **Smarts**

1. Join the gym closest to your home or office—it's always easier to get into the workout habit if the gym is conveniently located.

2. Use walking as a way to extend your workout time outside the gym. For instance, when you can spend only 20 minutes at the gym, walk later that evening to up your exercise.

3. Pare down your makeup and hair routines. Consider a short haircut and minimal makeup.

4. Do sit-ups, push-ups and other exercises that require no equipment at home. Use gym time for weight training, classes or aerobic machines.

5. Visit the gym during "off-peak" (mid-morning and afternoon and after 8:00 in the evening) hours as much as possible.

6. Keep a gym bag of sneakers, exercise clothing and a combination lock packed and ready to go. If possible, keep one at work and one at home.

7. Use the gym as a social club, a place to meet with friends or colleagues.

8. Splurge for several sessions with a personal trainer. If money is tight, schedule one session and ask for a tailor-made fitness plan.

9. Use the gym for recreation as well as exercise. If there is a basketball court, schedule a game with friends.

older blame those extra pounds on a declining metabolism (it is true that your metabolism can slow down as you age), researchers at the University of Vermont in Burlington found that a lagging resting metabolic rate—the energy your body expends to sustain such basic functions as breathing and heartbeat—is due primarily to a loss of muscle mass, rather than to a direct or inevitable metabolic meltdown as we age.

Beginning in the mid-20s, the average adult loses half a pound of muscle every year, or five pounds of muscle per decade. This relatively small number becomes significant because each pound of muscle burns 35 calories a day when you're resting; by comparison, a pound of body fat burns only two calories per day when you're not exercising. Muscle simply requires that much more energy for maintenance. So by adding muscle mass (through strength training) and burning body fat (through aerobic exercise), you'll burn calories faster all day long, which will help you lose excess weight.

Strength training doesn't have to be hard or time-consuming. Research has found that performing one set of strength-training exercises is effective in building strength. To add muscle, all you need to do is one set of strength-training exercises, consisting of eight to 12 repetitions, for each major muscle group in the legs, arms, back, chest and abdomen two or three times per week. You should use enough resistance that your muscles feel fatigued, but not in pain, afterwards. You can use free weights, weight machines (such as Nautilus or Cybex) or exercise bands (or rubber tubing) for these exercises, depending on what appeals to you. The good news is that progress comes fairly quickly: Research suggests the average adult can expect a 25 to 30 percent improvement in strength within a few months of starting a resistance-training program.

How to Stretch Your Limits

It's often the forgotten fitness factor, but developing and maintaining flexibility also is important for a fit body, especially as you get older. In fact, loss of flexibility is another hazard associated with aging: As you age, you naturally lose flexibility as muscle fibers and tendons shorten. As a result, your body doesn't move as freely, which can make you uncomfortable and more prone to injuries, particularly in the lower back. Although you can't stop the aging process, you *can* prevent some of its muscle-restricting effects through stretching. It's best to target the major tight spots: the upper and lower back and shoulders, the chest, the quadriceps and hamstrings, the calves and the hips.

Before stretching, spend five to ten minutes walking, jogging or riding a stationary bike at a gentle pace to raise your body temperature and warm up your muscles, making it safer to stretch them. (Stretching a cold muscle increases the chances of tearing those fibers.) When performing each stretch, stretch to the point where you feel mild tension, not pain, in your muscles and hold for 30 seconds. This is called static stretching, and it's the safest method. Ballistic stretching, where you bounce to stretch a muscle, is dangerous because it rapidly places excessive tension on the muscle, which can cause injury.

A Sample Workout

Yes, working out five days a week sounds like a lot, but if you really want to lose weight or are truly sincere about fitness, four to five days is a must. With the three fitness factors in mind, here is what a sample workout schedule for a week might look like (of course, don't forget to begin each session with a warm-up and end with a cool-down):

> **Monday:** Brisk walking, jogging or stair-climbing for 30 minutes; 15 minutes of stretching
>
> **Tuesday:** Strength-training exercises for 20 minutes; 15 minutes of stretching
>
> **Wednesday:** Cycling, cross-country skiing or aerobic dance for 30 minutes; 15 minutes of stretching
>
> **Thursday:** Strength-training exercises for 20 minutes; 15 minutes of stretching

Friday: Brisk walking, jogging or stair-climbing for 30 minutes; 15 minutes of stretching

Saturday: Strength-training exercises for 20 minutes; swimming, skating or rowing for 30 minutes

Sunday: You could take the day off. Or you could get physical for the sheer fun of it—by playing softball or tennis, hiking with friends or family or going for a leisurely bike ride.

How to Hire a Personal Trainer

They used to be exclusively for the rich and famous. Nowadays personal trainers are an integral part of the national fitness scene, offering convenience, privacy, tailored motivation and customized exercise programs. But it's important to choose a trainer carefully. Just as you wouldn't trust your health care to just *any* doctor, you shouldn't put your exercise program in the hands of just *any* personal trainer.

As a starting point, you may be able to get referrals from friends, your doctor, local health clubs or sports medicine clinics. Once you've collected the names of a few candidates, check out their educational and training backgrounds: There's no single, standard form of qualification that's required, but many industry experts say a qualified trainer should have a college background in exercise science or physical education and be certified by the American Council on Exercise (ACE), the Aerobics and Fitness Association of America (AFAA) or the American College of Sports Medicine (ACSM). You'll also want to make sure the trainer has professional liability insurance, in case you get injured.

Before creating a program, a personal trainer should review your health and exercise history as well as any injuries or physical limitations you may have. Most of all, he or she should design a program that's tailored to your needs and goals. Keep in mind that prices vary considerably—from $25 to more than $100 per hour, depending on the trainer's experience, the location and the workout design. Once you've narrowed your choices, ask a prospective trainer for the names and phone numbers of a few clients and call them. Ask how satisfied they were with their training, whether they accomplished their fitness goals and whether the trainer was punctual, prepared, courteous and attentive.

Schedule an initial meeting with a promising trainer to gauge the rapport. One of the most basic, and important, factors in a successful match is whether you like each other. Will this trainer motivate you with positive feedback? Is he or she flexible in terms of scheduling? Are your exercise styles in synch? Do you think you'll get along workout after workout? Is this someone you can talk to openly and honestly? Do you think the trainer will be genuinely committed to helping you reach your goals? If the answers to all these questions are *yes*, you have probably found a good fit.

Make It Social

Just as many people find it easier to achieve weight loss success through group programs, working out with a spouse or a buddy can increase the likelihood that you'll stick with an exercise regimen. In a recent study, researchers at Indiana University found that 94 percent of married couples who enrolled in a fitness program together were still going strong after a year; among married people who exercised on their own, by contrast, only 57 percent kept at it a year later. If exercising with your spouse isn't an option, don't sweat it: Choose a friend, neighbor or relative you enjoy being with and feel comfortable talking to and who shares your commitment to getting fit.

To maximize your chances of success, formalize a plan from the beginning: Decide when and how frequently you'll exercise together and how long each session should last, and create a contingency plan in case one of you can't make it (should you go solo or arrange a make-up session?). If you feel your motivation waning at any point, let your partner(s) know what kind of encouragement would help you. Open communication is one of the keys to making the buddy or group experience work.

How to Choose a Health Club

If you've decided to go the health club route, selecting one can be a daunting proposition. As with most significant purchases, it's smart to shop around and check out the options. Make sure the club offers your activity of choice. Visit during the hours you're likely to exercise so you can gauge the club's crowd condition. Keep this checklist in mind as you make your tour:

- Given the facilities, the atmosphere, the equipment and the clientele, is this a place where you'd feel comfortable working out? Is there a good variety of equipment? Are staff members friendly and helpful?

- Is the equipment state-of-the-art and well maintained? Do the facilities seem clean?

- Do instructors have current certification from a nationally recognized organization such as ACE, AFAA or ACSM? Is there at least one CPR-trained employee on duty at all times? Does the club have a well-stocked first-aid kit that's easily accessible?

- Does the club offer a free orientation and instruction session on how to use equipment for new members? Are trainers required to follow or chart your progress? Also, ask members if they are satisfied with the facilities and their maintenance.

◼ Is there ample parking? Is child care available if needed? Are the club's hours convenient to your schedule? Also, are there several branches of the club, and if so, does your membership allow you to visit the other clubs free of charge?

◼ Has everything that's been promised to you verbally been put in writing? Before signing the contract, make sure you understand the terms, the fees and the duration of the agreement. (Agreeing to a lifetime membership is a bad idea, since this generally refers to the club's lifetime, not yours.) You should also have the right to cancel a membership agreement and obtain a full refund for at least a few days after signing up.

Great Gadgets
for Good Workouts

1. *Exercise mat:* A must for floor exercises like sit-ups or leg-lifts, an exercise mat is a great investment that provides comfort plus protection.

2. *Walking weights:* Light hand weights add resistance to any aerobic workout (try them in step class). Plus they double as free weights for a great upper-body toning routine.

3. *Body tube:* This tube provides extra resistance for almost any body-toning movements. Stirrup handles make for easy grasping and prevent slipping.

4. *Dyna bands®:* Resistance bands of varying intensity help firm, tone and stretch muscles. Use them to hold feet together while doing sit-ups or add resistance to leg lifts or arm stretches.

Something to Think About

Who has a body you admire, and why? Also consider whose exercise abilities you admire and why. Be as specific as possible. Now consider how this person's shape is similar to and different from yours. How realistic is it for you to achieve that body or that level of fitness? If you had to choose which fitness goals are realistic for you to develop (considering your current level), which would they be?

CHAPTER nine

WHO'S AFRAID OF EXERCISE?

does the thought of exercising conjure up images of sweaty, Lycra–clad hardbodies trying to outdo each other at a too-loud gym? Or perhaps the idea of joining an aerobics class makes you worry about looking like a klutz? If so, you're not alone: Many people think they'll be laughed at when they try new activities; in turn, that fear of looking clumsy or inept often prevents them from trying experiences they might enjoy.

Indeed, many people who are overweight are hesitant to exercise because of embarrassment, so they often put off beginning an exercise plan until they've lost a certain amount of weight. But as most people know, losing weight can be a long, hard road that is made that much longer and harder without exercise. Besides, this state of mind can create and perpetuate a vicious cycle that ultimately hinders your weight loss efforts: Because you're embarrassed, you don't exercise and, as a result, don't lose weight as quickly as you'd like. This, in turn, can set you up for emotional overeating (out of frustration), which makes you even more ashamed and less likely to exercise.

It's important to overcome any mental roadblocks you may harbor toward exercise now. Whether your resistance is because certain activities are difficult due to the extra weight you're carrying, you have little experience with formal exercise or you're simply anxious about how you'll look, it's time to set these worries aside.

Exercise is just as essential to losing weight and maintaining the loss as good eating habits. In fact, a noteworthy study of 150 people recruited from Kaiser Permanente in northern California found that those who had lost weight, as well as those whose weight had always been stable, exercised regularly. Months after losing weight, 90 percent of the people who had maintained their weight loss were exercising at least three times a week for 30 minutes or more; in contrast, only 34 percent of those who had regained their weight were getting regular physical activity.

In trying to get over your fear of exercise, it helps to realize that many people share your insecurities and won't be paying attention to how you look or how well you perform the moves in a class. In fact, they're probably too preoccupied with how *they* look. Once you begin exercising and those mood-enhancing brain chemicals start working their magic, chances are you won't feel as self-conscious. You'll begin to feel stronger, more powerful and happier. You'll start to experience the benefits of exercise firsthand, and your body esteem will rise.

Research from Brigham Young University in Utah found that participating in either a walking or resistance-training program for 12 weeks led to an improvement in body image among 60 sedentary women between the ages of 35 and 49, even though neither group of exercisers experienced significant changes in body weight. Interestingly, those in the resistance-training group saw their body image improve even more than the walkers. Researchers concluded that this is because strength training produces more noticeable gains in terms of the amount of weight one can lift, as well as changes in muscle tone and definition, whereas the changes associated with aerobic exercise are more internal.

So the key to overcoming your self-consciousness and feeling good about your body is to start exercising. If you're too timid at this point to join a gym or class, there are plenty of ways to work out with greater privacy, including riding a stationary bike in your home, taking a brisk walk through your neighborhood or following an exercise videotape in the comfort of your living room. Plus, many health clubs and community centers now offer classes specifically geared to individual needs: classes for the overweight, exercise novices and women only are just a few options. The upshot is that you really don't have any valid excuses for not exercising (unless, of course, your doctor has indicated it would be dangerous for you).

Bear in mind that the only way to become an exercise convert is to find activities that you truly enjoy and make you feel vibrant, healthy and strong. Otherwise, you're not likely to stick with an exercise regimen. In fact, research has found that 50 percent of people who embark on an exercise program drop out in three to six months.

What makes some people successful in sticking with it? Surprisingly enough, a person's level of fitness in starting a program makes little difference; neither does personality type. What does seem to help, according to researchers, is support from friends and family, setting realistic goals and maintaining a flexible attitude towards exercise. Taking an all-or-nothing approach is usually counterproductive. If you can find forms of exercise that appeal to you, along with ways to prevent monotony and keep your motivation high, and stick with them long enough to get past that six-month hurdle, the odds increase dramatically that you'll become an exercise convert over the long haul.

How can you tell if a particular form of exercise is right for you? Consider whether it's something you enjoy and whether it can conveniently fit into your life. You may love swimming in the ocean, but if you live in Denver this isn't a realistic option. Do you prefer to exercise on your own or with other people? Do you favor activities you already know how to do or would you like to learn new skills? Do you like strenuous forms of exercise, such as running or high-impact aerobics, or kinder, gentler alternatives, such as walking or cycling?

Beyond these considerations, the following guide spells out some of the advantages and drawbacks of several aerobic activities, along with basics on how to perform them properly to minimize the risk of injury, recommendations on complementary activities and how many calories you can expect to burn with each.

Walking

Advantage number *one*: You know how to do it, you can do it anytime, anywhere—on a track or treadmill, in a mall or the great outdoors—and it doesn't place a lot of wear and tear on your muscles or joints. Make sure that you walk fast enough to get an aerobic workout (a casual stroll won't do the trick) and maintain proper form: Your hips should be in line with your knees and shoulders, your shoulders should be relaxed and level, your head high and looking straight ahead. *Best complements:* Walking is gentle enough to do regularly, but you may want to complement it with non-weight-bearing activities such as cycling, rowing or swimming or low-impact options like like ice- or roller-skating.

The calorie-burning effects: Depending upon the pace, a 150-pound person might burn between 160 and 240 calories while walking for 30 minutes; those who weigh more would burn slightly more, while those who weigh less would burn slightly fewer calories. If you choose to walk more slowly, simply extend your walk an additional five or 10 minutes for the same calorie-burning effect.

Jogging/Running

These are high-impact activities, so they're not a good choice if you have ankle, knee or back problems. Otherwise, for those who are in good health (consult with your doctor if you're not sure) and aren't prone to such injuries, jogging offers a top-notch cardiovascular workout—and a first-class ticket to weight loss. For proper form, which is key to preventing injuries, keep your back straight and in line with your head, let your arms swing freely, and hit the ground with the heel of your foot first.

Best complements: Supplement your jogging routine with non-impact exercises such as bicycling or swimming.

The calorie-burning effects: Someone who weighs 150 pounds would burn approximately 390 calories in 30 minutes if jogging a 9-minute mile, 468 calories if running 7-minute miles. Again, if the pace is increased, there will be more calories burned in 30 minutes— and fewer if you choose a more leisurely pace.

Make Sure
the **Walking Shoe Fits**

1. Measure right. Have the sporting-good salesperson measure your foot's arch height, as well as its overall length, before recommending the best size.

2. Fit the bigger foot. If your feet aren't the same size (most people's aren't), fit according to the larger foot. Also, shop late in the day, when feet are swollen and at their largest.

3. Use the rule of thumb. The toe bed (the area between your big and little toes) should lie flat. You should be able to fit a thumbnail between your big toe and the tip of the sneaker.

4. Line it up. Make sure the shoe's arch matches up with your arch (the highest part of the sneaker should fit right underneath the highest point of your arch). The ball of your foot (the area just behind the toes) should sit comfortably in the widest part of the shoe.

5. Sole search. Heavy and tall people wear away soles faster than smaller folks. If you're heavy, choose shoes with midsoles (the layer between the insole and the shoe bottom) made of polyurethane. It takes longer to wear down a polyurethane midsole than one made of another material, such as ethylene vinyl acetate.

6. Get puddle protection. Wet walking shoes often stretch out and lose shape. If yours get wet, lightly scrub and rinse shoes in a mild detergent; toss in the washer in just cold water (no soap); then stuff with newspaper and air-dry.

7. Use smart storage. Store walking shoes in a cool, dry place (in plastic in the original box is a good idea). A too-cool or too-warm spot can cause leather to dry out and crack.

8. Choose the right socks. Wearing the right socks protects the life of the shoes (not to mention your feet from blisters). If socks are too thick, shoes will stretch out. Choose socks made of a medium-weight cotton blend, not thick wool, that fit snugly.

9. Lace up. Make sure the lace holes on both sides of the top tongue are about an inch apart. This prevents the holes from tearing and gives you the best fit.

10. Wear your shoes for walking only. Aside from the fact that wearing walking shoes in non-fitness situations is a fashion no-no, the extra wear isn't good for the shoes. If your walking shoes are your only comfortable pair, try dress shoes made by walking shoe companies.

Bicycling

Whether performed indoors or out, bicycling is a great way to work the muscles of lower body, especially the butt (gluteus maximus) and the fronts of the thighs (the quadriceps). For proper form, make sure the seat is high enough so your leg is almost straight when the pedal is in the lowest position; keep your back straight, but don't lock your elbows or squeeze the grips too tightly. To prevent a sore saddle, a common complaint, make sure the seat is level, an inch higher than handlebars and wide enough at the back so you're resting on your "sit" bones (at the back of your pelvis).

If it hasn't debuted at your local health club yet, expect to see the hottest fitness trend making an appearance soon: It's called spinning class, and participants pedal specially built stationary bikes while an instructor coaches them through stints of hill climbing, fast pedaling and pedaling from a standing position at a slower pace, as motivating music plays in the background. Spinning is a high-octane workout that's guaranteed to make you sweat.

Best complements: Unless you use an indoor model with movable handlebars, be sure to complement biking with activities that work your upper body, such as rowing, cross-country skiing or swimming.

The calorie-burning effects: Someone who weighs 150 pounds can burn approximately 130 calories in 30 minutes if cycling at a leisurely pace (5.5 mph) or 345 calories at a racing pace.

Cross-Country Skiing

You can use an indoor machine or cross-country ski outdoors for a great total body workout that builds cardiovascular fitness and muscular endurance and controls body fat. Cross-country skiing uses the shoulders, triceps, upper back, butt, hip flexors, quadriceps and calves. Best of all, it's a non-impact activity, placing little strain on the

---

REALITY CHECK

Wise Walking

1. **Try an adventure.** Instead of walking the same old streets, try a walking vacation, traveling from one country inn to another on foot.

2. **Challenge yourself.** Pick up your pace and pump your arms to pick up some speed.

3. **Keep a diary.** Consider tracking your walking progress (distance traveled, calories burned and terrain covered). Use your diary for inspiration: Describe beautiful areas you've walked, thoughts and ideas you've had while walking, even places you dream of walking.

4. **Muscle up your routine.** Incorporate strength-training into your walk by using hand weights and arm stretches. Do arm circles (forward and backward), forward punches and overhead stretches as you walk.

5. **Go with a group.** Organize a walking group. Choose two or three days a week when your group will walk (in the morning, during lunch hour or after work).

body and offering minimal risk of injury, particularly on level terrain. A tip on form: While leaning slightly forward, take short, smooth gliding motions with one leg, then the other, almost like a shuffle. It's easier if you master the leg movements first, then add the arms, using the opposite arm and leg together. With practice, you'll be able to coordinate the movements.

Best complements: To round out your exercise program, try swimming, rowing, or aerobic dancing.

The calorie-burning effects: While cross-country skiing for 30 minutes, someone who weighs 150 pounds can burn approximately 280 calories.

Aerobic Dance

The moves can be fun, the music energizing, the workout downright fantastic. But the high-impact (jumping, pounding) variety can be hard on your joints, especially if you're considerably overweight; similarly, step aerobics can aggravate knee problems. Over all, low-impact aerobics are less jarring and pose a lower risk of injury. There are currently a wide range of classes available, from cardiofunk to slide aerobics to boxing aerobics, so shop around to find one that suits your fitness level. You can also choose from dozens of aerobics videotapes, if you'd prefer to do aerobics in the privacy of your home, at your own pace.

Best complements: Complement this with low-impact activities such as cycling or swimming.

The calorie-burning effects: With 30 minutes of aerobic dancing, someone who weighs 150 pounds can burn between 210 and 275 calories, depending on the intensity.

Jumping Rope

It's one of the highest-impact activities around, so jumping rope is not recommended if you have ankle, knee or back problems or are considerably overweight. But it is a great cardiovascular workout and an excellent way to condition your lower body relatively quickly. It's best to jump rope on a soft surface, such as a carpet, to cushion the impact. Keep rope circles small, not wild, and don't jump more than an inch off the ground. Also, try using your jump rope for isometric arm exercises: Double the rope over into a loop (if rope is long, continue doubling until loop is slightly longer than shoulder width); holding the loop at chest level, slowly pull ends to exert near-maximal force. Keep the rope stationary; release and repeat 10 times.

Best complements: To balance your workouts, supplement rope-skipping sessions with non- or low-impact activities such as cycling, swimming, skating or rowing.

The calorie-burning effects: Depending on the number of skips per minute, someone who weighs 150 pounds might burn 165 to 200 calories with just 15 minutes of jumping rope.

Rowing

When performed correctly, rowing is a great whole-body exercise for developing cardiovascular

Aerobics Pro **Fake-Out**

- *Search out a beginner's class.* Not every challenging workout looks like an audition for *A Chorus Line*. Many beginner-level classes are easy on the choreography, but every bit as tough as the more advanced classes.

- *Get behind someone who knows the moves.* Instead of trying to mirror-image the instructor, mimic the student in front of you.

- *Take a tutorial.* Arrive a few minutes before class and let the instructor know you're having trouble following complex choreography. Many instructors will take the time to preview any difficult steps they're planning to use.

- *Don't stare at your reflection.* Sure, it helps to check your position in the mirror occasionally, but if your focus is on your reflection, you're likely to get confused.

Keep your eyes on the person ahead of you or on the instructor.

- *Speak up.* If some moves were confusing, simply ask the instructor to demonstrate them after class.

- *Keep moving.* If you can't get a complicated step, jog in place until the instructor moves on. Don't feel flustered or embarrassed—you can always catch up with the instructor later and request help.

---

fitness and muscular endurance. It targets the butt, hips, calves and thighs, shoulders, upper back and biceps. Because it's a non-impact activity, rowing is easier on the joints than, say, jogging or high-impact aerobic dance. Whether you do it in an actual boat or a rowing machine, think of it as a two-part motion: squatting with your legs and rowing with your arms. Lead back with the elbows, keeping them close to your body, and complete the pull-in to your chest last.

Best complements: To work different muscles, try skating, jogging, cycling or stair climbing.

The calorie-burning effects: A recent study found that healthy adults in their 20s and 30s burned an average of 303 calories in 30 minutes while using a rowing machine at a somewhat high intensity.

Stair Climbing

You can do this by walking up and down stairs in your home or office building, but it's easier on your joints if you do it on a machine. You can get a great aerobic workout that strengthens the lower body, especially the butt, the fronts and backs of the thighs, the shins and the calves. For best results and to prevent "Stairmaster butt" (over-working muscles that can result in increasing, rather than reducing, their size) keep your posture upright—don't slouch or lean onto the handrails!—and take slow, deep pedal strokes. Don't give up on your first try; it may take several attempts to master the movement.

Best complements: Supplement these sessions with rowing, cross-country skiing or aerobic dancing for counterbalance.

The calorie-burning effects: Most machines tell you how many calories you expend in a given time frame, depending on your weight. A recent study found that healthy adults in their 20s and 30s burned an average of 314 calories in 30 minutes while using a stair machine at a somewhat high intensity.

Swimming

Swimming is one of the safest forms of exercise. Water's natural buoyancy cushions the body, making swimming safe for pregnant women (although any pregnant woman should check with her physician before starting any exercise regimen), overweight people and individuals with joint injuries. (Water aerobics classes are another option, now being offered at many health clubs and community centers.) Yet despite its mildness, swimming is a total-body workout, exercising all the major muscle groups in your upper and lower body. In fact, a study at the University of Toledo found that running on land and in deep water are comparable in terms of their effects on

cardiorespiratory fitness. If you're interested in swimming for fitness, try local colleges and high schools, motels and community centers, as well as the obvious YMCAs and health clubs for available pools. To bypass crowds, swim during off-peak hours and choose the "slow" lane if you're a beginner.

Best complements: Good cross-training choices are cross-country skiing, rowing, jogging and skating.

The calorie-burning effects: Depending on the stroke used, someone who weighs 150 pounds could burn 260 calories (if doing a slow crawl) to 330 calories (if doing the breast stroke) in 30 minutes of swimming.

Skating

In-line skating is a fun aerobic activity that's great for toning your rear and thighs, as well as for burning calories. In fact, it's one of the fastest-growing sports, now surpassing soccer, baseball, tennis and football in total number of participants. But in-line also carries a high injury rate; it's best to take a lesson or two to learn the basics and essential to outfit yourself with the appropriate gear— helmet, wrist guards, elbow guards and knee guards. For proper form, keep your knees bent, your elbows close to your body and your weight on your rear wheels. Maintaining balance can be harder than it looks. Ask your local in-line skate dealer about classes that will instruct you on the proper moves, including how to fall correctly.

Best complements: Jogging, bicycling, aerobic dancing and rowing are good choices for additional calorie-burning exercises that target different muscles.

The calorie-burning effects: Skating offers a first-rate workout. For a 150-pound person, 30 minutes of ice- or roller-skating can burn 220 calories.

Yoga

It won't do much for aerobic fitness or calorie-burning, but yoga offers plenty of other advantages: enhanced flexibility and strength, improved posture and a sense of relaxation. Because the many poses involved are unique and have specific breathing patterns, it's best to take a class to learn them correctly. Yoga postures also focus on correct breathing techniques, which some experts say may account for its link to helping lower blood pressure.

Best complements: A great addition to any aerobic exercise program, yoga or other flexibility-enhancing classes are especially recommended if you regularly participate in activities—such as jogging—that tend to make your muscles tight.

Avoiding Motivational Crises

Even the most committed exercisers can lose motivation at times. That's why it's essential to map out a plan of action that will minimize the likelihood that you'll experience a workout fallout. As a starting point, engage only in activities that you truly enjoy and skip the ones you don't to prevent exercise from feeling like a chore. In addition, take these steps to help you maintain motivation and become hooked on the pleasure of movement:

- **Set realistic short-term goals.** Consider goals that are personally meaningful to you, not ones that someone else told you to strive for. Break large goals (such as losing a certain number of pounds) into action-oriented, smaller ones (such as walking a total of 10 miles this week) and use these as a bridge to your larger aims. After all, success breeds success.

- **Keep an exercise diary.** To help monitor your progress, jot down your goals, exercise strategies and workout details (such as time and distance) in a journal. Also write down the benefits you see, both physically and mentally. This will serve as proof positive that your exercise program is making a difference, which can help you stay on track.

- **Make it fun and social.** Remember how much fun it was to play tag or kickball with the neighborhood kids when you were a child? Remember how your parents had to practically drag you back inside after dark? You can re-create the fun of exercising as an adult by joining up with friends or family members. Hiking some challenging hills with spectacular views or biking to a nearby lake and having a picnic can make the experience so pleasurable that it may not even feel like exercise. (If your friends are couch potatoes, consider joining a local walking or biking club.)

- Pace yourself. There's nothing wrong with being ambitious from the outset, but trying to do too much too quickly can set you up for burnout and injuries. Start small and increase the intensity and/or duration of your workouts gradually.

- Mix up your routine. Performing the same workout day after day in the same setting can be monotonous for anyone. If you participate in a wide variety of physical activities, on the other hand, this will keep your fitness life interesting and prevent boredom from setting in. This is called cross-training, and it also helps prevent overuse injuries that can result from too much stress on a particular muscle group.

- Give yourself a pep talk. What you say to yourself can influence your progress dramatically. Making negative comments about your attempts to exercise or lose weight can be self-defeating. A more constructive approach is to offer encouraging words—telling yourself that you *can* walk those three miles, that this tennis match offers a chance to try out your new serve. You might inspire yourself.

- Find a role model. Think of someone whose exercise habits you admire—for instance, a formerly overweight neighbor who you see race-walking every morning, rain or shine. Try to emulate that person's success. Tell yourself that if he or she can do it, you can do it.

- Picture success. When motivation wanes, visualize yourself sprinting toward the finish line in a 10-K race, performing a perfect flip turn at the end of the pool or rowing across a nearby lake. Many elite athletes use creative visualization techniques to enhance their performance, and you can use the same principles in your training. This sort of mental rehearsal will boost your confidence, which can, in turn, help you stay focused on achieving your goals.

- Reward yourself. Give yourself a pat on the back for your fitness accomplishments, and offer yourself special treats when you reach your short- and long-term goals, such as a sports massage after being able to jog five miles or a new exercise outfit after attending aerobics classes religiously for a month. This will reinforce your commitment.

- Don't make too much of lapses. If you fall off the fitness wagon, don't beat yourself up about it. Setbacks are inevitable in any major lifestyle change. If you miss a day unexpectedly, don't be hard on yourself. One lost day won't thwart your weight loss efforts. What's important is keeping an eye on the big picture.

How to Overcome Aerobics-Class Phobia

There's no question: Joining an aerobics class can be a rattling experience, particularly if you're a novice. But, simple as it sounds, the best way to get over an aerobics-class phobia is to join a class. If you just participate and deal with your uncomfortable feelings a few times, your fears will gradually recede. Think of short-term discomfort as a small price to pay for getting fit and losing weight, especially since the unease is not likely to last for long. In the meantime, here are some strategies to make the initial foray a little less scary.

First of all, be sure you know what you're getting into—shop around for a beginning class. If you're truly petrified of looking like a klutz, it may help to watch a class a few times before joining in or watch an aerobics video at home so you can master the basic moves on your own. It also may help to tell the instructor beforehand that you're a newcomer to aerobics; he or she may be able to give you a little extra attention without making you feel foolish. Stake out a spot where you'd feel comfortable in the class: It's often easier to follow along in the front, but if you can't stand the thought of being so visible, find a spot in the back of the room or somewhere in the middle. Bringing a friend can also make you feel more at ease.

To calm your nerves, spend a few moments before class breathing deeply and thinking about something that makes you feel good about yourself. Or remember a time when you felt as though you could do anything you set your mind to. Visualize that scenario, stand tall with your back and shoulders straight, your head held high, and try to recapture that can-do feeling in the way you move. This will help you feel more grounded physically and emotionally.

reality check

REALITY CHECK

Cold Weather "Warm-Up"

1. Shovel snow, but go slow—especially if you've been sedentary. This winter chore burns plenty of calories while saving you money on a plowing service.

2. Build a snowman. If you don't have kids of your own, borrow a neighbor's. Don't forget the artistic accessories: corn cob pipe, buttons, hat and lump of coal.

3. Go ice skating. Even if you've never done it before, rental skates and lessons are available at most commercial rinks.

4. Go sledding, or start a snowball fight.

5. Join a mall walking club. Many malls open their doors before business hours to let walkers do laps and window shop in a safe, weatherproof environment. Contact your local mall's managing agent for details.

6. Invest in an exercise video. Rent a few to find one you like before buying.

During the class, don't compare yourself to other people. Remember: everyone has to start somewhere, and even exercisers who have the moves down pat probably faced an awkward start the first time they joined a class. Learning new skills always takes time, so be patient with yourself. If you feel uncoordinated the first time, don't quit: You'll get the hang of it slowly but surely. In the meantime, take pride in the fact that you're making the effort and doing something healthy for your body and mind. And focus on how good you'll feel afterward.

Sore Muscles R$_{x}$

If your workout was a tad overzealous, consider these must-haves for easing the aches.

1. *A hot water bottle.* Grandma's low-tech answer to aches and pains actually works.

2. *Arnica gel.* A homeopathic remedy available in many pharmacies, arnica gel has been used to relieve overtaxed muscles.

3. *Stretching.* While you may be tempted to baby overworked muscles, a careful stretch can actually relieve some of the discomfort.

4. *Ibuprofen.* This anti-inflammatory is designed to bring down swelling so muscle tissue can heal.

5. *Massage.* Whether it's done by your spouse or a

trained professional, a good rubdown can help work out muscle kinks and soreness.

6. *Bath salts.* Epsom or Dead Sea salts are a great way to relieve discomfort while giving yourself a luxurious treat.

7. *Keep going.* Stiffness and soreness may be uncomfortable, but they will dissipate with continued regular exercise.

Something to Think About

Think about a sport or activity that you've always wanted to try but were afraid to. What stopped you from doing it? What exactly were you afraid of? What do you see as the worst—and best—possible outcomes?

. . . .

. . . .

. . . .

. . . .

. . . .

. . . .

. . . .

. . . .

. . . .

. . . .

. . . .

. . . .

. . . .

CHAPTER ten

THINKING LIKE A FIT PERSON

When it comes to losing weight and getting fit, you could be standing in your own way without realizing it. One of the biggest obstacles to slimming down—and staying that way—is how you think and feel about yourself. Embarking on a program to get in shape can feel like a long, lonely journey that's peppered with unexpected potholes and detours. It can be a lot easier and more pleasant, though, if you make some adjustments to your attitude and behavior.

Sound impossible? It isn't. The key is to explore some of the psychological issues that may be at the heart of your battle with the scale and find ways to overcome them. After all, the relationship between individuals and their weight doesn't exist in a vacuum. It is a highly charged emotional issue and often serves as a reading against which people measure their self-worth. For some, weight can become a cloak they hide behind or a pair of spectacles that color their life experiences.

Veils of Shame

Many people with an enduring weight problem blame their extra pounds on a shortage of willpower, a lack of control over their eating habits or an unwillingness to exercise—and these all may be contributing factors. But often emotional or psychological issues are at the core of a person's struggle with excess weight.

One of these is shame, which can involve a feeling of not measuring up to some cultural ideal, of not being fit enough to be admired and of not being worthy of other people's respect, love and attention. Shame arises from a discrepancy between how you see yourself and how you want to appear. It often involves the fear that people will reject you if they discover the *real* you, that they will come to see you for the flawed, disgraceful creature that you truly (think you) are. Feelings of shame don't apply only to your body; they can extend to your entire idea of self, too.

We live in a weight-obsessed, fitness-conscious culture, where thin bodies are valued over many other attributes. Consequently, you may feel ashamed when you can't achieve the lean physiques that comprise the prevailing definition of attractiveness. Consciously or not, you may feel ashamed that your figure doesn't look like a fashion model's or that you don't have sinewy biceps to rival the aerobics instructor's at the health club. Feelings of shame can also surface if you regain weight you've lost on a diet, in which case your body becomes an emblem of failure for the world to see.

Although both women and men experience feelings of shame in some form or another, psychologists say that women are more likely to feel it in the context of their bodies. Women know that their bodies are constantly being scrutinized—by others as well as by themselves. In fact, recent research from the University of Wisconsin found that the more young and middle-aged women internalized cultural standards of what constitutes a desirable body, adopting these as their own personal standards, the more likely they were to feel body shame and the less likely they were to feel body esteem.

Cultural beauty standards aren't the only cause of shame, however. The roots can often be traced back to childhood—particularly if your parents were highly critical and difficult to please, controlling or distant. A sense of shame often goes hand in hand with a negative body image, and the combination can develop as a result of being teased, criticized or ostracized for being overweight by family members or peers as a child. Indeed, there's plenty of evidence that shameful body attitudes, as well as our eating habits, are passed down from our parents. Research has found, for instance, a strong correlation between a mother's unhappiness with her body and her daughter's dissatisfaction with her own. These feelings essentially become learned behaviors.

In adulthood, this sense of body shame is an unpleasant secret many women harbor; it is seldom discussed with friends or loved ones because many women are too ashamed to admit they feel ashamed of their bodies. Yet this feeling can color their entire life, from their sex life and health to their behavior and outlook, sometimes leading to self-loathing. Not surprisingly, several studies have found a link between shame and eating disorders, including compulsive eating and bingeing and purging; for people suffering from shame, eating often becomes a way to satisfy their hunger and emotional needs in private. But eating compulsively usually ends up perpetuating feelings of shame, self-disgust and being out of control.

If they wrestle with shame too long, women, in particular, are susceptible to passivity, depression, loneliness, perfectionism or social isolation, according to psychologists. After all, feeling ashamed because you feel fat or unattractive can cause you to avoid participating in potentially rewarding situations. It might prevent you from going to an office pool party because you can't bear the thought of being seen in a bathing suit. Or it may stop you from joining an aerobics class because you feel too embarrassed to stand next to the lithe, Spandex-clad bodies.

If you can find a way to break out of the clutches of shame, you will increase your chances of controlling your weight and feeling generally happier with your life. Granted, banishing feelings of shame won't be easy, since they're often so ingrained; plus, many people aren't even aware that they have them. To get in touch with those feelings, it may help to keep a journal in which you chronicle the ways in which shame seems to control your life and record experiences in which you feel embarrassment or self-hatred. Acknowledging such feelings and where they come from can help release their hold on you. Then look at this phenomenon as a problem to be solved: How can you develop a mindset that will help you overcome these feelings?

A logical starting point is to think about your personal goals when it comes to losing weight or getting in shape and ask yourself why you want to achieve them. Are you doing this for yourself—or because someone else is pressuring you? Changing your lifestyle for another person rarely results in success; the desire and commitment have to come from *you*.

Dealing with Saboteurs

Changing your habits is hard even when you're feeling strong and committed. When the people who are closest to you undermine your resolve—by offering you tempting treats, by monitoring your every meal as if they were the food police or by trying to convince you that you look fine the way you are, so you should forget about exercising or losing weight—changing your habits can feel like Mission Impossible. Worse yet, it may feel as if the very people you count on for support—your spouse or partner, your parents, your friends and colleagues—want to see you fail in your endeavor to slim down and shape up.

In most cases, this sort of sabotaging behavior is neither intentional nor mean-spirited. It may simply be that it hasn't occurred to your partner that bringing you a box of your favorite chocolates to cheer you up won't do the trick; in such instances, you need to be honest and tell him that flowers, for example, would be appreciated more. Or perhaps it hasn't dawned on your mother that the rich macaroni and cheese you loved as a child no longer suits your tastes or eating habits, so you need to tell her so. Similarly, having a prepared response at the tip of your tongue—such as "No, thank you. I already ate."—can prevent you from falling prey to food-pushers at work or at parties.

Other times, the best of intentions simply run amok, as often happens when friends or family members who want to be supportive end up policing your every bite and movement. Besides making you feel as if you're under a microscope, such behavior can set you up for eating in secret or refusing to exercise. When people police your eating habits, it also can add to any feelings of shame you may have. It's up to you to end it by telling people specifically what's helpful to you

(continued on page 107)

How to Shed the
Victim Mentality

Before you can truly gain control of your weight and adopt a healthier lifestyle, you may need to give your attitude a makeover. You may need to stop your unhealthy ways of thinking and start thinking like a fit person. Here's how:

Old attitude: **I can't accept myself as I am.**

New attitude: **I am a kind, loving person with lots of admirable qualities.**

Try to become aware of what you say to yourself on a daily basis. Psychologists call this self-talk, and it can either bolster your self-confidence and self-image or tear it down. Using positive self-talk, or affirmations, can serve as the antidotes to the self-damaging messages you ordinarily give yourself. It may feel phony at first, but think of these declarations as tools for change. By repeating positive, affirming statements to yourself, you will gradually become more receptive to them and will come to believe them. You might say to yourself, "I, (insert your name here), deserve my own care and appreciation" or "I, (insert your name

here), am capable of resisting this cheese Danish because I am a strong, self-respecting woman." Develop statements that strike an inspiring chord and use them.

Old attitude: **My weight is responsible for what's gone wrong in my life.**

New attitude: **I am responsible for my eating and exercise habits from this day forward.**

In order to stop feeling like a victim, it's important to stop thinking like one. Your weight may not be entirely within your control—genetic influences certainly play a substantial role—but you *are* responsible for your eating and exercise habits. Besides, setting unrealistic expectations, such as believing that becoming thin will solve all your problems, is a surefire ticket to disappointment and regaining weight.

Rather than denigrating yourself for not eating a better diet or exercising more until now, or blaming your unhappiness or sedentary habits on your weight or other external factors, focus on taking charge from this moment. Coax and encourage yourself to make healthy changes, and give yourself a pat on the back for each day that you do. Instead of telling yourself what you *should* do or what you *have to* do, think in terms of *choosing* to eat more healthfully or exercise more because it's good for your health and psyche.

Old attitude: **If I eat healthfully, I've been good or virtuous; if I don't, I feel bad or guilty.**

New attitude: **I expect to have days when I fall off my plan; what's important is that I learn from them.**

Don't label yourself by the food you consume (in positive terms if you eat healthfully, in negative terms if you don't). This sort of self-flagellating, all-or-nothing thinking is self-defeating and can become an excuse to overeat if you can't resist eating a "bad" food. Setbacks are inevitable with any lifestyle change; the key is to figure out why you overate on a particular day, then to return to your eating plan and learn from the experience. Keeping a food diary is a great way to discover your own patterns.

Old attitude: **The ideal figure is that of a fashion model's and that's what I'll strive for.**

New attitude: **I will strive to have the healthiest, fittest body that I am able to have.**
Fit bodies, as you've already heard, come in a wide range of shapes and sizes. Truth is, the images of women that are often idealized in the media are *unnaturally* thin, if not biologically impossible for most women to attain. It's far healthier and more productive to aim for a shape that's realistic and comfortable for *you* and to let go of such comparisons. Start noticing when and how you compare yourself negatively to other people. Rather than focusing on your perceived shortcomings, try concentrating on your strengths and how you would like to enhance them. Imagine how you would feel about your body and yourself if you achieved that ideal, and start acting as if it were reality now.

and what's not; don't expect them to read your mind. And to reinforce the sort of positive encouragement you've come to value, be sure to voice your appreciation—that way, you'll promote more of the same.

If you suspect that a saboteur in your life actually has a vested interest in keeping you heavy—possibly because he or she feels threatened by the idea of your changing or inadequate by comparison—it helps to realize that this has to do with that person's psychological issues, not yours.

Acknowledging this can cushion the emotional impact on you. Still, at some point, you may need to confront such issues. While it's true that your weight and your exercise habits are your business, they do affect those around you. An office buddy, for example, may feel saddened by the thought that you won't be taking mid-afternoon coffee-and-cookie breaks together anymore. Again, it's best to address the matter directly: Reassure the friend that you value your relationship and explain how you feel when he or she undermines your goals. You might point out that improving your health can only be positive for you and your relationship and perhaps suggest a healthier alternative, such as taking a walk together to rejuvenate yourselves in the afternoon. What it comes down to is that these saboteurs may be afraid of losing you in some way, in which case a little reassurance and inclusion often goes a long way toward easing their fears.

Sometimes, too, you can be your own worst enemy in your efforts to lose weight. For many people, specific situations—whether it's getting stuck in traffic, going to a party or coping with stress at work—can threaten their dietary vigilance. One of the keys to navigating such stumbling blocks without falling off your food plan is to think ahead. If you carry healthy snacks with you, such as a bag of cut-up carrots, a piece of fruit or some rice or popcorn cakes, you'll be less tempted to stop at the donut shop that seems to beckon from the side of the road. If you know you're going to a dinner party, have a nutritious snack beforehand to take the edge off your hunger. If you get yelled at by the boss, instead of heading for the vending machine go outside and take a walk around the block. The idea is to identify situations that are troublesome for you and figure out how to handle them ahead of time.

What's most important is to stop blaming other people or situations for your weight and reclaim responsibility. No one can force you to eat (or not to) or to exercise (or not to); dedication to leading a healthy lifestyle has to come from within. So start setting limits, exercising discipline and behaving like a fit, thin person. That means befriending your body the way it is now and striving for what you want. The goal is to stop obsessing about your weight, your shape, and your eating habits and to become more fully invested in your life. Instead of waiting until you get fit, start accepting yourself now. Cut back on how much you observe and criticize your body and begin treating yourself well simply because you deserve it.

Being nurturing toward yourself is a far more effective way to instill motivation and foster change than self-punishment, which is likely to make you feel worse and rebel, psychologists say. Besides, if you put off looking for a new job, taking a much-needed vacation, or buying new clothes until you like your body more, you might just wait . . . and wait. And you'll set yourself up for a monumental letdown when you actually reach your goal. After all, you'll still be the same person. Your life won't be problem-free. And you will have waited so long to be kind to yourself!

On the other hand, if you treat yourself well while you're making these lifestyle changes, you won't feel as deprived. You will feel as though you have an ally in yourself, which can help you reach your goals. Besides, very few things have to be put off until you lose weight: If you've been coveting a velvet dress at a local boutique, why wait until you can squeeze into a size 6 when you can always have it made smaller? If you've delayed asking your boss for a raise, remind yourself that the quality of your work is what has earned it for you, not the size of your waistline.

How to Develop a Healthier Attitude Toward Food

Many people have a love-hate relationship with food: Eating may be pleasurable, but they consider food their nemesis. It doesn't have to be that way. On the contrary, it is possible to enjoy eating without relinquishing your control—if you have the right attitude. Here's how to get it:

- *Eat when you're hungry.* It's a back-to-basics concept: From now on, try to eat only when you are physically hungry. If you have a difficult time distinguishing physical from emotional hunger, some experts recommend waiting 10 minutes before giving in to a craving. If it's just a craving, it's likely to pass; if you're truly hungry, it won't, in which case you should eat. Monitoring what and when you eat is one of the best ways to control your weight.

- *Throw out your lists of forbidden foods.* There's no such thing as a good food or a bad food. All foods are fine in moderation. If fudge brownies are your all-time favorite treat, rather than depriving yourself, indulge occasionally. That way you'll minimize the urge to cheat or binge. Try to aim for a low-fat, balanced diet over time.

- *Rediscover the pleasure of eating.* By offering yourself a variety of nutritious fare, including different flavors and textures, you will help yourself develop an appreciation for the sensory and nourishing experience of eating. Make meals a special time, during which you do nothing else, and try to eat slowly, savoring each bite—that way you're more likely to enjoy the experience. Plus, you'll give your body ample time to register fullness. Don't try to join the clean-plate club: The goal is to eat until you are satisfied, not stuffed.

- *Find other ways to relieve bad moods.* If you've turned to food for emotional comfort in the past, start cultivating other mood-relieving methods. Distract yourself with an enjoyable activity, whether it's exercising, listening to music or calling a friend.

- *Don't skip meals.* Many dieters skip meals in the mistaken belief that it will help them peel off pounds. It won't. Skipping meals—as well as consuming too few calories—sends your body into starvation mode, causing it to conserve energy and to burn calories more slowly. Meal skipping can also lead to a binging episode. A better strategy is to eat regularly to keep your metabolism working efficiently.

Losing weight and getting and staying fit are lifetime commitments without a clear beginning or end. So try to be patient and keep an eye on the big picture: on taking good care of yourself physically and emotionally, on eating well and exercising regularly. As you begin to notice the positive effects such changes have—bringing you increased energy, a greater sense of body confidence, a more even emotional keel and a greater sense of self-efficacy, among others—you're bound to feel motivated to continue your newly developed healthy habits. And little by little, self-damaging emotions such as shame will slip into the past.

REALITY CHECK

Self-Esteem Pointers

1. **Respect yourself.** If you call yourself "thunder thighs" when you're on the treadmill, stop. You wouldn't put up with a stranger calling you names, would you?

2. **Accept yourself.** Remember that it's important to remain respectful and compassionate toward yourself, as well as toward others.

3. **Don't attach moral values to eating decisions.** Some people make the mistake of equating good eating decisions with good character and bad eating with moral flaws. Remember: the scale doesn't measure virtue—just pounds.

4. **Be responsible.** Recognize that you are the only one who controls your choices and actions. It's easier to get where you're going when you realize you're in the driver's seat.

5. **Stop magnifying your flaws.** When you look in the mirror, do you see your lovely eyes—or your "enormous" hips? Focus on your strengths instead of your perceived shortcomings.

Something to Think About

Spend some time reflecting on who is responsible for your weight and why. Make a list of times when you've blamed someone else—or particular situations—and why. Now think of ways in which you could have reclaimed responsibility in those situations.

CHAPTER eleven

LOVING YOUR BODY

Things are beautiful if you love them.

—Jean Anouilh, French playwright

if you've ever suffered a wardrobe crisis—trying on everything in your closet, never satisfied that anything looks good enough—or avoided looking in a full-length mirror, you are personally familiar with how body image can affect your everyday life. For many women, fat is a state of mind: Their emotional well-being is predicated on the numbers reflected on the scale; their outlook on life hinges on whether or not they feel slim and attractive. Yet even women who are thin and beautiful don't always see themselves that way. Feeling fat or feeling thin has less to do with actual body size than it does with perception—and it's a perception that can profoundly influence your life.

It's no wonder: Your body is where you live, first and foremost, and how you think and feel about this home is critically important to your physical and emotional well-being. If you feel happy with your body, you are more likely to like and feel comfortable with yourself on the inside; if you don't, that's another story. According to research conducted by Thomas Cash, Ph.D., a professor of psychology at Old Dominion University in Norfolk, Virginia, body image constitutes about one-quarter of a person's self-esteem. Studies have also found that body attitudes are a larger, more crucial aspect of a woman's idea of herself and her sense of self-worth than a man's.

Surveys indicate that the vast majority—by some calculations, up to 85 percent—of American women are unhappy with at least some aspect of their bodies, regardless of whether they're overweight or within the normal range. The spectrum of body-image issues can range from mild dissatisfaction with one's body or feeling somewhat unattractive to having such an extreme preoccupation with one's physical appearance that it interferes with the person's life. At the far end of the continuum is a condition called Body Dysmorphic Disorder (BDD), also known as "imagined ugliness." People suffering from BDD are preoccupied with an imagined defect in their physical appearance, and that preoccupation can be so severe that it can lead to social isolation, such as being housebound, or an inability to function on the job. They may be so convinced that people will gawk at their misshapen head or excessively large nose—when, in fact, these features are quite normal—that they shy away from being seen in public. Looking at their own reflection is almost like looking in a funhouse mirror. Although it is not known how prevalent the disorder is, some psychologists estimate that 2 percent of Americans may be extremely preoccupied with a perceived flaw in their appearance that other people would not notice.

If your body image falls anywhere on the negative side of the spectrum, it can have deep and lasting effects on your state of mind and your health. Research has found that body-image disturbances are linked to eating disorders, low self-esteem, anxiety, loneliness and depression. Feeling bad about your body can also lead to slouching or other forms of poor posture, which can create muscular imbalances, back problems, and decreased energy, among other ills.

The Weight of Our Discontent

Why do so many women have a bad body image? Many researchers blame such disturbances on sociocultural factors. Women have always been judged more closely by their looks than men have, and they are held up to more stringent standards of beauty—standards that are extremely difficult to obtain.

Complicating the picture, the cultural ideal of beauty for women has historically changed with the times. Women's body types, unlike men's, have gone in and out of style just as fashions have. As far back as the 1880s, the hourglass figure was preferred for women—large breasts and hips, with corseted waists to accentuate curves. Then the "ideal woman" gradually transformed into the flapper of the 1920s, complete with slim hips and a flat chest (which was often bound). Three decades later, the comeback of curves was heralded by Marilyn Monroe in the 1950s, an ideal that eventually gave way to Twiggy in the sixties. Even in the last decade alone, the female shape in vogue has varied from a lean, sculpted, athletic figure—such as that of actress Linda Hamilton or supermodel Cindy Crawford—to the return of the waif in the style of model Kate Moss. Meanwhile, the standards for men's physiques have changed little over the years; a wide range is still considered acceptable. Given the fact that women have tried to alter their bodies so that they fit the current view of attractiveness, it's no wonder so many are so critical of their natural-born shapes.

Cultural standards alone don't determine your body image, however. How you think and feel about your body develops from your accumulation of life experiences—how your parents related to you, whether your peers accepted or

How Accurately Do You See Your Body?

When it comes to seeing one's body for how it really is, many people have a sizable gap between perception and reality. In fact, research from the University of South Florida has found that the vast majority of women overestimate their body size, believing their bodies are on average 25 percent larger than they are. What's more, 40 percent of women perceive at least one part of their body to be at least 50 percent larger than it actually is. The researchers concluded that "the more inaccurate women are about their body size, the worse they feel about themselves."

Is this true for you? To find out if you have a distorted body image, perform these exercises:

1. First, unravel a ball of string and make a loop that you think reflects the circumference of your waist and tie it in a knot; make another loop that you believe reflects the circumference of your hips and tie it in a knot. Put these aside, but don't confuse the two measurements. Now take a piece of string and actually wrap it around your waist, mark it, and tie it into a loop; wrap another piece of string around your hips and do likewise. Compare your estimated dimensions with your real dimensions and see how off base you are.

2. Place several sheets of newspaper on the floor and draw an outline—crime-scene style—of what you think your body silhouette would look like if you were lying down. Next, lie down on several adjacent sheets of newspaper and have a friend or family member trace an outline of your body. Now compare the two to see how accurate your perceptions are.

rejected you, all the positive and negative feedback you've received about yourself and your body from important people in your life, among other factors. In addition, the way your parents felt about their own bodies—whether they denigrated or valued them—can influence how you feel about yours. Their skewed perceptions can become *your* skewed perceptions.

In short, a wide array of factors have contributed to your body image, and it has undoubtedly changed as you've entered and left various stages of your life. The way women think and feel about their bodies often fluctuates as their bodies change during puberty, pregnancy and menopause—milestones that happen to coincide with increased fat storage.

For people who are overweight, there has traditionally been a belief among some experts that one of the best ways to improve body image is to lose weight, thereby changing your body. But this is no guarantee. After all, even thin people don't always accept or like their bodies. And studies on this subject have yielded mixed results. Besides, given the fact that so many diets fail, and that so many dieters regain lost weight, it may be easier to change one's body image than to change one's body.

Recently, there has been something of a backlash against dieting. Sparked in part by mounting medical evidence that highly restrictive diets don't work, the current anti-dieting movement maintains that a *diet* teaches people to disregard their natural biological cues of hunger and satiety. In light of this, when they stop dieting they don't know when to stop eating. Indeed, many weight control experts now believe that dieting promotes mood swings, self-rejection and weight cycling (i.e., losing weight, regaining it, losing it again, and so on), among other negative effects.

That's not to say that you shouldn't try to lose weight. Even shedding small amounts of excess weight can bring important health benefits, such as a drop in blood pressure and blood cholesterol. But the emphasis is on shifting to a healthier lifestyle rather than simply dieting as a quick fix. The current wisdom is that if you eat a healthy, low-fat diet and get plenty of exercise regularly, your weight will take care of itself.

How to Shape Up Your Body Image

But there's good news: You don't have to wait for your body to change for your body image to improve. Research now suggests that it's possible to feel better about your body and yourself even if you lose little to no weight. The secret lies within your mindset.

In a study at the University of Vermont, 51 overweight women participated in eight weekly, two-hour group therapy sessions, during which they discussed the harmful effects of a negative body image, identified behavioral rituals (such as repeatedly inspecting their bodies in mirrors) that promote preoccupation with appearance and learned ways of coping with body discomfort in real life. As homework, the participants practiced various strategies—including replacing negative statements about their body with positive ones and exposing themselves to distressing situations—for coping with situations that were troubling to them. At the end of the study, researchers found that attitudes and behavior related to a bad body image improved substantially. Overall self-esteem, overeating habits and eating-related guilt also improved considerably for the women. Although many of the study's participants worried that learning to like their bodies more would hamper their efforts to lose weight—or, worse, cause them to abandon all self-control and gain weight—it turns out their fears were unwarranted: There was no significant association between body-image changes and weight.

Not only will improving your body image enhance your sense of well-being, but there's some suggestion that it could even facilitate weight loss. According to a study published in the *International Journal of Obesity*, a 10-week Australian program designed to discourage dieting behavior and help women accept their bodies proved successful on several fronts: At the end of the program, as well as two years later, the women experienced significant improvements in body image, self-esteem, feelings of depression and attitudes toward eating; what's more, they also lost weight.

However, if you're in the process of losing weight or have recently slimmed down, don't be surprised if your body image lags behind the reality. Sometimes it takes your mind a while to catch up with your changing body. Particularly with a significant weight loss, your body image may trail behind how you actually look, in which case even positive comments from other people can make you feel uncomfortable. In fact, studies have found that formerly overweight women often retain negative thoughts and feelings about their bodies, and some psychologists speculate that this may partly explain why so many people regain weight. It may help to use visualization techniques to help your mind grow accustomed to your new shape: Imagine yourself at your optimal weight and how you would feel and move; then practice walking or entering a room with that image in mind. This is an instance where putting on rose-colored glasses can benefit you.

Of course, in reshaping your body image, it's also important to readjust your expectations by making a distinction between cultural ideals and what's reasonable for you to achieve. After all, few of us can afford to spend four hours a day exercising as some celebrities do. Besides, comparing yourself to other people simply fuels a negative body image. And cultural standards of beauty can only torment you if you adopt them as your own. Instead, try to broaden your vision of beauty by noticing all the different body types that surround you and identifying at least a few qualities that are appealing about each. Once you can appreciate their unorthodox attributes, you'll be more apt to appreciate and respect your own. But don't define yourself solely by your body; try to build your self-image around other aspects of your life—your intelligence, your personality traits, your gratifying relationships, your work competence or your artistic abilities, for example.

In other words, try to put your appearance in its place. Focus on what your body can *do* rather than just on how it looks: Take pride in the fact that your body has given life to beautiful children if you're a mother, that it gives great hugs, or that it now lets you walk a 10-K course without feeling exhausted. Getting regular aerobic and strength-training exercise will help you feel physically and emotionally stronger, and it can lift your spirits as well. If you can begin to love and care for your body unconditionally, just as you would a child, it is possible to develop a fondness for the body you have and to enjoy all the emotional benefits that accompany that acceptance.

How to Promote
Body Acceptance

Do you wish you lived in a different body? Since you don't, you might as well start appreciating the one you have. The following mind-body techniques can help you begin to feel more comfortable in your own skin.

- *Visualize your ideal self.* Spend some time imagining how you would walk, dress and carry yourself if you really loved your body. Alternatively, remember a time when you felt completely accepting of your body and comfortable in it and try to re-create the experience in the expression on your face, in your posture and body language and in the way you think about your body. Then try acting as if you really love and accept your body for an entire day and see how it feels. You'll probably like it. Feeling beautiful really starts with how you treat yourself in your mind.

- *Start a body-image diary.* Each day write down whatever negative thoughts you have about your body, then try to refute them; think of these as erroneous assumptions that must be corrected. Also consider what else may have been bothering you. Sometimes people blame their bodies—or project negative feelings onto them—when they're really upset about something else, perhaps an argument with a spouse or boss. Learning to identify the true source of emotions behind body-loathing can help such feelings dissolve.

- *Come to your body's defense.* Imagine how maligned and abused your thighs, hips or butt must feel when you call these areas flabby, ugly or big. Start noticing when you speak to yourself harshly about your body and rally to its defense by replacing negative statements with positive or neutral ones, by complimenting your body instead of degrading it. If you've been carrying on about the width of your hips, remind yourself that those hips helped you give birth (if you're a mother). If you often make self-deprecating remarks about your butt, point out to yourself that your husband appreciates its ampleness (if that's the case) or that it looks great in a pair of jeans. If you practice short-circuiting these negative thoughts, it will gradually become automatic, even in potentially distressing situations. Psychologists often call this principle "stress inoculation"—and they contend it does work.

- *Stop hiding.* Wearing baggy clothes may seem like a good way to camouflage your body, thus minimizing your discomfort, but it can actually help you maintain a negative body image. If you've been doing this habitually, practice wearing body-hugging jeans instead of baggy trousers in situations where you're likely to feel less self-conscious (at home, for example). Gradually, work up to more difficult situations, such as a party.

In coming out of hiding, look beyond fashion, though: If you really want to improve your body image, it's important to confront situations or activities you've been avoiding and work through your discomfort. Just as people can overcome a fear of heights by gradually exposing themselves to such fears—this is called "desensitization"—you can overcome feeling bad about your body by facing anxiety-provoking situations such as joining a new exercise class. Confront these insecurity-triggering situations one at a time. It will be that much easier if you prepare yourself mentally, by relaxing and imagining yourself coping successfully with a scenario ahead of time, if you give yourself a pep talk to help you get through it and if you reward yourself afterward with praise and a treat. With each successful encounter, your body- and self-confidence will improve.

- *Focus on your assets.* Force yourself to make a list of the body parts you *do* like and highlight those aspects. (If you get stuck, ask a friend or family member what they think your best features are.) If you think your hands are your strongest point, treat yourself to a manicure; if it's your complexion you like most, treat yourself to a scarf in a flattering color and wear it around your neck. Choose clothes and colors that enhance your best characteristics and give yourself affirmations on a regular basis while gazing in the mirror: Make eye contact with yourself and say aloud, "I really have a dynamite smile" or "My eyes really sparkle when I wear blue"—or whatever positive statement you genuinely feel. The idea is to train a kinder, gentler eye on yourself. Just as smiling can boost your mood, complimenting your body can help you start to feel good about it.

- *Sign up for movement therapy.* Just as your mindset may require some retooling when it comes to body image, your movement habits may benefit from a little readjustment. Some body-image experts recommend participating in mind-body disciplines—such as yoga, tai chi, the Pilates technique, dance therapy, or the Alexander or Feldenkrais method—to help you begin to feel more comfortable with the way your body moves, with your breathing and with your sense of grounding. With all of these techniques, proper instruction is important, so look for a qualified instructor in your area.

Self-Esteem **Boost**

1. Accept sincere compliments. Most compliments are truly from the giver's heart. Don't squander that; a simple "thank you" is all that's needed.

2. Treat yourself like an honored guest. Make all your meals worth the effort and calories.

3. Be a picky eater. If you crave a piece of chocolate, don't settle for supermarket candy—insist on one perfect imported chocolate.

4. Speak up. If a friend repeatedly leans on you for favors she never returns,

let her know you're annoyed. You deserve to be listened to and treated with respect.

5. Don't hide behind nondescript hair or makeup. Even if you're working on improving your appearance, you should take pride in the way you look right now. Taking care of your grooming sends a message to the world: I like myself and I expect others to like me, too.

Something to Think About

Think about the parts of your body you love or hate and why. How can you make peace with the parts you're not particularly fond of? . . . .

. . . .

. . . .

. . . .

. . . .

. . . .

. . . .

. . . .

. . . .

. . . .

. . . .

. . . .

. . . .

. . . .

CHAPTER twelve

THE STYLE FACTOR

tyle has nothing to do with size, and everything to do with knowing who you are and what makes you look and feel good. Some of the world's most stylish women—Elizabeth Taylor, for example—have gone through a revolving door of dress sizes, yet their style has remained constant and true. A smart, stylish woman knows which colors, patterns, jacket shapes, skirt lengths and pants styles, among other things, she can—and *can't*—wear. And she sticks to these options, regardless of the number on the scale.

Style isn't about finding, and settling for, clothes that "just fit." It's also not about looking like some waif-thin model in an outfit that's absurd or choosing designer apparel on the assumption that if it's expensive and has a famous name on the label, then it *must* be stylish.

Your personal style is about selecting clothes that fit your life, your likes and, yes, your body. If you're trying to lose weight, whether it's 10, 20, or 30 or more pounds, that will certainly influence the choices you make. But you also need to take into account your job, whether it's corporate or creative; if travel is involved or work is done out of the house, your home and social life; and the area of the country where you live and its climate.

Add to that list your personal preferences—certain styles of clothing (classic or trendy, for instance) and accessories, colors and details—and your individual style begins to come together, make sense, have meaning and, ultimately, reflect the real you.

Reality Testing the Runways

Every day, images of underweight, pubescent girls parade across TV screens and magazines covers. This media feeding frenzy promoting the thin-is-the-ideal message has altered the mind-set of a society struggling to balance the scales. Also, among the behind-the-fashion-scene collaborators are designers and manufacturers intent on selling fantasy wear for fantasy figures (despite the fact that statistics show an estimated 65 million American women, or 40 percent, currently fit in the size range of 14 to 24, a category coined "plus size" by the industry).

Further controlling a woman's options are trends that promote designers' visions of what is considered "hot"—such as torso-tight dresses, hip-hugging pants, slit-to-there shirts and skirts—even when critics and the buying public's reactions are less than lukewarm. The general consensus on runway looks? Much of it makes little-to-no fashion sense for anyone with a real-life waist, hips or thighs.

So where in the world of 14-year-old, size two supermodels parading in see-through $500 blouses does a grown woman with 25 pounds to lose belong? It certainly doesn't appear to be in the spotlight—yet there are signs that things are slowly changing.

The Large(-size) Picture

Designers and manufacturers have started to recognize that there literally is a broader-sized audience for whom shapeless (read: oversized-to-obscure) dressing doesn't cut it anymore. They recognize that women carrying a few extra pounds or those in weight transition want clothing that transcends the five-, 10- or 15-pound fluctuation.

Since the industry has begun to realize that size needn't preclude style, there has been a proliferation of large-size shops within many major department stores, including Macy's, Bloomingdale's, Saks Fifth Avenue and Nordstrom. Designer lines are giving women on the edge of losing it (a few pounds or more, that is) the fashion edge they've been seeking.

The mantra of these women: the 4-Fs, or fit, function and figure-flattery. These elements are the secrets to successful dressing while slimming down or maintaining the status quo. Clothes that provide ample coverage, yet streamline a woman's shape, can do wonders for self-confidence. Versatility also plays an important part in the weighting game: The more smoothly clothes move from one point on the scale to another, as well as from day to night and season to season, the easier it is to maintain a sense of style and consistently feel good about yourself.

Making Friends with Your Mirror

It all starts in front of your full-length mirror. Being able to accept what you see, whether it's a wide waistline or thick thighs, allows you to let go of your old self-image— the overweight one that didn't deserve to look stylish.

Acceptance comes from a place deep inside that recognizes you have power over your body, rather than the reverse. Because the number on the scale doesn't match the one in your head doesn't mean it won't; it only means it doesn't *right now.*

Weight issues are often closely linked to self-esteem. If yours is in need of a boost, try separating your size from your identity—and seeing what you're all about. Does an extra 10 or 20 pounds make you less lovable, intelligent, friendly or funny? Once you can shift the focus from your weight to the traits that make you unique, you'll find it easier to forgive your figure and yourself.

The next step to style involves learning to work with what you've got by highlighting what you like and minimizing what you don't. Think of it as maximizing your appearance from head to toe. Are you secretly proud of your long, slim legs, but less than thrilled with the shape of your stomach? There's an easy answer: A stitched-down pleat-front skirt that falls above the knee provides a leggy effect while visually flattening below-the-waist bulge. Maybe you have a great bustline, but a not-so-great bottom line. Downplay a large derrière by wearing A-line or flared skirts (never pleated or form-fitting) and loose-fitting pants (anything tight is like a stoplight), and play up what's on top with a top that subtly calls attention to your curves.

Proportions can make—or break—the best outfit, and good balance is crucial:

- **Structured yet shapely** over slim, or flowing if you're fuller above the waist.

- **Long over lean** if you're fuller below the waist.

- **Slim above and full below the waist** (or vice versa) if you're thicker throughout the middle.

As you start (or continue) to slim down, you may experience some changes in your proportions. Weight shifts and fluctuations are more common than you might imagine, but they don't have to make your style take a detour. Here are some of the new-body basics to brush up on:

If you have 50+ pounds to lose:

- **Get real.** What are your expectations of slimming down? Do you imagine suddenly being able to wear everything? The reality is that while you'll certainly have much more fashion freedom at your slimmer size, your body shape is still constant.

- **Shop before you drop.** Don't wait until you drop down to your goal weight before buying new clothes. Purchasing a great-where-you-are wardrobe basic, such as a classic white men's shirt (the oversized fit generously allows for transition from one size to the next), validates that you deserve to look good **now**, rather than being worthy only when you reach a magic number on the scale. (Plus, the better you feel about yourself in clothes, the more motivated you'll be to get into that smaller size.)

- **Stay in touch.** With your body, that is. Being aware of the good and not-so-good points, plus those areas where you tend to gain and lose first, are your best clues to dressing for slimming success.

If you have 25 pounds to lose:

- **Re-think your image.** Dropping 25 pounds lifts your ego, and it gives you opportunity to really look at yourself and examine your fashion sensibilities. This is the time to critique your past fashion picks to determine whether you really loved them or simply settled for "something in your size." While style can have many influences, it's best when it's consistent and true-to-you.

- **Bridge the gap.** Twenty-five pounds is roughly two dress sizes—certainly a substantial weight loss, but not necessarily enough to throw your entire wardrobe away for a new one. Smoothly span the size range with a few well-chosen pieces. Stretchy (not clingy) knits, wrap-waist styles and A-line and flared shapes are the looks that easily keep pace with your changing waistline and see you through thick and thin.

- **Lose the flab.** Slimming down and firming up are two entirely different animals. If you're not ready to commit to exercise, "fake" firmness by opting for separates with body-sleeking Spandex.

If you have 10 pounds to lose:

- **Let your clothes be your scale.** The less weight you have to lose, it seems, the more stubbornly it clings. But don't live your life by the scale: You'll know quickly enough if a waistband feels tight or a button refuses to stay buttoned up. Feeling comfortable in your clothes is a key component to style confidence.

- **Keep "big" sizes out of sight, out of mind.** If you're not giving away the clothes that are big on you now, relegate them to the back of your closet. That way you won't be tempted to let your weight slip, knowing there are clothes you can always fall back on.

- **Get into shape.** No, this isn't about bodybuilding, but body "sculpting." Why not show off your hard-won shape with clothes that subtly highlight your curves? If you've recently rediscovered your waistline, opt for a waist-length jacket or cropped top to show off a little middle. Or if you're happy once more with your hips, consider low-slung pants or a skirt.

Building a Transitional Wardrobe

The mainstay of any successful weight loss wardrobe is a core group of basics that easily interchange with other separates you own. The good news is a big budget (or closet) isn't required. What is needed are classic shapes in season-spanning, fine fabrics (including cotton, rayon, lightweight wool, silk and good synthetics, all of which are supple, drapable and figure-flattering), with built-in, size-adjusting details (such as drawstring and wrap waistlines—*not* elastic, which causes fabric to balloon out below the waist, adding unwanted inches to your hips).

Look through your closet to determine which separates you need. All seven pieces suggested mix and match with each other effortlessly, providing colors are complementary.

Larger-Size **Sources**

Be on the lookout for these body-friendly clothing lines:

- Elisabeth by Liz Claiborne
- Danskin Plus
- Eagle's Eye
- Hearts Delight
- Lane Bryant Design
- Venezia Jeans Clothing Co. denim and sportswear

- New Options Plus
- Channa, Inc.
- Nostalgia II
- Just Desserts dresses
- Jerry & Me knitwear
- Select
- Harbour Vue
- Cynthia
- Blue Clover Jeanswear
- Saks Fifth Avenue Salon Z
- Emanuel Ungaro
- Mary McFadden Studio
- Givenchy
- Gianni Versace

- Andrea Jovine
- Forgotten Woman
- Adrienne Vittadini
- Dana Buchman
- Ellen Tracy
- Resortwear by Rain
- InStyle
- High Society
- La Cera
- Bodyslimmers by Nancy Ganz
- Goddess bras
- Fine And Fancy Lingerie
- Intimates lingerie and sleepwear
- Carol Wior swimsuits

Start with these seven separates:

1. **Long jacket.** Go for a semi-shapely cut (even if you have weight to lose, a gently-fitted style subtly defines your waist, which, in turn, makes you look more svelte) in a fingertip-length, to ensure ample coverage of hips and derrière. It's the perfect pro-portion for both short and long skirts, slim and full-leg pants.

2. **Classic white shirt.** A great lightweight layering piece (a must-have for women in size transition), a men's-style shirt provides an oversized effect. It can be worn under a suit, over a T-shirt and leggings (even a bathing

and-down (soft and full, another variation of the theme) slims as it skims past pounds you'd rather not see.

7. **Leggings.** Overall, you'll look slimmer when you opt for sleek, body-hugging leggings over stiff, bulky jeans. Leggings, especially, call for the long-over-lean proportion.

Quality Control

In a transitional wardrobe, where a few well-chosen pieces are the starting point for innumerable looks, quality counts. Why? Because everything that's paired with them will instantly look richer and more polished. Plus, less-than-meticulously-made clothes can play up just what you don't want the world to see. Cheap fabrics can look stiff and bunch up, tacking on "inches," while poorly finished seams and buttonholes can give way to the strain of excess weight. You can hardly go for a streamlined effect when your jacket or skirt won't lie flat or your shirt is gaping open.

Color It Special

Hit or myth: Black is the most slimming color you could wear. The real truth is, the best pound-paring palettes can range from neutrals (like taupe) to brights (lime green) to darks (navy or brown, the new "black").

   The one caveat: the color placement. A single shade (or two or three in the same tone) worn top to toe makes for the slimmest illusion, as it creates that unbroken, body-lengthening line.

REALITY CHECK

Patterns and Other "Fattening" Habits

Here's a hit list of details to avoid if you're busily down-scaling:

- Big floral patterns
- Bold prints
- Big patch pockets
- Oversized buttons, touches and trims
- Horizontal patterns
- Trouser cuffs
- Bulky fabrics

suit), knotted at the waist over a skirt or pants . . . just about any way you can imagine.

3. **Tunic-length sweater.** This follows the same principle as the long jacket, but is less structured and more relaxed. It works over both short and long hemlines.

4. **Classic crewneck T-shirt.** It's the inner secret to layering without adding bulk.

5. **Straight or A-line skirt.** A strong vertical line (or softened version) visually adds height to your frame, downsizes your width.

6. **Straight- or full-leg trousers.** These follow the same theory as the skirt. Straight-up-

Remember these other coloring guidelines (they apply to makeup, too): Put darker shades on bigger areas (deep colors cause the background to recede), lighter shades on the areas you want to bring out. Consider color-blocking, too. The strategic placement of a positive-negative (or contrasting) color combination can instantly "pare" pounds.

Accessories to the Facts (and Other Wardrobe Traps)

The last word in style: Accents. Earrings, necklaces, pins and rings. Bracelets. Bags. Sunglasses. Stockings. Shoes. Anything and everything that pulls your outfit together. Make it personal, give it the proper importance and it becomes the perfect finish to your stylish statement. The best way to pull it all together while you're losing it, pound by pound, inch by inch: Just keep the scale of the accessories similar and in proportion to your body. If you're big-boned, for instance, you'll need big-to-bold jewelry to look in sync (a delicate little necklace will just look lost on you). Conversely, if you're petite with a few pounds to lose, you need accessories that don't overwhelm your frame.

Some extras that are worth avoiding:

- **A big, wide belt.** It cuts your figure in half, so you look shorter and squatter.

- **Patterned hosiery.** Thin-ribbed is the exception. Anything else can cause legs to "spread," looking wider than they really are.

- **A big, heavy bag.** It's true: a bag that's overweight can visually weigh *you* down, too. (Ever notice women on the street slumping over from their heavyweight bags?)

- **Too clunky or too delicate shoes.** Either one can ruin your thinner image. Clunky shoes can look like ballasts if you're not top-to-toe slender, and dainty styles can make you appear heavier than you are above the ankles.

- **A head-hugging hat.** A hat or cap that rests flat against a full face only emphasizes its round shape. The better choice: a softly brimmed hat or flowing scarf, which "trims" inches from full cheeks.

Dressing well is one way you can be good to yourself, today and tomorrow. Whether you're a size 16 or six, just keep following these techniques and tips and you'll find a style that's *your* perfect fit.

Something to Think About

Ideally, what would make shopping a pleasant experience? Make a list of the stores you prefer shopping at—jot down what makes the experience a pleasure. . . . .

. . . .

. . . .

. . . .

. . . .

. . . .

. . . .

. . . .

. . . .

. . . .

. . . .

. . . .

. . . .

. . . .

. . . .

part 4

THE CLEVER COOK

CHAPTER thirteen

COOK, KNOW THYSELF

do you think of food as a friend, a pleasure and a comfort that's soothing and nourishing? Or is it an enemy you must face daily, challenging your willpower and causing you to weigh more than you want to?

You probably love *and* hate food. On the one hand, you, as well as the rest of society, celebrate food's pleasures in glossy magazine photos and tempting advertisements; on the other, you deem certain foods—often the same ones that are so pleasurable—as sinful indulgences.

If you regard certain foods, like butter and chocolate, as villains and view others, like broccoli and oat bran, as saviors that boost longevity, what do you make of olive oil and wine, two foods that end up on both the "savior" and "villain" list? If your head is spinning from all these confusing, contradictory food signals, rest assured: you are not alone.

America's Culinary Heritage: Guilt

Ambivalence about food is a particularly American phenomenon, with roots going back as far as the first European settlers, the Pilgrims. With their belief that earthly desires must be suppressed in the service of God, Puritans frowned upon taking pleasure in the act of eating. Eating for anything but sustenance was deemed immoral, and overweight individuals were considered weak. Today, the national tendency to scarf down dinner or eat meals on the run—removing much of the enjoyment from the process— finds its roots in the Puritan ethic.

Each subsequent group of immigrants who settled in this country brought their own traditions and attitudes toward food. For most, who came here fleeing poverty in their own countries, America was a land of abundance, where they could put meat on the table every night and eat daily the kinds of foods reserved only for special occasions in the old country. (Ironically, the grain- and vegetable-rich, low-meat diet they left behind is the one health experts urge us to adopt today.) America was the land of endless territory, expanding boundaries and, by extension, heaping plates.

Out of this immigrant patchwork grew our nation's "big-food" traditions: the abundant Sunday dinner, whether lasagna in Brooklyn or fried chicken in Birmingham; the church and synagogue socials teeming with rich baked goods; birthday parties featuring endless candy and cake; and, of course, the groaning Thanksgiving table. Not eating one's fill was somehow un-American.

Depending on the decade in which you grew up, images of starving children in Europe, Asia or Africa may have been conjured to prompt you to finish your dinner. What's more, your parents may have contributed to your guilt quotient: The "if you loved me/your mother, you'd eat" mentality was commonplace. Whether or not you liked what was on your plate, you were taught to eat all your food to make Mom happy or, perhaps, love you more. You ate not to satisfy yourself, but for others.

And every night, in homes across the country, parents urged their children to join "the clean plate club." The only requirements for membership: No food could go to waste, and children had to leave the dinner table stuffed, whether they came to the table hungry or not. If you look carefully, you may still find remnants of your family's attitudes influencing your eating habits today.

Food and Science

The nation's fascination with science and faith in technology also shapes our attitudes toward food. Early in this century there was an obsession with vitamins and minerals, as researchers began to discover the basic elements of nourishment. Later on, when physical exams found rickets and other diseases of malnutrition in soldiers enlisting to fight World War II, the concept of a "balanced diet" became critical. The four food groups were born, and—technology to the rescue—the era of fortified foods began.

In fact, for the greater part of this century, the chief message scientists, health experts and advertisers have conveyed about food has been to *eat more:* drink more milk for strong bones, eat meat daily for vigor, build a strong body with lots of sliced white bread. Many of us grew up absorbing those messages, and they remain part of our belief system.

In recent decades, however, the pendulum has swung to the other extreme: Now, obesity has become the nation's chief nutrition problem, and experts are cautioning us to *eat less.* In typical American fashion, we have tended to make that admonishment an all-or-nothing proposition. For example, when scientific research indicated that a high-fat diet could contribute to the risk of heart disease and cancer, fat became public enemy number one in this country. It had to be eliminated—not just reduced, but cut out altogether.

And, once again, we've turned to technology to rescue us from our fate. As science uncovers the bad news, we count on technology to supply the good: Witness the proliferation of vitamin-fortified, low-fat and fat-free foods that let us satisfy our cravings without the accompanying guilt. No wonder it's so easy to be seduced.

Unfortunately, "fat-free" isn't necessarily the answer. If you're like most people, you've probably uncovered the dirty little secret about "fat-free": you can eat an entire box of fat-free brownies and still want more. Fat-free simply doesn't supply the satisfaction or mouth feel of one super-rich brownie.

Enjoying Eating Again

With all these conflicting impulses surrounding food, it's tough to feed yourself and feel satisfied. But it *is* possible to break the unhealthy habits you learned as a child and develop a sane, balanced view toward eating and food. The first step is to acknowledge you need to eat to live, and that eating is supposed to be enjoyable. Make a resolution to eat consciously: Slow down and savor each meal, giving it your full attention.

When you sit down to eat, make sure your environment is pleasant and serene. Make it a rule to turn the TV off, and don't answer the phone. Classical music playing softly in the background can help you to eat more slowly, and using good china, cloth napkins and candles can make even the most mundane supper seem like a gourmet feast. Arrange the food on your plate as attractively as you can. Even a brown stew can look wonderful in the right bowl, or with a sprig of herbs or a fat-free yogurt garnish— think of how delectable it looks in a food magazine.

Even if you have small children, start by setting aside one night a week to use "the good

Just a Taste

If you find yourself taking "just a taste" during meal preparation, you could take in a lot of calories without noticing. Here's how a one-tablespoon taste adds up, calorie-wise, for some popular dishes.

Item	Calories/tablespoon
Chocolate chip cookie dough	60
Vanilla frosting	57
Macaroni and cheese	22
Butterscotch pudding	21
Beef stroganoff	20
Mashed potatoes	17
Pork fried rice	17
Chili con carne	16
Chicken chow mein	14
Tomato sauce with meat	10

stuff." You'll be pleasantly surprised by how well-behaved kids can be when you catch them off guard and treat them like grown-ups.

Also, work on conquering the deprivation mentality. Be choosy when you buy food for yourself and your family; think quality, not quantity. By all means, use low-fat and fat-free foods; find the ones you like best and use them regularly. But think of them as just one of many types of tools to help you lose weight rather than a solution to your weight problem.

When you're limiting calories, fat or portions, focus on flavor and texture. Don't force yourself to eat something you don't like just because it's "good for you." Instead, experiment with other nutritious foods and recipes until you find something that pleases your palate. Make sure every mouthful is exquisitely delicious; remind yourself that life is too short to eat bad—or even mediocre—food.

"But wait," you say, "if food tastes that delicious, I won't be able to stop eating it." In fact, you might find just the opposite. With all your senses stimulated—your eyes by the appealing setting, your ears by the music, your nose by the wonderful aromas, your tongue by the interesting tastes and textures—you'll probably need less food to feel like you've had enough. Trust yourself and try it.

When the meal is finished, even though it may go against your (or your Mom's) frugal impulses, don't eat what the kids leave behind. Encourage healthy eating habits, and don't nag them to finish all the food on their plates. How about

making their portions smaller to start with, and let them have seconds if they want more?

Most importantly, let yourself (and your children) have an occasional treat. No person can resist eating something indulgent once in a while. Believing that your willpower will always be rock-hard is a set-up for failure—as well as for feeling frustrated with yourself when you can't meet your impossibly high standards.

Begin to treat food as a friend, and you'll find that it satisfies you more.

What's Your Cooking Style?

Whether you love or hate to cook, you've developed your own ways of preparing a meal. In fact, your cooking style can affect what happens when you sit down to eat. Do any of the following sound like you?

■ Are you a **"speed-scratch"** cook, who puts together meals with components prepared elsewhere (for example, a pizza made from a pre-baked crust with packages of tomato sauce, shredded cheese and sliced pepperoni)? While cooking this way saves time, you could end up with a lot more fat, calories and salt than you bargained for since you didn't do the cooking.

Best options: Read labels carefully, so you know what you're getting—and measure, to make sure you're really eating what the label defines as "one serving." Or, take a cue from cooks with big families and prepare some of those easy-assembly components yourself.

Set aside Sunday afternoon for "big-batch" cooking: perhaps a pot of tomato sauce, roast beef or chicken, batches of steamed chopped greens, vegetable soup, a pound of pasta twists, a baked pizza crust and a bag or two of washed salad greens. Keep these in your fridge in single-serving containers, and dip into them throughout the week to create your own meals in minutes.

■ Are you a **"tireless taster,"** who sneaks spoonfuls of a dish as it cooks? While you might need a tiny taste to check seasonings, each spoonful adds up. By the time dinner is on the table, you might have already eaten the equivalent of a serving or two.

Best options: Use only a teaspoon for tasting, or get in the habit of spitting out what you've tasted. If you find yourself tasting unconsciously, keep something in your mouth as you work, like a celery stalk or pencil. You'll have to take it out of your mouth to eat. Or cook with an audience. You'll be less inclined to snack if you know family or friends are watching.

■ Are you a **"hyper-hold-out"** who won't put a morsel in your mouth until the meal you're preparing is on the table and you're uncontrollably ravenous?

Best options: Drink some skim milk, or nibble on a healthy snack as you cook— say, some carrots or low-fat crackers—so you won't be tempted to gorge when dinner is served. Or have a snack before you start cooking to ward off hunger pangs.

■ Are you a **"feed the troops"** cook, who always makes big batches so there will be leftovers? This is a great time-saving technique—if you're disciplined enough to measure out just what you need and truly put away the rest. If not, this method may put too much temptation in your way.

Best options: Use recipes that serve only the amount of people for whom you're cooking. If you must make a big batch, portion it into leftover containers before you sit down to eat, and freeze them when they're cold. That will prevent you from helping yourself to seconds.

Raising a Healthy Eater

Like all infants, you arrived in this world with healthy eating habits: you ate only as much as you needed, and stopped when you'd had enough. Cuddled in your mother's or father's arms, eating was a pure pleasure.

Somewhere between then and now, you've come to fear eating, feeling as though it's a constant battle between your hunger and your will. You worry you'll pass those feelings on to your children, especially if you have daughters, as no doubt your family imposed their food hang-ups on you. What can you do to prevent this? Here are some ideas for raising a child with a healthy appetite.

- **Love your child in other ways besides feeding her.** When your child is an infant, she comes to associate you, and your love, with food. As she gets older, it's easy to continue this food-love connection, by treating the meals you prepare as gifts of love from you (which, if she doesn't eat them, become rejections of you instead of the food). Avoid this trap by showing your love in other ways, such as reading her stories, going on special walks together, or crayoning in coloring books with her. Don't serve a special food as a reward or force a disliked food as punishment. Keep meal times neutral.

The Good, the Bad and the Ugly

Just a few examples of our country's continuing confusion about healthy eating:

- The latest National Health and Nutrition Examination Survey found that Americans are eating leaner: 34 percent of our daily calories come from fat, down from 42 percent in the sixties.

- Yet the same survey found that we're eating more calories—an average of 231 more per day. That's one reason why over a third of Americans are overweight today—one of the highest rates in the world.

- According to a 1996 survey by the Calorie Control Council, 88 percent of U.S. adults consumed reduced-fat foods and beverages on a regular basis. That's up from 67 percent five years ago.

- In 1995, we munched on an average of 21.3 pounds of snack foods per person—up from 19.8 pounds five years earlier. Potato chips topped the list, followed by pretzels and tortilla chips. We spent most on salty snacks ($6.7 billion) and cookies ($3.7 billion).

- Eighty-six percent of Americans ate at least one low-fat or nonfat food during a surveyed two-week period, according to the NPD Group, a consumer research company. That number has stayed fairly steady for several years.

- The NPD survey also found that French fries, hamburgers and chicken nuggets were the fastest-growing restaurant foods, and that more and more of us are eating our restaurant meals in our cars.

- Accept that you can't—and shouldn't—control the quantity of food your child eats. Your child's stomach will tell her when she has had enough; forcing food on her will teach her to suppress this critical food-regulating cue. If she doesn't learn what "enough" feels like, she'll have problems stopping eating later in life.

- Don't make one food "better" than another. Children don't eat a food because it's "good for them"; they eat it because it tastes good. Likewise, they quickly learn that broccoli isn't as desirable as cake, if they can't have the cake until they've finished the broccoli. If you've planned a dessert, serve it whether or not the broccoli is finished, and present it without fanfare, as just another course.

- Let your child snack between meals if she is hungry. Forcing her to deny her hunger "because it will spoil her dinner" only sends her the message that her natural feelings of hunger aren't to be trusted, and that eating occurs not because of hunger but because it's the proper time. That's setting her up to eat out of habit rather than need. Instead, have a good selection of healthy foods available so she can pick a snack she likes, and don't make a fuss if she doesn't eat much at dinner.

- Make eating times important and worthwhile. Don't have the TV on or allow toys or comic books at the table. Food should be the only focus.

- Avoid obsessing over the balanced meal. You aren't a bad parent if your child doesn't eat three square meals a day. In fact, most kids' appetites vary widely from day to day, but over the course of several days they'll probably get what they need somehow. Even the child who eats only peanut-butter sandwiches will eventually want something else.

- Don't put your child "on a diet" if he's overweight. It will only make him feel as if he doesn't measure up to your expectations of him. Instead, work on helping your child—and yourself—become more active. How about signing the two of you up for tennis lessons, or taking a post-dinner walk together a few nights a week?

Something to Think About

When you see an advertisement for fattening, luscious food, how do you feel?

. . . .

. . . .

. . . .

. . . .

Complete the following sentences:

I love food because ...

. . . .

. . . .

. . . .

. . . .

I hate food because ...

. . . .

. . . .

. . . .

. . . .

. . . .

CHAPTER fourteen

THE LEAN, MEAN KITCHEN

Unless you're one of the chosen few who has a staff of chefs and servants at the ready, you probably feel inadequate when it comes to those day-to-day activities of planning meals and purchasing and preparing food. You're certain you'd be healthier if only you knew the right techniques for cutting fat, if only you had the time to cook from scratch, if only you had fancier equipment, if only your spouse and kids didn't demand fattening treats . . . the "if only" list could stretch for miles, making the simple act of feeding yourself and your family seem like an impossible task.

Yet with a few simple strategies and techniques, you'll find that buying and cooking food isn't an obstacle to healthier eating habits or losing weight; it can even be a pleasure. You don't have to have Julia Child's cooking ability or Martha Stewart's kitchen. In fact, your own kitchen probably will do just fine. Chances are, however, that it's due for a makeover.

Is your kitchen loaded down with useless gadgets and appliances you rarely use? Are the cupboards booby-trapped with treats that tempt you every time you open their doors? When you need something, is it impossible to find?

A well-organized kitchen, stocked with a few essential tools and healthy foods in the pantry, can actually help you stick to your health and weight loss goals. The principle is simple: Make sure the healthiest foods and the equipment you'll need most are within plain view—and tuck the bad-for-you stuff and rarely used gadgets out of reach and sight. This process, called *stimulus control*, can play a big role in changing eating behavior.

Equipment: The Ideal Stuff

The well-stocked, low-fat kitchen doesn't require stacks of pots and pans or drawers full of gadgets. Here are some of the most important items—from the essentials to the useful luxuries—for low-fat cooking.

The Musts:

■ **Good knives and a sharpening steel.** Mandatory for any cook, high-quality knives help you breeze through the most time-consuming parts of healthy food preparation, such as chopping vegetables and trimming fat from meats. An all-purpose chef's knife and a paring knife should be all you need; choose high-carbon stainless steel, which keeps a sharp edge best.

- **A kitchen scale and measuring cups and spoons.** Be sure to purchase them in a full range of sizes. By using precise measurements instead of eyeballing, you'll learn portion control—and get better results from recipes, to boot.

- **A 10-inch nonstick skillet.** This size skillet will suffice for most 2-to-4-serving recipes, and it can dramatically cut the amount of fat you need for frying. Look for those made of heavy stainless steel with an aluminum core (the heavier they are, the more evenly they'll heat) or enamel-coated cast iron. A smaller omelet size is also handy. Another option: a large heavy nonstick saucepan or Dutch oven, to double as a cooking pot and skillet.

- **A steamer basket or rack.** You can buy an inexpensive, collapsible steamer basket at department and kitchen stores and fit it in your saucepans, or choose a saucepan with a perforated steamer insert. Either way, you'll be able to cook vegetables, dumplings and small pieces of fish or poultry virtually fat-free.

- **Baking sheets.** Not just for cookies, baking sheets are perfect for oven roasting foods you'd normally fry, such as potatoes, peppers or eggplant. Simply toss the foods with a little oil and spread in a single layer on the baking sheet. If you can find them, buy nonstick sheets, which will help you cut fat even further; heavier types or insulated sheets (hollow inside) will hold heat more evenly. A metallic, reflective surface like aluminum will help prevent foods from browning too deeply.

- **Nonstick bakeware.** Think 8-inch round pans, muffin tins and 9-by-5-inch loaf pans. They'll give your low-fat baking a boost, since you needn't grease the pan.

- **A roasting pan with a drip pan insert.** Available in kitchen stores, these pans allow you to roast meats and poultry as fat drips off (a great way to cook burgers, too).

- **A grater.** A grater is a good way to exert "sprinkle control" for cheese; grating citrus zest directly on dishes also provides a fat-free flavor boost. The four-sided box grater is easiest to find, but it's probably more convenient to use and clean a simpler, paddle-like hand grater. You can find either in kitchen stores.

- **Sealable plastic bags.** Cook big batches of the low-fat foods you love, such as soups or stews, and freeze leftover single-serving portions in these reusable bags. They'll stack easily and take up less room than plastic tubs. Don't forget to label and date them.

Nice to Haves:

- **A microwave oven.** Those who own them rave about their ability to steam vegetables quickly with little or no water and minimal nutrient loss.

- **A blender and/or food processor.** This is essential for making low-fat shakes, purees for soups and sauces. A food processor also makes short work of grating large quantities of hard cheese, shredding vegetables, grinding lean meat and making low-fat doughs.

- **A pressure cooker.** This old favorite has been given new life, particularly for vegetarians. A pressure cooker can shorten the cooking time for traditionally slow-cooked nutritious foods like dried beans and lean cuts of meat. An added bonus: fewer nutrients get lost during the shorter cooking time.

- **A fat separator and/or skimmer.** Spoon a sauce or gravy into a measuring-cup-like fat separator, and pour out all but the layer of fat on the surface. For larger-batch foods such as soup or stew, skim the surface with a spoon-like fat skimmer. (Alternatively, refrigerate the dish until the settled fat hardens and can be scraped off.)

- **A hand-held blender.** Sometimes called immersion blenders, these gadgets are wonderful for turning cooked vegetables and fruits into low-fat, tasty sauces and creamy soups in seconds—right in the pot.

- **Parchment paper.** Perfect for lining baking sheets and pans so that they don't need greasing. You can also tuck foods (try chicken breasts or fish topped with herbs) into a parchment paper packet and bake them on a baking sheet; the food will cook in its own steam and sealed-in flavorings.

- **An outdoor grill.** Grills add wonderful smoky flavors to meats, poultry, fish and vegetables without adding fat.

Outfitting the Pantry

Once your equipment is in place, ask yourself whether your pantry could use a little remodeling, too. You can use the principles of stimulus control to help you organize your cupboards and refrigerator. The goal: making nutritious meals come to mind every time you open a door.

Cabinets

Empty out one of your cabinets to clean it, and you'll discover all kinds of things you'd forgotten about. Time to get rid of those foods you haven't used in over a year; accept the fact that you probably won't ever use them. The same goes for overly rich food gifts like canned pâté and jarred fudge sauce. Toss anything beyond its expiration date and give the rest to a friend or a local soup kitchen.

Give the cabinets a good scrubbing and a fresh strip of washable shelf liner. Now that the shelves aren't so cluttered, they'll be easier to keep clean, so plan on repeating this "spring cleaning" at least twice a year.

Is there enough lighting in the kitchen to really see what's in the cupboards? The biggest shelves—those at eye level—should be well illuminated. Perhaps your overhead light could use some more wattage, or you can install some inexpensive wall lighting (check your hardware or home store for ideas). Fluorescent bulbs are an energy-efficient choice.

The only foods on your shelves now should be those you really need and use, and the healthiest items should be the easiest to find. Here's how to organize them:

- Put the most tempting foods, such as snack chips, at the back of a faraway cabinet, on the high shelves. If you don't see them, you're less likely to eat them. This is a good place to store high-fat treats you've bought for your children or spouse, too, if you'd like to steer them toward more nutritious eating.

- Keep less tempting staples, such as pasta, canned vegetables and dried beans, at eye level in the front of the cabinet. They'll be the first things you see—and will help spur healthy meal ideas.

- Nutritious snacks like dried fruit, whole-wheat crispbreads, popcorn and applesauce can go on lower shelves, where they're easy to spot when you're searching for a snack.

- Try putting spices and flavorings near some of your staple foods, to inspire you to prepare them creatively. Put bay leaves and thyme near the beans, or garlic powder or paprika near the popcorn.

- Don't store spices and oils in the cabinets by the stove. Though it's convenient, the heat will speed the oil's going rancid and the spices' losing their flavor.

Refrigerator

Refrigerators make wonderful hiding places for forgotten leftovers, moldy produce and strange condiments used only once. Turn off the power, open the door and ruthlessly get rid of them all. Remove the rest of the food and pack it in an insulated ice chest to keep cold while you work.

Wash the fridge inside and out with a mild soap or baking soda-and-water solution, and put a small box of baking soda in the back of a middle shelf to combat odors. Replace or clean the light bulb so the interior is brightly lit. Turn the fridge back on and wait for it to reach 40°F or lower before reloading. (You'll want to repeat this cleaning every two months or so.)

Before you replace all the food exactly where it was before, think about how often you find yourself staring into the fridge, looking for something to eat. Now, consider how might you arrange the shelves so that you can't fail to see the healthy stuff first:

- The top shelf is the premium spot. Here's where to place low-fat (1 percent) or skim milk, calcium-fortified orange juice and, most importantly, water (to remind you to drink at least six glasses daily).

- Put snacks on the second shelf, so you won't have to hunt when you have a craving. Make it easy to pick something nutritious: have carrots, celery and other veggies pre-cut, washed and ready to nibble. Keep a jar of salsa or fat-free dip nearby, along with fat-free yogurt and cut-up fruit.

  Make it a habit to store chopped cooked greens on the second shelf, too (try cooking them as soon as you get home from shopping, while you're putting away groceries). They can be sprinkled into almost any food—pizza, soups, stews, salads, stir-fries—or tossed with a little vinegar and garlic powder and eaten as a snack.

- Use the third shelf for storing vegetables, where you'll see them easily. Wrap them in "breathable" veggie bags to protect them from drying out (recycle the ones you buy pre-cut produce in); you can also use plastic bags you've perforated with a toothpick in a few places.

  The third shelf is also a good place to group ingredients to trigger meal ideas. For example, place tomatoes, zucchini, peppers and an onion next to lean ground turkey to inspire a veggie-packed chili. (Of course,

onions shouldn't be stored long-term in the fridge, and instead in a cool dark place, but keeping a single onion there a day or two to help meal planning won't hurt.) Fat-free cheeses and sauces can go next to the cooked pasta.

- Veggie drawers are the last place you should store vegetables—you won't see them unless you hunt. Instead, store tempting foods like peanut butter, candy or cookies here, out of sight. Or hide them in the back of one of the narrowest shelves, where they'll be hard to find behind the eggs and leftovers.

- Whole grains like brown rice and whole-wheat couscous and flour, which need refrigeration to delay rancidity, can go on the bottom shelves. Keep them in dated sealable plastic bags.

- Use the door to keep low-fat seasonings and flavorings handy, and put them in meal-inspiring groupings. Place soy sauce, garlic and spreadable fruit near each other, for example—they'll make a quick Asian-style barbecue sauce for chicken or pork.

Freezer

Too many of us use a freezer as a graveyard— a final resting place for leftovers that will never again see the light of day. Is your freezer loaded with mysterious packages? Perhaps the only identifiable container is that ice cream you bought

Drink Up the H$_2$O

1. Make a weak herbal tea.

2. Add some lemon, parsley or cucumber.

3. Try carbonated, flavored seltzers and mineral waters.

4. Fill a pitcher or water bottle and keep it nearby as you work.

5. Add garlic, lemon, parsley, herbs and spices to hot water for a refreshing "soup."

"for the kids" that you find yourself spooning into when you're hungry. Time for a spring cleaning; arm yourself with freezer containers, sealable plastic bags and plenty of freezer tape.

Turn off the freezer and unload its contents into a well-insulated freezer chest. Go through every package individually to determine whether the food is still edible. Packaged foods will have expiration dates; those strange leftovers won't. Throw out anything with freezer burn or ice crystals, anything that smells or looks funny and anything you know has been there longer than a year. Purge the freezer of too-tempting treats, or repackage them (see below). Rewrap what's left in freezer containers, sealable plastic bags or freezer wrap, and clearly label and date each item.

Wash the freezer with a baking soda–and–water solution and let it dry thoroughly before you turn it back on. Make sure the freezer is fully chilled to 0° F or below before you reload it. Twice a year should be enough for this cleaning task.

As you put back the food, take advantage of the freezer's uncluttered clean state to arrange the items strategically:

- Use the freezer door for storing frozen vegetables, in plain sight. Put your frozen chicken breasts or lean hamburger patties in next to the veggies, to remind you to use them together in your meals. The freezer is a good place to keep single-serving containers of nutritious foods you've cooked in a big batch, such as beans or whole grains, so you can easily thaw and add them to dishes.

- Reserve the front of the top shelf for those odd bits of fat-free seasonings that can really jazz up your cooking but are needed only in small amounts, such as chopped chile peppers, chunks of ginger root, dabs of tomato paste, strips of lemon and lime rind and lemon or lime juice (just freeze in ice cube trays, then store the cubes in sealable plastic bags).

- Use the front eye-level shelves for healthy frozen snacks like frozen seedless grapes, banana slices or strawberries and fruit-juice popsicles.

- Store any foods you have trouble resisting, such as coffee cake or tempting leftovers, in the back of the freezer. Wrap them individually in serving-size portions, and place them in opaque containers, taped shut. The time you need to open them could deter you when you have a craving.

- Use the lower shelves for storing items such as sliced whole-wheat bread, tortillas, halved bagels and low-fat muffins. It's easy to remove only what you need for a quick sandwich or breakfast, while the rest stays fresh. These shelves are also a good place for keeping a large sealable plastic bag to collect bones and other scraps for making stock.

At the Ready

Whether you've got a tiny kitchen or a restaurant-sized one, you actually need very little space to cook most efficiently. Designate a work station—a few feet of counter space where you can do most of your food preparation—and arrange your tools and equipment so that they're all within easy reach of that spot. A good place for a work station is within an arm's length of the sink on one side and the stove or oven on another. Here are some ideas for organizing around your work space:

- Frequently used appliances, such as the food processor, blender and kitchen scale, should go right on the counter, near your cutting board. If you don't have outlets for them all, consider buying an inexpensive "power strip" with multiple outlets and built-in overload ("surge") protection.

- Rarely used appliances (such as a cappuccino maker or hot air popcorn popper) can go in out-of-the-way cabinets, freeing valuable counter space for food preparation. The same goes for those gadgets that do little more than create clutter, such as cherry

REALITY CHECK

Making Progress

1. You can pass a plate of doughnuts at work without having one.

2. You find yourself enjoying your workout.

3. You can "eyeball" a portion size.

4. You look forward to your annual physical.

5. You'd rather walk than ride.

6. You prefer the flavor of skim milk (whole milk tastes too thick).

7. You know what the scale will say before you get on it.

8. You go to the gym to unwind.

9. You cancel your cable television service because you haven't been watching TV lately.

pitters or corn cob scrapers. If your space is limited, put them in a well-labeled box in the basement or donate them to a charity. If you haven't used them in a year, you can probably live without them.

■ Keep your most frequently used cooking tools in the most visible, easily accessible drawers and in the front of the cabinets closest to your work station. This is a good place to store those tools that can help you cook more healthfully, such as a fat separator, a steamer and nonstick cookware. They'll be easy to grab when you need them.

■ Another option if you have limited storage space is to hang what you use most on the wall. A simple pegboard-hook system (available at hardware stores) gives you lots of versatility for only a little money. You can hang your pots and pans there, as well as most of your gadgets.

Something to Think About

If you could have the perfect kitchen, what would it look like?

. . . .

. . . .

. . . .

. . . .

Now, make a list of what you can do to your present kitchen to make it more like the kitchen of your dreams.

. . . .

. . . .

. . . .

. . . .

Pick three things you can do to your kitchen next month to make it more like your dream kitchen.

. . . .

. . . .

. . . .

. . . .

. . . .

CHAPTER fifteen

AT THE MARKET

how do you keep your pantry and refrigerator stocked? Like most Americans, you probably go grocery shopping about twice a week. With more than 30,000 products on the average supermarket's shelves, your excursion is far from a simple one. But with a little planning, you can sail through the aisles unswayed by temptation— and come home only with what you need, without spending more than you'd hoped.

The Game Plan

The first step in making a successful supermarket trip is to recognize and plan for the temptations you'll face, both internal and external. Internally, you'll find your appetite stimulated as you mentally plan your future meals and snacks. The supermarket is not an easy environment for making decisions about food. You'll run into things you love to eat but hadn't planned on buying, and thoughts of straying from your list will inevitably come to mind, such as "Oh, I forgot to put chocolate pudding mix on the list."

Compounding those feelings are the external temptations that the store has lying in wait for you, such as sample tables with their enticing aromas, brightly colored packaging, abundant-looking food displays and on-sale specials that appeal to your bargain-hunting instincts. It's not a conspiracy to make you break your healthy eating intentions, it's simply marketing: Supermarket planners design their stores with the primary intention of inducing you to spend— often far more than you'd planned.

To avoid temptations on all fronts, you need to come up with a game plan before you leave the house. Here are some suggestions to help you create a shopping strategy:

- Bring a shopping list and stick to it. A list will help you stay in control, and you'll be better able to withstand the temptation to make an impulse buy (or "splurchase," as they're called in the grocery store trade).

- Make a list of reliable staples that can always translate into a few meals. This could include plain nonfat yogurt, frozen spinach, chicken broth, canned tuna, low-fat (1 percent) milk, high-fiber cereal, whole-wheat bread and pasta. Make several copies of the list and use one for each shopping trip, adding extras or crossing out as needed.

■ **Have your week's menus in mind when you make your list, so you won't need to make an extra trip later in the week.** A good place to start is the sale circular that arrives in your local newspaper; plan your meals around the produce that's on sale. Make fresh vegetables the main focus—say, a butternut squash soup if winter squash is a bargain, or spaghetti with fresh tomato and basil sauce when tomatoes are abundant. Then look in the meat section for any deals on meat, poultry or lean dairy products to jazz up a vegetable-based main course. Consider skinless chicken drumsticks to simmer with a spaghetti sauce or low-fat ricotta cheese to garnish a soup. Check your refrigerator and pantry, too, to see what could be used in your menus.

■ **Plan at least some of your meals around pre-cut bagged produce;** it can make healthy fare literally fast food. Try a stir-fry or Caesar salad kit (with your own fat-free Caesar dressing), or simmer pre-cut carrots, celery and spinach with chicken broth to make a tasty soup. Frozen vegetables are an even faster option for cooked dishes; they can be tossed into low-fat canned soup, or thawed and layered onto a pizza crust and topped with low-fat shredded cheese.

Coupons and Bulk Foods:
Should You or Shouldn't You?

If you go shopping with a fistful of coupons, remember that a coupon won't save you a dime if it persuades you to buy something you don't really need. Ditch those coupons for cookies or the latest fried snack chips.

As for buying large-size items, they are usually cheaper per pound, but not always—check the unit-price labels. Moreover, buying more than you need or can use might tempt you to eat more than you planned. Sure, a six-pack of rice cakes is a bargain, but will you be tempted to polish off a package in one sitting if you know there are five more around?

- Arrange the shopping list by aisles (produce, cereals, etc.) in the order they appear in the store, so you won't need to backtrack to pick up something you missed earlier. That could extend your shopping time and expose you to more temptations.

- **Leave the kids at home.** Studies show that you'll spend 29 percent more on groceries with a child in tow if you're female, 66 percent if you're a man. Those kid-sized shopping carts (that let your child stroll behind you with her own basket) are more than just entertainment—they're marketing tools so little shoppers can pick up their own favorite, oftentimes unhealthy, foods.

- **Eat a nutritious snack before you go, or shop after a meal.** If you're hungry, you're more likely to buy high-fat junk food and fewer fruits and vegetables.

- **Plan to spend as little time in the store as possible.** The average weekly shopper spends 107.8 minutes in the supermarket, according to tracking studies, and adds about $1.89 to the bill in "splurchases" for each minute spent in the supermarket beyond that limit.

- **Before you enter the store, look at your list.** If you need to pick up only a few things, grab a basket instead of a cart. Besides preventing you from buying more, you'll get some arm-strengthening exercise in the bargain.

On the Trail

At last, you're in the supermarket, armed with your list and steely determination. What awaits you? We've designed a strategy to get you through a typical supermarket:

- **First stop: Produce.** When you enter the store, you're greeted with brightly colored piles of pristine fruit, vegetables and flowers. You're meant to feel as if you've entered a fresh, new world, relaxed and ready to buy. All in all, if you're going to let yourself succumb to the supermarket's lures, this is the place. Don't hurry through; take your time inspecting the fruits and vegetables and seeing what looks good and is on special.

  Best option: Fill your basket with seasonal produce—it's freshest and cheapest—and throw in something new each visit. How about trying starfruit, kohlrabi or mustard greens? Even at premium prices, they're a pretty cheap splurge. Grab some fresh herbs to inspire your cooking; you can always hang up and dry what you can't use right away.

- **Next stops: Canned and Packaged Foods.** Spend the least amount of time in these center aisles, where the processed foods lurk. You'll find eye-catching promotional displays at every turn of your cart; don't be tempted by sale items you don't need. Ditto the products piled in the end-of-aisle displays; often, they only look like a bargain.

On the shelves, don't automatically grab for the items just below eye level—this premium position is usually granted only to items with the highest markups. Have you noticed that the most expensive—and least nutritious—cereals are placed at a kid's-eye level?

In general, steer clear of overly processed meal "kits" like macaroni and cheese, pizza-in-a-box and taco kits. These shortcuts are too often loaded with fat, calories, sodium and hard-to-pronounce additives (just the mystifying ingredients list should be a turn-off)—and most can be made nearly as quickly with fresh ingredients. One exception are the low-fat, reduced-sodium instant soups and couscous cups that make tasty quick lunches.

Best options: Leave your cart at the end of the aisle, fetch what you need and bring it back. You'll be less likely to load up on cookies, chips and canned spaghetti if you have to lug it back to your cart. Look for food processed as minimally as possible (canned tomatoes rather than tomato sauce, uncooked rice instead of flavored rice packets), low-sodium broths, high-fiber cereals, canned and dried beans, canned salmon or water-packed tuna, dried fruit, low-fat crackers, rice cakes and graham crackers.

If you have time to browse, the condiments aisle is a good place to get ideas for livening up your cooking. Many choices are fat-free, including chutneys, salsas, mustards and vinegars. The same goes for the natural foods aisle, where you might find some healthy snacks like whole-wheat crackers, fat-free chips and bean dips, along with healthier versions of convenience foods such as instant brown rice pilaf.

■ Next stops: Meats/Fish/Poultry. You can save money if you buy these big-ticket items when they're on sale or in big quantities—use what you need and freeze the rest. Trim off the skin and fat as soon as you get home, reserving the bones for stock (see pages 243–244 for more on freezing foods).

Best options: Choose meats with the smallest amount of visible fat. Cuts with "loin" or "round" in the title are generally leanest; the leanest cuts of beef are those labeled "select" (ask your butcher for help if you have trouble finding them). Boneless roasts, chops and skinless poultry may be pricey, but there's no waste. As for fish, don't turn up your nose at the frozen cuts; if there's no evidence of dryness (or ice crystals, which indicate thawing), they're often "fresher" and cheaper than the daily catch.

■ Next Stop: Deli. Here, you'll need restraint: Appetizing dishes like meat loaf and macaroni salad beckon from their well-lit displays. Resist the urge to fill your cart; it's not a cafeteria!

Best options: Buy a roasted or rotisserie-style chicken; peel off the skin and slice it

The Hamburger **Alternative**

In light of nutritional guidelines that advise Americans to seriously reduce their consumption of red meat, veggie burgers can be a healthful alternative. Packed with protein and low in fat, some of these burgers taste like the real thing. A study in *Vegetarian Journal* found that the veggie burgers currently available are significantly lower in fat and calories—and more tasty—than those available in the early 1990s. Eleven of the burgers tested by the *Journal* had no fat and anywhere from 70 to 190 calories.

Yet given that some veggie burgers have 12 grams of fat and 210 calories per patty, reading the label is still a must. Burgers made of nuts, seeds or soy—especially those topped with cheese—are higher in fat than those made from grains. But consider this: Even the fattier burgers provide health benefits beyond what meat can offer. They are excellent sources of fiber and are low in saturated fat (the type that stimulates the body's formation of artery-clogging cholesterol). Also, the soy-based burgers may contain compounds that lower cancer and heart disease risks. Here is a guide to the basic burgers now stocked on supermarket shelves:

- *Vegetable-based burgers:* Made mostly of mushrooms, beans, carrots and other ground-up vegetables, these burgers don't have the taste or texture of beef but are an excellent source of fiber and nutrients.

- *Imitation meat:* Made from soy or wheat protein, these have a hamburger-y taste and texture. Some are higher in fat than other types of veggie burgers but still lower in fat than lean ground beef.

- *Grain-based burgers:* These burgers tend to be lower in fat than other types of veggie burgers, but some are bland or taste like bread. You may need to sample a few different brands to find one you like.

- *Tofu and Tempeh:* High in protein, firm in texture, research has shown that foods made from soy protein, such as tofu and tempeh burgers, may significantly lower your cholesterol if your levels are high or moderately high.

into serving-size portions when you get home. Also, stock up on reduced-fat or fat-free lunch meat, roast beef or turkey breast; get it thinly sliced, so you can have the satisfaction of a well-stuffed sandwich. Try to stick to the least processed choices (chicken breast rather than chicken loaf, lean ham rather than bologna), and go for the fat-free versions if they're available.

If your deli has a salad bar and you're in a hurry, it might be worth the extra expense to grab some ready-to-eat fresh produce. Since you pay by the pound, get your money's worth by choosing the lightest-weight vegetables, such as sliced fresh mushrooms and interesting salad greens, and forego anything heavy or dripping in dressing. Skip the croutons and toppings; you can add some toasted bread cubes and your own fat-free dressing at home.

■ **Next stop: Packaged Meats.** In this section, you'll find an array of turkey-based lunch meats. They're tasty, but sometimes no leaner than the products they're replacing. Check labels: Lean ham may have less fat than turkey "ham"!

If the rows of cured meats such as hot dogs, sausages and bacon are tempting, be sure to read labels. In most cases, the poultry-based versions are the leanest—but remember, even if they're made from turkey, kielbasa or bacon are hardly low-fat fare. When you get home, cut them into small portions and freeze to use as needed for flavoring soups, sauces or stews.

One item that's unsafe at any speed: those pre-packaged lunch kits with crackers and slices of cheese and ham. Instead of paying for all that packaging (and a fatty, protein-heavy lunch), why not create your own easy "lunch kit" with pre-cut veggies, a few slices of fat-free lunch meat, and some whole-wheat crispbreads?

Best options: Anything marked "fat-free"; the choices are many, from hot dogs to turkey "ham" to sausage patties.

■ **Next stop: Frozen Foods.** This aisle is full of seductions for the time-strapped. While it's handy to have some frozen entrées in the freezer (read the labels and select the most nutritious ones), the brightly packaged pie crusts, ravioli and freezer cakes make it a little too easy to splurge.

Best options: Pick up some frozen vegetables to stock your freezer so you'll always have veggies on hand. Unsweetened frozen fruit is good, too, for easy desserts or pureeing into a quick sauce. Get your calcium-fortified orange juice here (instead of from the refrigerator case) and reconstitute it yourself; you'll save money and packaging and lighten your grocery bags.

■ **Last stop: Dairy.** By design, this is often at the farthest part of the store from the entrance, so shoppers coming in "just for milk"

On-the-Road **Tips**

1. Ask and you shall receive. Simply request your special meal—vegetarian, heart-healthy, fruit-only and kosher meals are the most popular requests—when you make your airplane ticket reservation.

2. Bring your own food. Planes get delayed, special meals get forgotten and roadside restaurants can be junk-food wastelands. Health-conscious travelers tote apples, rice cakes, cut-up veggies and other alternative snack foods so that travel mishaps don't lead to dietary snafus. If the kids demand snacks in the car, make each one of you a special "snack bag" with single portions of healthy snacks so you won't be tempted to share theirs.

3. Keep an eye out for farmers' markets and grocery stores in the towns you drive through—terrific sources for fresh fruit and veggies to snack on. Local tourism boards can tell you where to find them.

4. Be choosy. You don't have to eat junk food just because you're in an airport, train or bus station or with the kids. Search out the frozen yogurt, fruit and healthful sandwiches. On the road, look for the fast-food chains you know have healthy options, such as salad bars, baked potatoes, grilled chicken sandwiches or rotisserie fare—or a diner, where you can always order breakfast cereal and fresh fruit or a sandwich made to order.

5. On the airplane or cafeteria tray, pass on the butter and salad dressing. You can automatically reduce the fat content of your meal by leaving the greasy condiments untouched.

6. Keep your perspective. Before succumbing to the cake on your airplane tray or the dessert rack, ask yourself: Would I go out of my way to eat this if I were at home?

7. Turn the mini-bar in your hotel room from a menace into an amenity. Instead of snacking on overpriced chips and chocolate, use the mini-bar to store skim milk, carrot sticks and other perishables. Or simply return the key to the front desk.

8. Always pack sneakers. Even if your hotel doesn't have a gym or pool, the front desk can probably tell you where you can safely walk or jog.

9. Turn off the TV. *Wheel of Fortune* doesn't look any different on the hotel's TV than it does on yours. Use the time to exercise, have a leisurely dinner, plan tomorrow's itinerary or get a better night's sleep.

10. Plan ahead for breakfast. Order from the card hanging on the doorknob before you go to bed—not from room service when you wake up hungry. If your only choice is a "family" restaurant nearby, order oatmeal or breakfast cereal à la carte and skip the truckers' breakfasts.

will be tempted into buying something else on the way there. The choices will be awe-inspiring: yogurts in every flavor, cheeses in every size, sliced or shredded, and flavored cottage cheeses and sour cream dips. Chances are, you'll confront a sophisticated display of "gourmet" cheeses, too, strategically packaged in appetizer-sized chunks.

The plethora of choices isn't an accident: you're meant to be dazzled by the volume of it all and numbed by the act of picking through it to find what you need. And if your eyes happen to alight on something else you didn't need but wouldn't mind buying, so much the better for the supermarket. Time to put on blinders and stick to your shopping list.

Best options: Stock up on low-fat dairy products: skim or 1 percent milk, low-fat buttermilk (1.5 percent or lower), diet margarine, light ricotta and reduced-fat cheeses.

Choose plain nonfat yogurt and unflavored cottage cheese; they'll give you the most versatility. For example, you can add your own chopped fresh herbs for an easy vegetable dip or filling for a pita sandwich, drain the yogurt in a coffee strainer to make spreadable yogurt cheese, or puree cottage cheese and toss with cooked pasta and a sprinkle of Parmesan cheese.

Don't buy cheese to snack on or serve as an appetizer. Why blow all those calories and fat before dinner has even begun? Instead, scan the gourmet cheese bin for full-flavored types, like Parmesan and Roquefort, to use as a flavoring or topping—you'll need only a little bit to add big flavor. Stroll virtuously past the ice-cream display, often strategically placed just before the checkout line to encourage spontaneous purchases. If you really crave a frozen dessert, opt for a sorbet.

Create a list of healthy food resources and keep it as a handy reference.

. . . .

. . . .

. . . .

List your favorite markets and food stores, where you can buy the foods you need—including the freshest produce and leanest meats. Think beyond the supermarket: butchers, farm stands, produce markets, etc. Include addresses and phone numbers.

. . . .

. . . .

. . . .

List phone numbers of sources for information about healthy food. Examples: consumer hotlines, mail order sources for healthy ingredients, consulting dietitians.

. . . .

. . . .

. . . .

. . . .

. . . .

. . . .

. . . .

part 5

THE GOODS

CHAPTER sixteen

ENERGY-BOOSTING BREAKFASTS

Sure, you've heard that breakfast is the most important meal of the day—but do you really believe it, or are you one of the millions of Americans who skip it? If you are, you should rethink your reasons because science is proving Mom's favorite admonition true. Research shows that people who eat a good breakfast are, among other things, more likely to eat healthfully for the remainder of the day—important news if you're trying to lose weight. A bonus: Many breakfast foods are naturally low in fat and high in fiber.

If the thought of eating early in the day leaves you cold, start small—a piece of fruit or some toast will help you ease into the habit. Cereals are one of your best options; many are high in fiber and fortified with essential nutrients (be sure to check the nutrition label on the box). Top your cereal with a cup each of skim milk and sliced strawberries—and you've got a third of your calcium and more than 100 percent of your vitamin C for the day. If you stroll down the cereal aisle at your grocery, you're sure to find one brand, hot or cold, that appeals to you.

If you're out of the house at the crack of dawn, you need something portable that's not covered with icing or full of fat. Small bagels or muffins are bake-shop options, or spread part-skim ricotta on a slice of raisin bread for a half-sandwich to go. Yogurt travels well, too.

After crazy weekday mornings, weekends deserve leisurely breakfasts. Rich yet light Cottage Cheese Pancakes are family pleasers. You may prefer to linger over the Sunday paper and a cup of coffee with our lightened version of traditional Scones. Or if bacon and eggs are your weakness: Scramble up egg substitute with any leftover veggies and a grating of extra-sharp cheddar; and try turkey bacon—it's quite flavorful, and the smell of it sizzling on the griddle is sure to rouse sleepyheads!

Making time to eat in the morning should be a priority. Whether you're looking to reap breakfast's proven health benefits or to increase your energy level for the day ahead, get what you're seeking in a nutritious breakfast. Try some of the low-fat choices that follow.

Scones

makes
12 servings

Per serving:
82 Calories,
2 g Total Fat,
0 g Saturated Fat,
18 mg Cholesterol,
132 mg Sodium,
14 g Total Carbohydrate,
1 g Dietary Fiber,
2 g Protein,
40 mg Calcium.

POINTS per serving: 2.

Light in texture and delicately flavored, these scones are a real treat with a cup of Earl Grey or English Breakfast tea.

1 cup + 2 tablespoons all-purpose flour

1 tablespoon sugar

1 teaspoon baking powder

½ teaspoon freshly grated nutmeg

¼ teaspoon baking soda

¼ teaspoon salt

½ cup dried currants

½ cup plain low-fat yogurt

1 egg

1 tablespoon margarine, melted and cooled

1. Preheat the oven to 425° F. Spray a nonstick baking sheet with nonstick cooking spray. In a large bowl, combine the flour, sugar, baking powder, nutmeg, baking soda and salt. Add the currants; toss to combine. In a small bowl, combine the yogurt, egg and margarine. Stir the yogurt mixture into the flour mixture.

2. Lightly flour a work surface and rolling pin. Turn out the dough and knead briefly; roll out and cut into 12 triangles with a sharp knife, or cut into 12 rounds with a biscuit cutter. Place on the baking sheet. Reduce the oven temperature to 400° F; bake until golden brown, 12–15 minutes. Cool on a wire rack.

Sweet and Spicy Oatmeal
with Dried Cranberries

makes
2 servings

Cooking with juice is a great way to make hot cereal for those who don't like milk. If you prefer a more traditional flavor, use 2 cups water and omit the orange juice.

Per serving:
261 Calories,
3 g Total Fat,
0 g Saturated Fat,
0 mg Cholesterol,
545 mg Sodium,
54 g Total Carbohydrate,
5 g Dietary Fiber,
7 g Protein,
257 mg Calcium.

1 cup orange juice

1 cup water

¼ teaspoon cinnamon

⅛ teaspoon salt

⅛ teaspoon ground nutmeg

1 cup old-fashioned rolled oats

¼ cup dried cranberries

POINTS per serving: 5.

In a medium nonstick saucepan, bring the orange juice, water, cinnamon, salt and nutmeg to a boil; reduce the heat. Stir in the oats and cranberries. Cook, stirring as needed, about 5 minutes; let stand until the oatmeal reaches the desired consistency.

HINT

Hate milk, but want to make sure you get your calcium? Drink calcium-fortified orange juice (you'll also cover your Vitamin C requirement).

Ricotta Parfaits

makes
2 servings

Parfaits taste better when they are made the night before, so that flavors meld together. If you like, substitute plain nonfat yogurt or cottage cheese for the ricotta.

Per serving:
306 Calories,
9 g Total Fat,
5 g Saturated Fat,
25 mg Cholesterol,
106 mg Sodium,
44 g Total Carbohydrate,
5 g Dietary Fiber,
16 g Protein,
253 mg Calcium.

POINTS per serving: 6.

⅔ cup part-skim ricotta cheese

½ cup crushed pineapple

1 tablespoon sugar

1 mango, peeled and cubed

¼ cup + 2 tablespoons wheat germ

In a small bowl, combine the ricotta, pineapple and sugar. Spoon a few tablespoons of the ricotta mixture into 2 parfait glasses; top each with one-sixth of the mango and 1 tablespoon of the wheat germ. Repeat the layers 2 more times. Refrigerate, covered, at least a few hours or overnight.

make ahead

Baked French Toast

A little maple syrup and some fresh fruit make this a satisfying breakfast treat. Use a sturdy bread—some whole-wheat bread can fall apart when you dip the slices in the egg mixture.

makes
2 servings

Per serving:
343 Calories,
14 g Total Fat,
3 g Saturated Fat,
213 mg Cholesterol,
557 mg Sodium,
41 g Total Carbohydrate,
5 g Dietary Fiber,
16 g Protein,
160 mg Calcium.

POINTS per serving: 6.

2 eggs

½ cup skim milk

2 teaspoons confectioners' sugar

½ teaspoon vanilla extract

¼ teaspoon cinnamon

4 slices firm whole-wheat bread

1 tablespoon stick margarine, cut into bits

2 tablespoons maple syrup (optional)

1.   Preheat the oven to 425° F. Spray a baking sheet with nonstick cooking spray (butter-flavored is nice).

2.   In a medium bowl, lightly beat the eggs with a fork; blend in the milk, sugar, vanilla and cinnamon.

3.   Soak the bread, 1 slice at a time, in the egg mixture. Place the bread on the baking sheet. Sprinkle the margarine over the bread. Bake until lightly golden and slightly puffy, about 8 minutes. Serve with the maple syrup, if using.

one pot

rush hour

Veggie Omelet

makes
1 serving

If you enjoy eggs, invest in a good nonstick omelet pan. Try ¼ cup chopped shiitake mushrooms instead of the red bell pepper for another tasty filling.

Per serving:
163 Calories,
9 g Total Fat,
2 g Saturated Fat,
212 mg Cholesterol,
528 mg Sodium,
6 g Total Carbohydrate,
1 g Dietary Fiber,
14 g Protein,
41 mg Calcium.

POINTS per serving: 4.

½ onion, chopped

¼ red bell pepper, seeded and chopped

1 egg

2 egg whites

2 teaspoons reduced-calorie margarine

¼ teaspoon salt

¼ teaspoon freshly ground pepper

1. Spray a small nonstick omelet pan or skillet with butter-flavored seasoning spray. Sauté the onion and bell pepper until tender, about 5 minutes; remove and set aside.

2. In small bowl, beat the egg, egg whites and 2 tablespoons water until frothy.

3. In the omelet pan, melt the margarine until a drop of water sizzles. Pour the egg mixture into the pan, tilting to cover the bottom (it should set immediately at the edges). Cook until the underside is set, about 1 minute, lifting the edges with a spatula to let the uncooked egg flow underneath. Sprinkle the onion and bell pepper evenly over 1 side of the omelet; with a spatula, fold the other side over the filling to enclose. Slide the omelet onto a plate and serve, sprinkled with the salt and pepper.

one pot

rush hour

Banana-Coconut Fruit Smoothie

With the wide array of exotic-flavored yogurts available, you can make a different combination every day of the week. If you want an extra boost, try a cappuccino-flavored yogurt.

makes

I serving

One 8-ounce container aspartame-sweetened coconut-flavored nonfat yogurt

½ banana, sliced and frozen
½ cup orange juice
2 ice cubes

In a blender, puree all the ingredients. Pour into a tall glass and serve immediately.

Per serving:
231 Calories,
0 g Total Fat,
0 g Saturated Fat,
5 mg Cholesterol,
141 mg Sodium,
47 g Total Carbohydrate,
3 g Dietary Fiber,
9 g Protein,
265 mg Calcium.

POINTS per serving: 4.

HINT

Have you discovered what a satisfying snack frozen fruit is? Try grapes, orange sections and sliced peaches, as well as bananas.

rush hour

Tropical Breakfast Wrap

Tortillas make for great "totable" breakfasts, since they can be wrapped around almost anything. Experiment with scrambled eggs, peanut butter or, for a savory breakfast, fat-free refried beans and cheese. Make these the night before a morning that you know is going to be hectic.

Two 6" flour tortillas
¼ cup pureed nonfat cottage cheese
2 teaspoons sugar

¼ teaspoon vanilla extract
½ mango, peeled and thinly sliced
½ banana, sliced

1. Heat the tortillas according to package directions. Meanwhile, in a small bowl, combine the cottage cheese, sugar and vanilla.

2. Spread 2 tablespoons of the cheese mixture down the center of each tortilla; top with the mango and banana slices. Roll tightly and wrap in plastic. Refrigerate until "set," at least 4 hours.

make ahead

HINT

To make pureed cottage cheese, just blend nonfat cottage cheese in a food processor or blender until it's smooth and creamy. This spread is also a tasty substitute for cream cheese.

Egg and Cheese Muffin

English muffins come in such a wide variety of flavors—including cranberry, oat bran, sourdough and blueberry—so you can create all kinds of breakfast sandwiches.

makes
1 serving

1 slice reduced-fat American or cheddar cheese

1 honey-wheat English muffin, split and toasted

1 teaspoon stick margarine

⅓ cup fat-free egg substitute

¼ teaspoon salt

¼ teaspoon freshly ground pepper

Per serving:
244 Calories,
9 g Total Fat,
3 g Saturated Fat,
10 mg Cholesterol,
803 mg Sodium,
26 g Total Carbohydrate,
3 g Dietary Fiber,
20 g Protein,
311 mg Calcium.

POINTS per serving: 5.

1. Place the cheese on one half of the muffin.

2. In a small nonstick skillet, melt the margarine over medium heat. Add the egg substitute and scramble, stirring gently, until set. Place over the cheese and sprinkle with the salt and pepper; cover with the other muffin half. Serve at once.

Easy Banana-Raisin Bran Muffins

makes
6 servings

Per serving:
183 Calories,
4 g Total Fat,
1 g Saturated Fat,
0 mg Cholesterol,
250 mg Sodium,
36 g Total Carbohydrate,
1 g Dietary Fiber,
4 g Protein,
17 mg Calcium.

POINTS per serving: 4.

When you buy packaged or convenience foods, check the nutrition labels. Choose those foods that aren't loaded with fat, cholesterol or sodium; look for muffin mixes with 1 to 3 grams of fat per serving. Add your favorite fruit and some wheat germ to boost the nutrition.

One 7-ounce box bran muffin mix (1–3 grams fat per serving)	1 banana, chopped
2 egg whites	¼ cup raisins
	¼ cup wheat germ

1. Preheat the oven to 400° F. Spray a nonstick 6-cup muffin tin with nonstick cooking spray.

2. In a medium bowl, combine the muffin mix, egg whites and ½ cup water, stirring until just blended; fold in the banana and raisins. Spoon the batter into the muffin cups, filling each two-thirds full. Bake until a toothpick inserted in the center comes out clean, 15–20 minutes. Cool in the pan on a rack.

one pot

make ahead

HINT

Don't have a 6-cup muffin tin? Use a 12-cup tin; fill the outer cups with the batter, the inner ones with water (this keeps the heat evenly distributed throughout the pan).

Crunchy Apple Spice Yogurt

This satisfying breakfast "dessert" is perfect for the person who craves a morning sweet.

makes
1 serving

1 baking apple (Rome works well),
   cored and chopped

2 tablespoons golden raisins

¼ teaspoon cinnamon

One 8-ounce container aspartame-
   sweetened vanilla nonfat yogurt

¼ cup wheat-and-barley nugget cereal

Per serving:
380 Calories,
1 g Total Fat,
0 g Saturated Fat,
5 mg Cholesterol,
319 mg Sodium,
85 g Total Carbohydrate,
10 g Dietary Fiber,
13 g Protein,
294 mg Calcium.

POINTS per serving: 6.

1.   In a small microwavable dish, combine the apple, raisins, cinnamon and 1 tablespoon water. Microwave, covered, on High 1½ minutes. Set aside to cool for about 5 minutes.

2.   Fold the yogurt into the apple mixture, then top with the cereal.

Waffle Sundae

makes
2 servings

Per serving:
286 Calories,
3 g Total Fat,
1 g Saturated Fat,
12 mg Cholesterol,
323 mg Sodium,
56 g Total Carbohydrate,
4 g Dietary Fiber,
10 g Protein,
277 mg Calcium.

POINTS per serving: 5.

Make several batches of yogurt cheese in advance and use it as a topping or spread.

½ cup yogurt cheese★

1 tablespoon maple syrup

½ teaspoon vanilla extract

1 kiwi fruit, peeled and chopped

1 orange, peeled and sectioned

1 banana, sliced

2 low-fat waffles, toasted

In a small bowl, combine the yogurt cheese, maple syrup and vanilla. In another small bowl, combine the fruit. Spread the yogurt cheese over the waffles; top with the fruit.

★*To prepare ½ cup yogurt cheese, spoon 1 cup plain nonfat yogurt into a coffee filter or cheesecloth-lined strainer; place over a bowl. Refrigerate, covered, at least 5 hours or overnight. Discard the liquid in the bowl.*

Cottage-Cheese Pancakes

These satisfying pancakes, garnished with nonfat or light sour cream and fresh berries taste wonderful. If you're serving more than two, don't double the recipe—make a new batch each time.

makes
2 servings

⅔ cup nonfat cottage cheese

2 eggs, separated

¼ cup all-purpose flour

1 tablespoon canola oil

¼ cup nonfat sour cream

2 cups strawberries, blueberries or raspberries

Per serving:
303 Calories,
10 g Total Fat,
1.5 g Saturated Fat,
325 mg Cholesterol,
369 mg Sodium,
31 g Total Carbohydrate,
4 g Dietary Fiber,
24 g Protein,
140 mg Calcium.

POINTS per serving: 6.

1. In a sieve or fine-mesh strainer over a small bowl, drain the cottage cheese until dry, about 5 minutes.

2. In another small bowl, whisk the egg yolks until lemon-colored. In a medium bowl, thoroughly combine the flour and cottage cheese. Stir in the yolks.

3. In a medium bowl, beat the egg whites until stiff; with a rubber spatula, fold gently into the flour mixture.

4. In a large nonstick skillet, heat the oil until a drop of water sizzles. Drop the batter by tablespoons, and brown on both sides. Serve, topped with the sour cream and berries.

CHAPTER seventeen

LUNCHES

When you're trying to lose weight, lunch can be a hazardous meal. If you stay home, do you eat the same fat-laden lunch meat or PB&J sandwiches that you make for your kids? If you work at an office, especially if it doesn't have a pantry or kitchen, how do you find a nutritious alternative to take-out?

Salads are an easy option, especially if you base them on grains or beans instead of on lettuce (they're more filling, too). If you have some rice from last night's dinner, toss it with cubed left-over meat, chopped broccoli or carrots, diced pears, and small grapes or dried fruits; or mix in some black beans, cheddar cubes and salsa.

A small thermos is a great way to get some warmth, as well as nutrition, when you tote a hearty vegetable or bean soup. In the summer, bring a chilled fruit soup or gazpacho.

If you can't abandon the idea of a satisfying sandwich, think beyond cold cuts and loaf bread. Mash white beans into a paste with a touch of olive oil and herbs, or make a "mayo-less" tuna salad. Both work well in pitas or lavash—one of many Middle Eastern flatbreads. Experiment with taco shells, flavored English muffins and tortillas, as well.

Grilled Veggie Wrap

makes
2 servings

Vegetable sandwiches are a great way to pack in nutrition without any fuss. Beware of restaurant- or deli-grilled vegetables, since these tend to be swimming in oil.

Per serving:
231 Calories,
8 g Total Fat,
4 g Saturated Fat,
10 mg Cholesterol,
272 mg Sodium,
32 g Total Carbohydrate,
5 g Dietary Fiber,
9 g Protein,
99 mg Calcium.

POINTS per serving: 4.

1 small (¾-pound) eggplant, cut
   lengthwise into ¼" slices
Two 6" flour tortillas
1½ ounces goat cheese

½ cup watercress
4 oil-packed sun-dried tomato halves,
   drained and cut into strips

1. Preheat the broiler. Spray the broiler rack with nonstick cooking spray (Italian-flavored is nice); place the eggplant on the rack and spray the top with more spray. Broil until tender, about 5 minutes on each side.

2. Heat the tortillas according to package directions. Spread the cheese down the center of each tortilla; top with the eggplant, watercress and sun-dried tomatoes. Roll the tortilla carefully.

one pot

make ahead

HINT

Flavored nonstick cooking sprays are a boon to busy health-conscious cooks. In addition to olive oil and butter-flavored sprays, those with Italian, Asian, Cajun or even mesquite barbecue flavors are available.

Italian Hero

Experiment with different types of fillings—such as eggplant salad and giardiniera, the Italian salad of pickled cucumbers, onions, peppers, cauliflower florets and carrots—that are available in the Italian condiment section of supermarkets. Look for items packed in water or vinegar.

makes
2 servings

2 small hero rolls

2 jarred roasted red peppers, drained and sliced

2 ounces part-skim mozzarella, sliced

½ cup oil-packed artichoke hearts, rinsed, drained and halved

½ cup arugula, washed and trimmed

Per serving:
320 Calories,
11 g Total Fat,
3 g Saturated Fat,
16 mg Cholesterol,
570 mg Sodium,
45 g Total Carbohydrate,
6 g Dietary Fiber,
16 g Protein,
259 mg Calcium.

POINTS per serving: 6

Preheat the broiler. Spray a baking sheet with nonstick cooking spray. Split the hero rolls lengthwise and scoop out the inside bottom half of each roll, discarding the bread. Layer the bottom halves with the peppers and mozzarella. Place on the baking sheet; broil until the cheese melts, about 3 minutes. Top with the artichoke hearts and arugula. Cover each bottom half with its top half.

vegetarian

rush hour

one pot

make ahead

Mediterranean Tuna Salad

makes
2 servings

Although higher in fat than water-packed white tuna is, light tuna in olive oil has such a succulent, rich flavor that it's worth an occasional treat.

Per serving:
154 Calories,
9 g Total Fat,
4 g Saturated Fat,
19 mg Cholesterol,
521 mg Sodium,
16 g Total Carbohydrate,
2 g Dietary Fiber,
6 g Protein,
149 mg Calcium.

POINTS per serving: 3.

One 6-ounce can solid-pack light tuna packed in olive oil, drained

1 tomato, chopped

½ red onion, chopped

1 tablespoon fresh lemon juice

⅛ teaspoon freshly ground pepper

2 large sourdough pitas, split

In a medium bowl, combine the tuna, tomato, onion, lemon juice and pepper. When ready to serve, divide the salad between the pitas.

rush hour

make ahead

HINT

Be sure to use light tuna that's packed in olive oil, not vegetable oil. The flavors are completely different.

Curried Chicken Salad Sandwich

Chicken tenders are the inner strips of the chicken breast; if you prefer, simply slice a skinless boneless chicken breast into strips. For extra crunch and color, chop in a Granny Smith apple.

makes
2 servings

2 teaspoons canola oil

1 tablespoon minced onion

1 teaspoon curry powder

½ pound chicken tenders

½ cup plain nonfat yogurt

1 tablespoon nonfat sour cream

1 tablespoon mango chutney

½ teaspoon salt

2 tablespoons raisins

4 slices whole-grain bread

Per serving:
392 Calories,
10 g Total Fat,
2 g Saturated Fat,
70 mg Cholesterol,
898 mg Sodium,
42 g Total Carbohydrate,
5 g Dietary Fiber,
35 g Protein,
192 mg Calcium.

POINTS per serving: 8.

1. In a medium nonstick skillet, heat the oil. Sauté the onion until translucent, about 2 minutes. Stir in the curry; cook 30 seconds longer. Add the chicken; sauté until cooked through, about 5 minutes. Transfer to a medium bowl; let cool.

2. Meanwhile, in a small bowl, whisk together the yogurt, sour cream, chutney and salt. Fold into the chicken mixture; add the raisins.

3. When ready to serve, place a slice of bread on each of 2 plates; spread each with the chicken salad and top with the remaining bread.

rush hour

one pot

make ahead

Tofu "Egg" Salad

makes
4 servings

If you're looking for a delicious way to get soy into your diet, and if you'd like to avoid the dietary cholesterol and fat in eggs, this salad is the way to go.

Per serving:
238 Calories,
7 g Total Fat,
0 g Saturated Fat,
0 mg Cholesterol,
345 mg Sodium,
33 g Total Carbohydrate,
7 g Dietary Fiber,
13 g Protein,
106 mg Calcium.

POINTS per serving: 4.

2 tablespoons reduced-calorie mayonnaise

1 tablespoon Dijon mustard

½ pound reduced-fat firm tofu, pressed★ and diced

1 celery stalk, diced

1 onion, chopped

½ red bell pepper, seeded and diced

8 slices whole-grain bread

8 spinach leaves, cleaned

1. In a small bowl, combine the mayonnaise and mustard.

2. In a medium bowl, combine the tofu, celery, onion and pepper; stir in the mayonnaise mixture and toss gently to coat. Refrigerate, covered, 1 hour.

3. To assemble the sandwiches, place 1 slice of bread on each of 4 plates. Top each with a spinach leaf and one-fourth of the tofu mixture, then another spinach leaf and another slice of bread.

vegetarian

make ahead

★*To press tofu, place the tofu between two flat plates. Weight the top with a heavy can or similar object; the sides of the tofu should be bulging slightly but not cracking. Let stand 30 minutes–1 hour, then pour off and discard the water that accumulates. Use immediately or refrigerate, covered, up to 2 days.*

**MEDITERRANEAN
HALIBUT**

**VANILLA-SNAP
SANDWICHES**

Thanksgiving Burritos

Kids love these turkey spirals because they're sweet and easy to handle.

makes
2 servings

2 tablespoons whole-berry cranberry
    sauce

1 tablespoon reduced-fat mayonnaise

Two 6" flour tortillas

6 slices cooked turkey breast

In a small bowl, combine the cranberry sauce and mayonnaise. Spread the mixture down the center of each tortilla, then place the turkey on top. Spread with the remaining mayonnaise mixture and roll tightly. Cut in half on the diagonal.

Per serving:
278 Calories,
5 g Total Fat,
I g Saturated Fat,
71 mg Cholesterol,
265 mg Sodium,
27 g Total Carbohydrate,
I g Dietary Fiber,
29 g Protein,
56 mg Calcium.

POINTS per serving: 6.

rush hour

Tabbouleh Salad with Hummus

makes
4 servings

The traditional grain for tabbouleh—bulgur—is wheat that has been hulled, steamed and dried. Besides its delicious flavor, bulgur also has a short cooking time, making it a real winner.

Per serving:
246 Calories,
10 g Total Fat,
1 g Saturated Fat,
1 mg Cholesterol,
370 mg Sodium,
31 g Total Carbohydrate,
8 g Dietary Fiber,
10 g Protein,
99 mg Calcium.

POINTS per serving: 4.

Tabbouleh:

½ cup bulgur (cracked wheat)

½ teaspoon salt

1 cucumber, peeled, seeded and chopped

1 red bell pepper, seeded and chopped

2 scallions, sliced

1 cup chopped parsley

3 tablespoons fresh lemon juice

1 tablespoon olive oil

Hummus:

1 cup drained rinsed canned chickpeas

¼ cup plain nonfat yogurt

3 tablespoons fresh lemon juice

2 tablespoons tahini (sesame paste)

Pinch garlic powder

¼ teaspoon hot red pepper sauce (optional)

1. To prepare the tabbouleh, in a medium bowl, combine the bulgur and salt. Add ¾ cup water; cover and let stand about 30 minutes. Stir in the remaining ingredients; cover and chill about 2 hours.

2. To prepare the hummus, in a food processor, puree the chickpeas, yogurt, lemon juice, tahini, garlic powder and pepper sauce (if using).

3. Arrange the tabbouleh around the edge of a plate; in the hole in the center, place the hummus. Serve with raw vegetables and pitas.

vegetarian

make ahead

HINT

This chickpea mixture is too thick for a blender. If you don't have a food processor, use a potato masher to make the hummus.

Wild Rice Salad

With so many kinds of rice on supermarket shelves, it's easy to experiment with the various types. If you find wild rice too chewy, then try jasmine, wehani or basmati—each with its own distinct flavor and texture. Just be sure to adjust the cooking times according to package directions.

2 cups low-sodium chicken broth
⅔ cup wild rice blend
¼ cup chopped mixed dried fruit
2 tablespoons orange juice
1 tablespoon olive oil

1 tablespoon mango chutney
1 cup cubed smoked turkey
1 celery stalk, chopped
4 scallions, sliced

makes
2 servings

Per serving:
347 Calories,
9 g Total Fat,
1 g Saturated Fat,
15 mg Cholesterol,
1,026 mg Sodium,
50 g Total Carbohydrate,
6 g Dietary Fiber,
17 g Protein,
69 mg Calcium.

POINTS per serving: 6.

1. In a medium saucepan, combine the broth and rice. Bring to a boil, then stir once or twice. Reduce the heat and simmer, covered, about 25 minutes, adding the dried fruit for the last 10 minutes. With a fork, fluff the rice; set aside to cool.

2. In a small bowl, whisk the orange juice, oil and chutney. Pour over the rice; fold in the turkey, celery and scallions. Serve at room temperature or chilled.

HINT

Always use a fork to fluff rice—using a spoon will make it clumpy.

one pot

make ahead

Spinach Salad with Apples, Walnuts and Cheddar

makes

2 servings

Per serving:
220 Calories,
10 g Total Fat,
3 g Saturated Fat,
15 mg Cholesterol,
259 mg Sodium,
23 g Total Carbohydrate,
6 g Dietary Fiber,
12 g Protein,
311 mg Calcium.

POINTS per serving: 4.

Popeye was right: Spinach is a real nutritional powerhouse, and this is the best way to eat it—raw. This tasty salad is a good source of iron, folic acid and vitamin C.

1 tablespoon orange juice

1 tablespoon strawberry jelly

1 tablespoon raspberry vinegar

2 tablespoons vegetable oil

1 bunch spinach, cleaned and torn into bite-size pieces

1 apple, peeled, cored and chopped (try Gala, Braeburn or Granny Smith)

⅓ cup shredded reduced-fat extra-sharp cheddar cheese

2 tablespoons walnuts, toasted*

1. To prepare the dressing, in a small microwavable bowl, combine the orange juice and jelly. Microwave on High until the jelly is melted, 15 seconds. Whisk in the vinegar and oil.

2. Place the spinach and apple in a large bowl; toss with the dressing. Serve, sprinkled with the cheese and walnuts.

microwave

vegetarian

rush hour

To toast walnuts, place in a small nonstick skillet and cook, stirring constantly, until lightly browned and fragrant, about 3 minutes.

Chicken Caesar Salad

This classic salad was born when Tijuana restaurateur Caesar Cardini had very little to feed his restaurant guests after a long Fourth of July weekend. He mixed the few staples he had on hand with a little ingenuity to create this favorite.

makes
2 servings

2 anchovies in olive oil, drained

3 tablespoons grated Parmesan cheese

2 tablespoons fresh lemon juice

2 teaspoons olive oil

1 garlic clove, minced

4 cups torn Romaine lettuce

12 cherry tomatoes, halved

1 red onion, sliced

1 cup cubed cooked chicken breast

½ cup seasoned croutons

Per serving:
269 Calories,
8 g Total Fat,
3 g Saturated Fat,
66 mg Cholesterol,
412 mg Sodium,
18 g Total Carbohydrate,
5 g Dietary Fiber,
28 g Protein,
116 mg Calcium.

POINTS per serving: 5.

1. To prepare the dressing, in a small bowl, mash the anchovies; combine with 2 tablespoons of the cheese, the lemon juice, oil and garlic.

2. In a large bowl, combine the lettuce, tomatoes and onion; toss with the dressing, then toss with the chicken, croutons and the remaining 1 tablespoon cheese.

rush hour

make ahead

Southwestern Salad

makes
4 servings

Southwestern food has strong, vibrant flavors; it's a natural for low-fat cooking. Serve this with baked tortilla chips.

Per serving:
130 Calories,
1 g Total Fat,
0 g Saturated Fat,
0 mg Cholesterol,
337 mg Sodium,
28 g Total Carbohydrate,
7 g Dietary Fiber,
8 g Protein,
61 mg Calcium.

POINTS per serving: 1.

One 19-ounce can black beans, rinsed and drained

1 cup thawed frozen corn kernels

8 scallions, sliced

½ cup Mexican-style stewed tomatoes

2 teaspoons fresh lime juice

1 teaspoon ground cumin

In a large nonreactive bowl, combine all the ingredients. Refrigerate, covered, until chilled, at least 2 hours.

vegetarian

make ahead

spicy

HINT

Substitute salsa for the stewed tomatoes for extra kick.

Mediterranean Salad with Feta

Fat-free feta cheese makes following the traditional Mediterranean diet even healthier. Serve this with—or in—pita breads.

makes
4 servings

4 tomatoes, chopped

4 kirby cucumbers, chopped

2 yellow bell peppers, seeded and chopped

3 ounces fat-free feta cheese

1 tablespoon fresh lemon juice

1 tablespoon olive oil

½ teaspoon kosher salt

Per serving:
129 Calories,
4 g Total Fat,
1 g Saturated Fat,
0 mg Cholesterol,
472 mg Sodium,
16 g Total Carbohydrate,
6 g Dietary Fiber,
9 g Protein,
146 mg Calcium.

POINTS per serving: 2.

In a large nonreactive bowl, combine all the ingredients. Let stand, covered, at least 30 minutes.

HINT

What's nonreactive, and why use it? Acidic foods—tomatoes, vinegars, buttermilk, citrus juices and fruits—can discolor and develop very strange flavors when they react with certain materials, primarily metals like steel, unseasoned cast iron and aluminum (anodized aluminum is fine). Use glass, enamel-coated metals or plastic.

vegetarian

make ahead

CHAPTER eighteen

AFTERNOON-SLUMP SAVERS

does a snack alarm go off in your body a couple hours after lunch? Next time you're tempted to reach for a candy bar, ask yourself these questions to determine whether your 3:00 afternoon snack is due to habit or you really do need a pick-me-up.

If you're hungry ...

1. Your stomach growls, or you feel weak and distracted.

2. The feeling has been building for the last hour or so.

3. You would be happy to eat almost anything.

4. The feeling creeps up while you're doing something enjoyable or intellectually engaging.

5. You haven't been thinking about food.

If you're eating out of habit ...

1. You could go another hour or two without food.

2. The feeling comes on suddenly, say, after you walk past a bakery.

3. Only one food will do—think chocolate, chips, pastries.

4. The feeling comes when you're bored, lonely or stressed.

5. You're reading a magazine with pictures of food, watching TV food commercials or smelling something cooking.

If you determine that you are truly hungry, reach for one of the healthful nibbles described in this chapter. If you're eating out of habit, take a break in a different way.

If you can sneak 10 minutes, take a walk around the block. Stroll to the water cooler, the rest room or a colleague's office.

For a truly energized afternoon, try a technique from yoga. *Kapalabhati*, or the cleansing breath, is performed by first placing your hand on your belly and inhaling through your nose. Then, push your belly forward, expanding it fully; exhale and tighten your stomach muscles while pushing the air out. Repeat several times, being sure to relax; and as you inhale, push your belly out and slightly tilt your lower back. Don't overdo it (a little goes a long way!), and consult your doctor first if you suffer from any medical condition.

Opt for a New Age approach to increase your energy and concentration throughout the afternoon by escaping through your senses. Keep a small bottle filled with an essential oil, such as jasmine, lavender or orange, in your desk drawer and breathe in the soothing fragrance.

At the very least, stretch out your entire body—you won't need to even get up from your chair. Gently roll your head from side to side, shrug your shoulders, twist your torso, extend your legs and rotate your ankles. You're sure to feel rejuvenated.

Healthy Trail Mix

Packaged trail mixes can be high in fat; our salty-sweet version has little fat yet satisfies most cravings. Opt for a cereal without a sugary coating; we like a mixture of corn and rice squares or bite-size shredded wheat.

2 cups cereal

2 cups (about 60) small pretzel twists

1 cup (about 24) dried apricot halves, chopped

¼ cup semisweet chocolate chips

In a medium bowl, combine all the ingredients; divide among 4 snack-size resealable plastic bags.

makes
4 servings

Per serving:
247 Calories,
4 g Total Fat,
2 g Saturated Fat,
0 mg Cholesterol,
423 mg Sodium,
53 g Total Carbohydrate,
4 g Dietary Fiber,
5 g Protein,
23 mg Calcium.

POINTS per serving: 4.

make ahead

rush hour

Peanut Butter–Caramel Sandwiches

makes
4 servings

Per serving:
165 Calories,
4 g Total Fat,
1 g Saturated Fat,
0 mg Cholesterol,
215 mg Sodium,
26 g Total Carbohydrate,
1 g Dietary Fiber,
8 g Protein,
18 mg Calcium.

POINTS per serving: 3.

This mini-meal is guaranteed to get you through the afternoon slump, or try the peanut butter-cheese spread on toast at breakfast to jump-start your day. Look for the popcorn cakes in the rice-cake aisle; if you can't find them, use your favorite flavor rice cake.

⅔ cup nonfat cottage cheese

2 tablespoons peanut butter

4 caramel popcorn cakes

1 banana, sliced

4 teaspoons chocolate syrup

In a mini food processor, puree the cottage cheese and peanut butter. When ready to serve, spread on the corn cakes. Top with banana slices, and drizzle with the chocolate syrup.

make ahead

rush hour

Sun-Dried Tomato–Tofu Dip

Savory, rich sun-dried tomatoes add a great depth of flavor to tofu. Look for dry-pack sun-dried tomatoes in small tubs in the produce department. Serve this with raw vegetables, or spread it on whole-grain crackers.

1 cup silken tofu

1 tub (2.6 ounces) julienned sun-dried tomatoes with herbs

1 teaspoon dried basil, crumbled

In a food processor or blender, puree all the ingredients. Transfer to a serving bowl; or refrigerate, covered, up to 1 week.

makes
6 servings

Per serving:
52 Calories,
2 g Total Fat,
0 g Saturated Fat,
0 mg Cholesterol,
260 mg Sodium,
8 g Total Carbohydrate,
2 g Dietary Fiber,
4 g Protein,
30 mg Calcium.

POINTS per serving: 1.

HINT

Substitute a few cloves of roasted garlic and a box of frozen chopped spinach (thaw it and squeeze out all the moisture) for the sun-dried tomatoes and basil.

make ahead

rush hour

Cheese and Crackers

makes
4 servings

Per serving:
166 Calories,
4 g Total Fat,
2 g Saturated Fat,
16 mg Cholesterol,
453 mg Sodium,
21 g Total Carbohydrate,
1 g Dietary Fiber,
12 g Protein,
111 mg Calcium.

POINTS per serving: 3.

If you adore the flavor of cheese spreads but deplore their fat, this snack is for you. We make the most of full-fat cheddar's intense flavor yet minimize the fat by pureeing it with cottage cheese. Experiment with jalapeños, herbs and spices, and other cheeses for a variety of spreads.

1 cup nonfat cottage cheese
½ cup shredded extra-sharp cheddar
   cheese

20 fat-free crackers
1 apple, cored and sliced

In a food processor or blender, puree the cottage cheese and cheddar. When ready to serve, spread on the crackers and apple.

make ahead

rush hour

Banana-Apple Crumble

Cooking really brings out the sweetness of fruit. Try different fruit combinations, such as pears and dried cranberries, to discover how satisfying these crustless fruit pies can be. This makes an excellent company dessert when served with a scoop of frozen yogurt.

makes
I serving

Per serving:
188 Calories,
2 g Total Fat,
0 g Saturated Fat,
0 mg Cholesterol,
31 mg Sodium,
46 g Total Carbohydrate,
6 g Dietary Fiber,
2 g Protein,
25 mg Calcium.

POINTS per serving: 3.

1 Granny Smith apple, peeled and
    sliced
½ banana, sliced

¼ teaspoon cinnamon
2 tablespoons low-fat granola

In a small microwavable dish or casserole, combine the apple, banana and cinnamon. Add 1 tablespoon water; cover with plastic wrap, vented on one side. Microwave on High until the fruit is tender, 1½–2 minutes. Remove the plastic and sprinkle with the granola.

HINT

To serve four, use 4 apples and 2 bananas, but up the cinnamon to I teaspoon and granola to ⅓ cup; microwave 4–5 minutes.

microwave

rush hour

CHAPTER nineteen

FAMILY DINNERS

o balance these entrées and help your family get their daily quota of five fruits and veggies, add a salad to the meal. Some tips for making the salad of your dreams:

- Save time by buying salad greens and veggies that are already cut and cleaned. Two that only need a quick rinse to be salad ready: cellophane bags of triple-washed spinach, and Mesclun, the mixture of salad greens available in many supermarkets.

- Greens will last longer if you wash them, but never hold a bunch of greens under running water—it just pushes in the grit. Instead, cut off the root end and immerse the leaves in cold water. Swish them around a bit, then let the grit sink. Lift the greens out, then dry.

- A salad spinner is the easiest way to dry and store greens. Don't overload it, though, or you won't get all the water off the leaves.

- If you don't have a salad spinner, blot the greens between paper towels. Wrap them loosely in dry paper towels, then seal tightly in a plastic bag. They'll keep for about 1 week.

- Expand your definition of salad beyond greens: Drizzle chopped veggies with a low-fat vinaigrette.

- Boost texture, flavor and nutrition by tossing in cheese cubes, chopped nuts, diced fruit or croutons.

- Speedy, easy dressing: Mix ¼ cup broth, a tablespoon or so of vinegar or fruit juice, a bit of oil, mustard and herbs in a glass jar. Cover and shake to blend.

- Drizzle dressing on individual servings rather than over the entire salad bowl. Take any leftovers to work the next day, tossing in some diced meat, as well as dried fruit and nuts.

Minestrone

makes
4 servings

Use the veggies listed here as inspiration: Toss in sliced zucchini, shredded cabbage, whatever you have on hand.

Per serving:
272 Calories,
4 g Total Fat,
1 g Saturated Fat,
0 mg Cholesterol,
659 mg Sodium,
48 g Total Carbohydrate,
8 g Dietary Fiber,
10 g Protein,
100 mg Calcium.

POINTS per serving: 4.

1 tablespoon olive oil

1 onion, chopped

1 garlic clove, crushed

3 cups low-sodium vegetable broth

One 15-ounce can cannellini beans, rinsed and drained

One 14½-ounce can diced tomatoes

1 carrot, thinly sliced

⅔ cup cut green beans

1 cup rotelle

1 teaspoon dried basil

1 teaspoon dried oregano

½ teaspoon salt

¼ teaspoon freshly ground pepper

1. In a large nonstick saucepan, heat the oil. Sauté the onion and garlic until softened, about 5 minutes.

2. Stir in the broth, cannellini beans, tomatoes, carrot and green beans; bring to a boil. Reduce the heat and simmer, covered, until the carrot is tender, about 10 minutes. Add the rotelle and herbs; cook until the rotelle is tender (check package directions). Season with the salt and pepper.

vegetarian

make ahead

one pot

English Muffin Pizzas

Not only can these be put together in a snap, but kids love them.

makes
4 servings

4 English muffins, split and toasted

2 tomatoes, thinly sliced

1⅓ cups shredded part-skim mozzarella cheese

1 red onion, very thinly sliced

12 large black olives, pitted and sliced

2 teaspoons dried oregano

½ teaspoon salt

¼ teaspoon freshly ground pepper

8 teaspoons grated Parmesan cheese

Per serving:
288 Calories,
10 g Total Fat,
5 g Saturated Fat,
25 mg Cholesterol,
915 mg Sodium,
34 g Total Carbohydrate,
1 g Dietary Fiber,
16 g Protein,
425 mg Calcium.

POINTS per serving: 6.

Preheat the broiler. Arrange the muffins on a baking sheet; top with the tomatoes, mozzarella, onion and olives. Sprinkle with the oregano, salt and pepper, then with the Parmesan. Broil 4–6" from the heat, until the cheese just starts to melt, 2–3 minutes. Serve at once.

vegetarian

rush hour

one pot

Beef Stew with Herbed Dumplings

makes
4 servings

Per serving:
388 Calories,
14 g Total Fat,
5 g Saturated Fat,
75 mg Cholesterol,
592 mg Sodium,
33 g Total Carbohydrate,
4 g Dietary Fiber,
32 g Protein,
109 mg Calcium.

POINTS per serving: 8.

When the thermometer dips, nothing's more warming than a bowl of beef stew. Make a double batch of the stew and freeze it to serve, with or without the dumplings, next month. For even more color, toss in a handful of thawed frozen green peas just before you top with the biscuits.

1 pound beef chuck, trimmed and
    cubed
2 carrots, chopped
2 onions, quartered
2 celery stalks, chopped
1 parsnip, chopped
1 tablespoon all-purpose flour
1½ cups low-sodium beef broth
½ teaspoon dried thyme, crumbled
½ teaspoon salt
¼ teaspoon freshly ground pepper

For the dumplings:

¾ cup all-purpose flour
½ teaspoon baking powder
⅛ teaspoon baking soda
Pinch salt
½ teaspoon dried thyme, crumbled
4 teaspoons reduced-calorie margarine
⅓ cup buttermilk

one pot

make ahead

1. In a large nonstick Dutch oven, brown the beef, stirring constantly, about 5 minutes. Stir in the carrots, onions, celery and parsnip; sauté about 5 minutes. Remove from the heat and stir in the flour; add the broth, thyme, salt and pepper. Simmer over very low heat until the beef and vegetables are tender, about 1½ hours.

2. To make the dumplings, sift the flour, baking powder, baking soda and salt into a bowl. Mix in the thyme; cut in the margarine until the mixture resembles coarse crumbs. Stir in the buttermilk, 1 tablespoon at a time, to make a soft but not sticky dough (you may not need to use all of it). Lightly flour a work surface and rolling pin. Turn out the dough and knead briefly; roll out and cut into 8 rounds with a biscuit cutter. Place the dumplings on the stew. Cook, covered, until the dumplings are cooked through and the beef is very tender, about 8–10 minutes.

Quick Classic Meat Loaf

The secret to cutting the cooking time in half: Bake this meat loaf in a ring mold. Sautéed vegetables and bread soaked in milk add flavor and moisture—and they stretch the meat as well.

makes
6 servings

3 slices whole-wheat bread
¼ cup skim milk
2 teaspoons olive oil
1 cup chopped mushrooms
1 carrot, finely chopped
1 celery stalk, chopped

½ onion, chopped
1 teaspoon salt
1 pound lean ground beef (10% or less fat)
2 egg whites

Per serving:
268 Calories,
12 g Total Fat,
5 g Saturated Fat,
70 mg Cholesterol,
798 mg Sodium,
14 g Total Carbohydrate,
2 g Dietary Fiber,
27 g Protein,
53 mg Calcium.

POINTS per serving: 6.

1.   Preheat the oven to 350° F. Spray a 6-cup ring mold with nonstick cooking spray. In a large bowl, combine the bread and milk; let stand about 15 minutes.

2.   Meanwhile, in a large nonstick skillet, heat the oil. Sauté the mushrooms, carrot, celery, onion and ¼ teaspoon of the salt until the vegetables are very soft, about 10 minutes. Let cool slightly. Add the sautéed vegetables, the beef, egg whites and the remaining ¾ teaspoon salt to the bread mixture; with moistened hands, gently combine. Transfer to the mold.

3.   Bake until no longer pink in center, about 30 minutes. Invert the loaf onto a large round platter; let stand 10 minutes before slicing.

HINT

Don't happen to have a ring mold lying around? Just shape the meat mixture into six balls and bake them in a muffin tin for about 25 minutes.

one pot

make ahead

Turkey Burgers

makes
4 servings

This burger of the nineties can take on many different twists just by adding a topping. Try salsa, chutney, caramelized onions or reduced-fat cheese.

Per serving:
235 Calories,
12 g Total Fat,
3 g Saturated Fat,
196 mg Cholesterol,
313 mg Sodium,
6 g Total Carbohydrate,
0 g Dietary Fiber,
24 g Protein,
41 mg Calcium.

POINTS per serving: 6.

1 pound ground skinless turkey

½ red onion, chopped

3 tablespoons seasoned dried bread crumbs

2 egg whites

2 tablespoons chopped parsley

2 teaspoons Worcestershire sauce

1. Preheat the broiler. Spray a broiler rack with nonstick cooking spray.

2. In a medium bowl, combine all the ingredients. Shape into four ¹/₂"-thick burgers. Broil 6" from the heat until the burgers are cooked through and the meat springs back when pressed lightly with a finger, about 5 minutes on each side.

rush hour

one pot

Pork Chops in Apricot Sauce

This sauce is thick, rich and gravy-like, and there's a good amount of it. Orzo makes a good accompaniment because it soaks up the sauce.

makes
4 servings

3 tablespoons all-purpose flour
½ teaspoon salt
¼ teaspoon freshly ground pepper
Four 4-ounce pork chops, ¼"-thick
2 teaspoons vegetable oil

2 carrots, julienned
1 red bell pepper, seeded and sliced
1 cup apricot nectar
1 tablespoon Dijon mustard
1½ tablespoons apricot spreadable fruit

Per serving:
232 Calories,
9 g Total Fat,
3 g Saturated Fat,
40 mg Cholesterol,
342 mg Sodium,
23 g Total Carbohydrate,
3 g Dietary Fiber,
14 g Protein,
36 mg Calcium.

POINTS per serving: 5.

1.   In a gallon-size sealable plastic bag, combine the flour, salt and pepper; add the pork chops and shake to coat. Shake off the excess flour; reserve any remaining flour.

2.   In medium nonstick skillet, heat 1 teaspoon of the oil. Add the chops; cook until golden, about 3 minutes on each side. Transfer to a platter.

3.   In the skillet, heat the remaining 1 teaspoon oil; sauté the carrots and bell pepper until softened, about 5 minutes. Add the reserved flour; cook, stirring, until browned, about 1 minute. Stir in the apricot nectar, mustard and spreadable fruit; cook, stirring, until thickened, 1–2 minutes. Add the chops; simmer until the chops are cooked through, about 4 minutes. Serve with the sauce.

rush hour

one pot

Turkey Cutlets with Cranberries and Apples

makes
4 servings

Turkey cutlets are so easy to cook! In about 20 minutes, you can have the flavors of Thanksgiving dinner.

Per serving:
261 Calories,
6 g Total Fat,
1 g Saturated Fat,
70 mg Cholesterol,
226 mg Sodium,
23 g Total Carbohydrate,
1 g Dietary Fiber,
29 g Protein,
19 mg Calcium.

POINTS per serving: 6.

3 tablespoons all-purpose flour

¼ teaspoon salt

⅛ teaspoon freshly ground pepper

1 pound turkey cutlets

1 tablespoon olive oil

2 teaspoons reduced-calorie margarine

1 Granny Smith apple, cored and thinly sliced

½ cup low-sodium chicken broth

½ cup whole-berry cranberry sauce

1 teaspoon grated orange zest

1.   On a sheet of wax paper, combine the flour, salt and pepper. Dredge the cutlets in the flour mixture, shaking off the excess flour; reserve any remaining flour.

2.   In a large nonstick skillet, heat 1½ teaspoons of the oil. Cook half the cutlets until golden, about 3 minutes on each side. Transfer to a platter and keep warm; repeat with the remaining oil and cutlets.

3.   In the same skillet, melt the margarine. Sauté the apple about 5 minutes; stir in the chicken broth, cranberry sauce, the reserved flour and the orange zest; cook, stirring as needed, until thickened, about 3 minutes. Pour over the cutlets and serve immediately.

rush hour

one pot

HINT

If you don't have time to make the cranberry glaze, simply melt some reduced-calorie margarine with fresh lemon juice and brush it on the cutlets before and after grilling.

Faux Sloppy Joes

Thanks to prebrowned Textured Vegetable Protein (TVP) crumbles, now widely available in supermarkets, your family will never know this is a meatless dish. The crumbles are also wonderful in tacos and chili.

2 teaspoons olive oil

1 green bell pepper, seeded and chopped

1 onion, chopped

One 12-ounce bag prebrowned Textured Vegetable Protein crumbles

One 14½-ounce can chunky chili-style tomato sauce

4 hamburger buns

In a large nonstick skillet, heat the oil. Sauté the pepper and onion until softened, about 5 minutes. Add the TVP crumbles and tomato sauce; cook until heated through, about 8 minutes. Serve in the buns.

makes
6 servings

Per serving:
176 Calories,
3 g Total Fat,
1 g Saturated Fat,
0 mg Cholesterol,
802 mg Sodium,
26 g Total Carbohydrate,
4 g Dietary Fiber,
14 g Protein,
88 mg Calcium.

POINTS per serving: 3.

vegetarian

one pot

rush hour

make ahead

Spicy London Broil

makes
4 servings

Per serving:
202 Calories,
9 g Total Fat,
4 g Saturated Fat,
47 mg Cholesterol,
68 mg Sodium,
1 g Total Carbohy-
drate,
1 g Dietary Fiber,
27 g Protein,
12 mg Calcium.

POINTS per serving: 5.

Although you might think of cinnamon as a sweet spice, it's a traditional Mexican flavoring in savory dishes. You don't really taste it, but it gives depth to the other spices. If you have any leftovers, wrap them in warmed tortillas with sautéed peppers and onions.

1½ teaspoons chili powder

½ teaspoon paprika

½ teaspoon ground cumin

⅛–¼ teaspoon freshly ground pepper

⅛ teaspoon cinnamon

One 1-pound London broil, about 1"-thick

1. Preheat the broiler. Spray a broiler rack with nonstick cooking spray.

2. In a small bowl, combine the chili powder, paprika, cumin, pepper and cinnamon. Place the meat on a sheet of wax paper and sprinkle both sides with the spice mixture; let stand about 15 minutes.

3. Broil 5" inches from the heat until cooked through, 5–7 minutes on each side. Let stand about 10 minutes before slicing thinly on an angle against the grain.

one pot

spicy

Pork Medallions with Chutney

We use mango chutney in this sophisticated dish because it's available in most super-markets, but if you run across other flavors, go ahead and experiment with them.

makes
6 servings

1½ pounds boneless pork tenderloin

¼ teaspoon salt

¼ teaspoon freshly ground pepper

1 tablespoon olive oil

1 tablespoon Dijon mustard

⅓ cup mango chutney

¼ cup chopped parsley

Per serving:
195 Calories,
6 g Total Fat,
2 g Saturated Fat,
66 mg Cholesterol,
154 mg Sodium,
9 g Total Carbohydrate,
0 g Dietary Fiber,
24 g Protein,
14 mg Calcium.

POINTS per serving: 4.

1.   Preheat the oven to 400° F. Slice the pork into medallions, about ⅓"-thick. Flatten each medallion slightly; sprinkle both sides with the salt and pepper.

2.   In a large nonstick skillet, heat 1½ teaspoons of the oil. Cook half the medallions about 2 minutes; turn and cook 1 minute longer. Transfer the medallions to a baking sheet. Repeat with the remaining oil and medallions.

3.   Brush the tops of the medallions with the mustard; spread with the chutney. Bake until the meat is cooked through, about 4 minutes. Transfer to a serving platter and garnish with the parsley.

rush hour

CHAPTER twenty

CHICKEN

When you start a healthy eating plan, chicken is one of the first items on your grocery list, and for good reasons. It's easy to prepare, inexpensive, high in protein and everyone likes it. Unfortunately, too much of a good thing can result in the dreaded "chicken fatigue" syndrome. Avoid this plague by creating exciting dinners with our tips.

1. Check out the poultry case in the supermarket, so you can experiment with the variety of chicken pieces available. Try breast fillets, roaster thighs, drumsticks, chicken tenders or ground chicken. And check the butcher's counter, too—he may offer marinated breasts at the same price as regular. Turkey parts, such as cutlets, breast tenders and sausages, make good substitutes for red meat in many dishes.

2. If you're on a budget, cut your own strips and chunks. Freeze the breasts for about 15 minutes to make them firm, less slippery and easier to slice into strips or cut into chunks. Or create cutlets: Place chicken breasts between two sheets of wax paper and pound them with a small skillet or rolling pin, so they are uniformly thin.

3. Use different cooking techniques.

   ■ If you usually grill chicken parts, try cooking a whole bird on a vertical roaster, which cooks chicken evenly while fat from the skin drains off.

   ■ To keep chicken breasts moist, cook them *en papillote*: Place chicken on a square of parchment or foil; top with julienned vegetables and seasonings, then bring up the sides of the foil, sealing and crimping the edges. Bake at 400°F until cooked through, about 20–25 minutes.

   ■ A great quick-cooking technique is stir-frying—and you don't have to stick to Asian ingredients. Add Mexican, Italian and Caribbean seasonings to vary the flavor.

- Poaching, or simmering in liquid, is an underrated cooking method that deserves more attention. It's virtually fat-free, and if you use wine, juice or broth instead of water, you really boost flavor. Take a journey around the world by trying these international bouquets (seasonings tied in cheesecloth and added to the poaching liquid):

  gingerroot, star anise and garlic for a Chinese accent;

  lemongrass, mint, cilantro, lime, gingerroot and chiles for Thai;

  chiles, allspice, curry powder, lime, gingerroot and coconut for Caribbean;

  bay leaf, parsley, thyme and black peppercorns for French.

- Add flavor with rubs, marinades and sauces.

Rubs (sometimes called dry marinades) are made by mixing a little liquid with spices or herbs to form a paste-like consistency. They impart intense flavor in a short time and keep the moisture in by giving the chicken a crust.

Marinades add flavor and moisture. Prick the chicken's flesh, place it in a sealable plastic bag and cover with just enough marinade to keep the chicken wet. For best results, marinate in the refrigerator for 4–6 hours.

- Lighten "fried" chicken by dipping pieces in beaten egg white, buttermilk or yogurt and then in bread crumbs, cracker crumbs or cornmeal mixed with grated cheese and dried herbs. To help the coating adhere, refrigerate the coated chicken for about 20 minutes; then bake until cooked through.

Chicken Fajitas

This new classic is a snap to prepare and is sure to please every palate. Substitute fish or beef for the chicken when you want a change of pace.

makes
4 servings

¼ cup chopped cilantro

¼ cup fresh lime juice

1 tablespoon olive oil

2 garlic cloves, minced

¾ teaspoon ground cumin

¼ teaspoon salt

¾ pound skinless boneless chicken breasts

1 green bell pepper, seeded and cut into thin strips

1 red bell pepper, seeded and cut into thin strips

1 onion, sliced

Four 6" flour tortillas

¼ cup salsa

¼ cup nonfat sour cream (optional)

Per serving:
231 Calories,
5 g Total Fat,
1 g Saturated Fat,
52 mg Cholesterol,
279 mg Sodium,
23 g Total Carbohydrate,
3 g Dietary Fiber,
23 g Protein,
68 mg Calcium.

POINTS per serving: 4.

1. To prepare the marinade, in a gallon-size sealable plastic bag, combine the cilantro, lime juice, oil, garlic, cumin and salt; add the chicken. Seal the bag, squeezing out the air; turn to coat the chicken. Refrigerate, covered, about 30 minutes, turning once or twice.

2. Preheat the broiler. Reserving the marinade, remove the chicken and place it on the broiler rack. Add the green and red bell peppers and onion to the marinade; seal the bag and shake to coat. Place the peppers and onion on the broiler rack with the meat. Broil 6" from the heat about 5 minutes. Turn the chicken and vegetables; broil until the chicken is cooked through and the vegetables are beginning to brown, about 5 minutes longer. Let the chicken stand about 5 minutes; slice on the diagonal into ¼"-thick slices.

3. Divide the chicken and vegetables among the tortillas; top each fajita with 1 tablespoon salsa and fold up. Serve with sour cream, if using.

one pot

spicy

HINT

Customize the heat level with your choice of salsa. If you go overboard, the sour cream will help cool things down.

Balsamic Chicken Thighs

makes

4 servings

The bold flavors of fennel, balsamic vinegar and Parmesan cheese turn economical chicken thighs into a rich treat.

Per serving:
284 Calories,
12 g Total Fat,
3 g Saturated Fat,
61 mg Cholesterol,
230 mg Sodium,
24 g Total Carbohydrate,
4 g Dietary Fiber,
20 g Protein,
125 mg Calcium.

POINTS per serving: 6.

3 tablespoons all-purpose flour

3 tablespoons grated Parmesan cheese

1¼ pounds (about 4) chicken thighs, skinned

1 tablespoon olive oil

1 fennel bulb, halved lengthwise and thinly sliced

1 red bell pepper, seeded and sliced

1 large onion, halved lengthwise and thinly sliced

½ cup orange juice

⅓ cup balsamic vinegar

1. In a gallon-size sealable plastic bag, combine the flour and cheese; add the chicken and toss to coat.

2. In a large nonstick skillet, heat the oil. Reserving the flour-cheese mixture, add the chicken. Cook until browned, 4–5 minutes on each side. Remove the chicken from the skillet.

3. Reduce the heat. Add the fennel, pepper, onion and the reserved flour mixture; sauté until the vegetables are very soft, about 10 minutes. Increase the heat. Add the orange juice and vinegar; cook, stirring, until slightly thickened, about 2 minutes. Add the chicken and stir to coat. Reduce the heat and simmer, covered, until the chicken is cooked through, about 15 minutes.

one pot

RICOTTA
PARFAITS

**EASY APPLE
DANISHES**

SPINACH SALAD

with Apples, Walnuts, and Cheddar

TURKEY CUTLETS

with Cranberries and Apples;
Steamed Vegetable Medley

Honey Mustard Chicken Fingers

Kids love this finger food, thanks to the sweetness of honey; adults love it, thanks to the sharp bite of mustard. Cracker crumbs make for a crunchy coating without frying.

makes
4 servings

2 tablespoons honey

2 tablespoons Dijon mustard

¾ pound skinless boneless chicken breasts, cut into ¼"-wide strips

16 saltine crackers, crushed

1. Preheat the oven to 400° F. Lightly spray a nonstick baking sheet with nonstick cooking spray. In a medium bowl, combine the honey and mustard. Add the chicken and toss to coat.

2. Spread the cracker crumbs in a shallow dish; dip the chicken in the crumbs a few strips at a time to coat, then place on the baking sheet. Bake, turning once, until just cooked through, about 18 minutes.

Per serving:
194 Calories,
4 g Total Fat,
1 g Saturated Fat,
52 mg Cholesterol,
244 mg Sodium,
18 g Total Carbohydrate,
1 g Dietary Fiber,
21 g Protein,
34 mg Calcium.

POINTS per serving: 4.

HINT

To keep from both your hands becoming thoroughly messy, use your left hand to transfer the chicken pieces from the mustard mixture to the crumbs; use your right hand to toss the crumbs over the chicken and move the chicken onto the baking sheet.

Jamaican Chicken

makes
4 servings

If you like this spicy rub, check out the array of different packaged seasoning blends available in supermarkets and gourmet-foods stores.

Per serving:
192 Calories,
6 g Total Fat,
1 g Saturated Fat,
69 mg Cholesterol,
353 mg Sodium,
7 g Total Carbohy-
drate,
1 g Dietary Fiber,
26 g Protein,
31 mg Calcium.

POINTS per serving: 4.

3 tablespoons fresh lime juice
4 teaspoons firmly packed brown
  sugar
1 tablespoon olive oil
2 teaspoons ground allspice
1 teaspoon ground ginger

2 garlic cloves, minced
½ teaspoon cinnamon
½ teaspoon salt
¼ teaspoon cayenne pepper
1 pound skinless boneless chicken
  breasts

1. In a small bowl, combine the lime juice, brown sugar, oil, allspice, ginger, garlic, cinnamon, salt and cayenne; mix to form a paste. Place the chicken on a plate and rub the chicken evenly with the paste; refrigerate, covered, at least 2 hours or overnight.

2. Preheat the broiler. Spray the broiler rack with nonstick cooking spray. Broil the chicken 6" from the heat until cooked through, 3–4 minutes on each side.

one pot

make ahead

spicy

Chicken with Garlic and Potatoes

Squeeze the roasted garlic from its skin to use as a rich spread for French bread. It's so rich and full of flavor that you'll never believe it's nonfat.

One 3-pound chicken, cut into eighths and skinned

1 pound small red potatoes, scrubbed and quartered

20 garlic cloves, unpeeled

2 carrots, sliced

1 teaspoon salt

2 sprigs rosemary

¼ teaspoon freshly ground pepper

2 tablespoons olive oil

Per serving:
405 Calories,
13 g Total Fat,
3 g Saturated Fat,
90 mg Cholesterol,
690 mg Sodium,
38 g Total Carbohydrate,
4 g Dietary Fiber,
33 g Protein,
66 mg Calcium.

POINTS per serving: 8.

1. Preheat the oven to 425° F. Spray a large roasting pan with nonstick cooking spray. In the roasting pan, combine the chicken, potatoes, garlic, carrots, salt, rosemary and pepper. Add the oil; toss to coat.

2. Bake, stirring occasionally, until the vegetables are tender and the juices run clear when the chicken is pierced in the thickest part with a fork, about 50 minutes.

one pot

CHAPTER twenty-one

FISH

In the last 15 to 20 years, fish consumption has doubled, but more than half of that fish is eaten in restaurants. Though we all know that most fish is exceptionally healthful—it's low in fat, especially saturated fat, and the fat that is there tends to be heart-healthy omega-3 oils—a lot of myths still surround this excellent source of protein.

The myth: Fish is hard to cook.

The reality: Fish can be one of the easiest, speediest foods in your repertoire. Flavorful fish like tuna, swordfish and salmon are delicious even if you don't have time to marinate: Just brush them lightly with oil; broil, grill or pan-fry them; then top them with a fruit or veggie salsa or a spoonful of honey mustard. You've just made dinner—in about 10 minutes.

The secret to succulent fish: Don't overcook. The rule of thumb is 10 minutes per inch of thickness (measure at the thickest part). Fish will continue to cook after you've removed it from the heat, so do *not* cook the fish until it flakes easily. When you test fish for doneness, which you should start doing after it has cooked about 8 minutes per inch, stick a sharp knife in the thickest part and peek in—it should just be opaque.

The myth: Cooking fish will stink up my house, my pans, my hands . . . .

The reality: Fish does have a distinctive odor, but it doesn't have to linger. Rub the cutting board, knife and your hands with lemon. If the smell remains in the pan, fill it midway with a half-and-half mixture of distilled vinegar and water. Boil, let cool, then wash the pan again.

If your stove's exhaust fan isn't cutting it and it's too cold to open windows to air out your house, try this: Line a small saucepan with heavy-duty foil and add ½ cup sugar. Cook it over medium heat until the smell of caramel permeates the air. When the syrup is cooled, just lift out the foil and toss.

The myth: Fish is expensive.

The reality: Nearly every supermarket has a fish department, and nearly every fish department has weekly specials. If you're flexible, you can often buy fish for less per pound than you can skinless boneless chicken breasts, pork chops and many cuts of beef. If you're not sure how to tell what's fresh, or how to cook something you've never heard of, ask the fish department's manager—or consult one of the many excellent fish cookbooks available.

The myth: Fish is full of toxins and mercury.

The reality: If you eat a variety of fish and if you buy your fish from a reputable market, you'll probably avoid this problem. Certain long-lived fish, such as swordfish, tuna and shark, can develop high levels of mercury over time, but the chances of accumulating mercury in your system are minuscule unless you eat the same tainted fish over and over.

Some tropical fish can harbor high levels of something called ciguatoxin. Steer clear of fish from tropical waters, especially grouper, barracuda, jack or red snapper (those from Florida and the Gulf of Mexico, however, are acceptable).

Scombrotoxin occurs in fish like tuna, mackerel, bluefish and mahi-mahi; it is a direct result of mishandling—letting fish sit out too long at room temperature. If you buy your fish from a trustworthy source and handle it properly when you get home, you should be fine.

Lemon-Lime Swordfish with Mango Salsa

Thick, meaty fish steaks, such as salmon or tuna, can be easily substituted for the swordfish.

makes
4 servings

¼ cup fresh lemon juice
¼ cup fresh lime juice
1 tablespoon olive oil
2 garlic cloves, chopped
¼ teaspoon salt
⅛ teaspoon fresh ground pepper
1 pound swordfish steak

Mango Salsa:

1 mango, peeled and chopped
1 red bell pepper, seeded and chopped
½ red onion, chopped
1 tablespoon fresh lemon juice
1 teaspoon olive oil
¼ teaspoon salt

Per serving:
211 Calories,
7 g Total Fat,
2 g Saturated Fat,
45 mg Cholesterol,
271 mg Sodium,
14 g Total Carbohydrate,
2 g Dietary Fiber,
24 g Protein,
20 mg Calcium.

POINTS per serving: 4.

1. To prepare the marinade, in a large nonreactive dish, combine the lemon juice, lime juice, oil, garlic, salt and pepper; transfer 2 tablespoons to a small nonreactive bowl. Add the swordfish to the marinade in the large dish; turn to coat. Refrigerate, covered, 1 hour, turning after 30 minutes.

2. Meanwhile, to make the mango salsa, in a medium bowl, combine the mango, bell pepper, onion, lemon juice, oil and salt. Let stand at room temperature to let the flavors blend, up to one hour.

3. Drain the marinade into a small saucepan; bring to a rolling boil 1 minute, stirring constantly. Remove from the heat.

4. Preheat the broiler. Spray the broiler pan with nonstick cooking spray. Broil the swordfish 6" from the heat, brushing occasionally with the marinade, until cooked through, about 5 minutes on each side. Serve with the mango salsa.

one pot

make ahead

Mediterranean Halibut

makes
4 servings

When you're pressed for time, use Italian-, Mexican- or Cajun-seasoned stewed-tomato blends; omit the capers, olives and herbs.

Per serving:
210 Calories,
7 g Total Fat,
1 g Saturated Fat,
32 mg Cholesterol,
568 mg Sodium,
13 g Total Carbohydrate,
2 g Dietary Fiber,
23 g Protein,
142 mg Calcium.

POINTS per serving: 4.

1 pound halibut steaks

1 tablespoon olive oil

1 onion, sliced

1 garlic clove, minced

Two 14½-ounce cans diced tomatoes

1 tablespoon drained rinsed capers

10 oil-cured black olives, pitted and chopped

1 tablespoon fresh lemon juice

1 teaspoon dried basil

1 teaspoon dried oregano

¼ teaspoon freshly ground pepper

1. Preheat the oven to 450° F. Place the halibut in an 8" square baking dish.

2. In a medium nonstick skillet, heat the oil. Sauté the onion and garlic until slightly softened, about 3 minutes. Stir in the tomatoes, capers, olives, lemon juice, basil, oregano and pepper. Reduce the heat and simmer, stirring as needed, until heated through and slightly thickened, about 8 minutes. Spoon the sauce over the fish. Bake until the fish is just opaque in the center, about 10 minutes.

rush hour

Maple-Glazed Salmon

Stove-top grills are an easy way to prepare this tasty dish, especially when it's too cold to stand on the patio and monitor an outdoor grill.

makes
4 servings

1 pound salmon steaks

¼ teaspoon salt

¼ teaspoon freshly ground pepper

¼ cup grapefruit juice

2 tablespoons balsamic vinegar

2 tablespoons maple syrup

2 garlic cloves, minced

1 tablespoon olive oil

Per serving:
208 Calories,
10 g Total Fat,
1 g Saturated Fat,
20 mg Cholesterol,
179 mg Sodium,
10 g Total Carbohydrate,
0 g Dietary Fiber,
19 g Protein,
27 mg Calcium.

POINTS per serving: 5.

1. Sprinkle the salmon steaks with salt and pepper. Preheat the grill or broiler. Spray the grill or broiler rack with nonstick cooking spray.

2. In a small nonreactive saucepan, combine the grapefruit juice, balsamic vinegar, maple syrup and garlic. Bring to a boil and cook about 5 minutes; stir in the oil.

3. Brush the steaks with the glaze; grill or broil until cooked through, basting frequently with the marinade, about 5 minutes on each side.

rush hour

Tuna Burgers

makes
4 servings

Per serving:
215 Calories,
7 g Total Fat,
2 g Saturated Fat,
89 mg Cholesterol,
460 mg Sodium,
9 g Total Carbohydrate,
1 g Dietary Fiber,
27 g Protein,
44 mg Calcium

POINTS per serving: 5.

If you love fish cakes and crab cakes, this is the perfect way to eat canned tuna. Since this recipe doesn't require special ingredients, it's a perfect addition to your fall-back collection for times when the cupboards seem bare.

1 egg

1 egg white

Two 6-ounce cans water-packed
   white tuna, drained and flaked

1 celery stalk, finely chopped

¼ cup + 2 tablespoons plain dried
   bread crumbs

4 scallions, sliced

1 tablespoon fresh lemon juice

1 garlic clove, minced

¼ teaspoon freshly ground pepper

1 tablespoon vegetable oil

1. In a medium bowl, lightly beat the egg and egg white. Stir in the tuna, celery, bread crumbs, scallions, lemon juice, garlic and pepper. With a ½-cup measure, shape into 4 patties.

2. In a large nonstick skillet, heat the oil. Add the patties and cook until golden brown, about 5 minutes on each side.

one pot

rush hour

Crispy Baked Codfish Sticks

Remember those fish sticks you ate growing up? Here's a healthier version that tastes just as good, if not better.

makes
4 servings

1½ pounds codfish, cut crosswise into 1" strips

1 tablespoon fresh lemon juice

1 teaspoon olive oil

⅓ cup all-purpose flour

3 tablespoons cornmeal

¾ teaspoon baking powder

¼ teaspoon salt

⅛ teaspoon cayenne pepper

Per serving:
209 Calories,
2 g Total Fat,
0 g Saturated Fat,
73 mg Cholesterol,
312 mg Sodium,
12 g Total Carbohydrate,
1 g Dietary Fiber,
32 g Protein,
51 mg Calcium.

POINTS per serving: 4.

1. Preheat the oven to 425° F. Spray a baking sheet with nonstick cooking spray. In a large bowl, combine the fish, lemon juice and oil; toss to coat.

2. In a shallow bowl, combine the flour, cornmeal, baking powder, salt and cayenne. Add a few strips of fish at a time; toss to coat. Transfer to the baking sheet and repeat with the remaining fish. Bake until golden brown and crispy, about 5 minutes on each side.

one pot

rush hour

CHAPTER twenty-two

PASTA

asta is one of the most misunderstood foods of the decade. First it was good for you, then it was bad, and now it seems to be beneficial again. The controversy surrounding this truly *complex* carbohydrate started when a report on Italian restaurant cuisine called Fettuccine Alfredo "a heart attack on a plate." Shortly thereafter, an article in *The New York Times* reported that some people have a faulty hormone system: When they eat large amounts of carbohydrates, they release too much insulin, which in turn prompts their bodies to store more fat. The truth of the matter is that insulin resistance appears to affect only one in four Americans, and it's usually a *result* of being overweight, not a *cause*.

Even with all this bad press, most nutritionists still recommend eating a diet high in complex carbohydrates and low in fat. Pasta can be a safe meal choice; it's the cheese, butter, heavy cream and oil, especially when served in typically large restaurant portions, that make it dangerous. To keep pasta the healthy food it is, keep these points in mind:

- Quantity counts. One cup cooked pasta (about 2 ounces of dry strands or ½ cup dry small or medium shapes) is considered an appropriate serving size. A bundle of spaghetti that is the diameter of a nickel will give you 1 to 1½ cups cooked pasta.

- Watch the sauce. Choose tomato-based sauces over those containing oil, cream or butter. If you use a jarred sauce, look for one with no more than 60 calories per ½ cup.

- Sauce pasta as you would dress a salad. The idea is to coat, not drown, the pasta.

- Stretch an oil-based or cream sauce by reserving some of the pasta cooking water or using hot broth. Add it back to pasta with about three-quarters the amount of the high-fat sauce you'd ordinarily use.

- Substitute evaporated skimmed milk for cream in your recipes.

- Substitute vegetables for meat in your recipes. Make lasagna with a large eggplant (cooked and chopped) instead of ground beef or Italian sausage.

- Use small amounts of high-flavor foods. Try aged cheeses like authentic Parmigiano-Reggiano or Pecorino Romano and oils infused with seasonings, since they carry lots of flavor.

- Create sauces with broths or vegetable purees. Sauté sweet onions, red bell peppers or mushrooms in a little olive oil; then add chicken or vegetable broth, and cook until slightly reduced.

Fettuccine and Meatballs

With so many different pasta shapes in supermarkets, rethink your idea of traditional spaghetti and meatballs! We used fettuccine, a wide ribbon pasta, that really holds the sauce.

makes
4 servings

Per serving:
400 Calories,
13 g Total Fat,
2.2 g Saturated Fat,
100 mg Cholesterol,
578 mg Sodium,
47 g Total Carbohydrate,
3 g Dietary Fiber,
31 g Protein,
76 mg Calcium.

POINTS per serving: 8.

Sauce:

1 tablespoon olive oil

1 onion, chopped

¼ carrot, minced

2 garlic cloves, minced

One 28-ounce can crushed tomatoes

2 tablespoons chopped fresh basil, or 2 teaspoons dried, crumbled

½ teaspoon salt

¼ teaspoon freshly ground pepper

Meatballs:

¾ pound lean ground beef (10% or less fat)

⅓ cup bread crumbs

1 egg

2 tablespoons minced onion

1 garlic clove, minced

¼ teaspoon salt

⅛ teaspoon freshly ground pepper

6 ounces fettuccine

4 teaspoons grated Parmesan cheese (optional)

1. In a large nonstick skillet, heat the oil. Sauté the onion and carrot until softened, about 5 minutes. Add the garlic; cook, stirring, about 1 minute. Stir in the tomatoes, basil, salt and pepper; cook, stirring as needed, until slightly thickened, about 20 minutes. Remove from the heat; let stand, covered, about 15 minutes.

2. Meanwhile, preheat the oven to 350° F. To prepare the meatballs, in a large bowl, lightly combine the beef, bread crumbs, egg, onion, garlic, salt and pepper; form into 24 meatballs. Place on a baking sheet. Bake until browned on the outside and slightly pink inside, 15–20 minutes. Add the meatballs to the sauce; cook, stirring as needed, until heated through, about 10 minutes.

3. Cook the fettuccine according to package directions; drain and place in a serving bowl. Serve, topped with the sauce; sprinkle with the cheese, if using.

make ahead

Perciatelli with White Clam Sauce

makes
4 servings

Per serving:
298 Calories,
5 g Total Fat,
1 g Saturated Fat,
3 mg Cholesterol,
380 mg Sodium,
50 g Total Carbohydrate,
2 g Dietary Fiber,
9 g Protein,
69 mg Calcium.

POINTS per serving: 6.

Perciatelli, a thick hollow spaghetti, is a good substitute for the traditional linguine because its thicker shape provides a more satisfying mouth feel. Cornstarch helps the sauce coat the pasta without adding extra oil.

½ pound perciatelli

1 tablespoon olive oil

2 garlic cloves, minced

1 tablespoon cornstarch

One 8-ounce bottle clam juice

½ cup dry white wine

Two 6½-ounce cans baby clams
(do not drain)

⅓ cup finely chopped parsley

2 teaspoons dried basil, crumbled

¼ teaspoon freshly ground pepper

3 tablespoons bread crumbs

1. Cook the perciatelli according to package directions; drain and keep warm.

2. In a medium saucepan, heat the oil. Sauté the garlic until lightly browned, about 1 minute. In a 1-cup glass measure, stir the cornstarch into the clam juice; stir into the garlic, then stir in the wine. Bring to a boil; cook, stirring constantly, until thickened, about 1 minute.

3. Add the clams and their liquid, the parsley, basil and pepper. Reduce the heat and simmer, covered, until the clams are heated through, about 5 minutes. Serve over the perciatelli, sprinkled with the bread crumbs.

rush hour

Fettuccine Carbonara

Evaporated skimmed milk is a great stand-in for real cream—it has a richer, thicker consistency than does regular skim milk.

makes
4 servings

½ pound fettuccine

½ cup evaporated skimmed milk

¾ cup fat-free egg substitute

¼ cup + 2 tablespoons Parmesan
   cheese

¼ cup low-fat (1%) milk

¼ teaspoon salt

¼ teaspoon freshly ground pepper

¼ teaspoon ground nutmeg

6 slices turkey bacon, cooked and
   crumbled

2 tablespoons chopped parsley

Per serving:
333 Calories,
7 g Total Fat,
2 g Saturated Fat,
23 mg Cholesterol,
640 mg Sodium,
48 g Total Carbohydrate,
1 g Dietary Fiber,
18 g Protein,
235 mg Calcium.

POINTS per serving: 7.

1. Cook the fettuccine according to package directions; drain and return to the pot.

2. Meanwhile, in a medium bowl, combine the evaporated skimmed milk, egg substitute, cheese, low-fat milk, salt, pepper and nutmeg.

3. Add the milk mixture, bacon and parsley to the fettuccine. Place the pot over low heat and cook, stirring quickly, until the mixture becomes creamy, about 1 minute. Do not overcook or the sauce may curdle. Serve immediately.

HINT

This sauce does not keep well—it really must be served at once. Keep the accompaniments simple; a salad of fresh greens always works. Also, set the table *before* you start cooking.

rush hour

Spaghetti Bolognese

makes
8 servings

Per serving:
330 Calories,
5 g Total Fat,
1 g Saturated Fat,
23 mg Cholesterol,
407 mg Sodium,
52 g Total Carbohydrate,
3 g Dietary Fiber,
14 g Protein,
83 mg Calcium.

POINTS per serving: 6.

Ground turkey goes a long way toward lightening this hearty meat sauce from Bologna; prebrowned Textured Vegetable Protein (TVP) crumbles would cut the fat even further. The long simmering is what gives the sauce its rich flavor.

1 tablespoon olive oil

1 onion, chopped

½ carrot, finely chopped

1 celery stalk, chopped

2 garlic cloves, minced

½ pound ground skinless turkey

½ cup dry white wine

2 teaspoons dried basil, crumbled

1 teaspoon dried oregano, crumbled

½ teaspoon salt

¼ teaspoon freshly ground pepper

½ cup low-fat (1%) milk

⅛ teaspoon ground nutmeg

2 tablespoons tomato paste

One 28-ounce can Italian tomatoes

1 pound spaghetti, cooked

1. In a large nonreactive saucepan, heat the oil. Sauté the onion, carrot and celery until softened, about 5 minutes, adding a little water if the vegetables begin to stick to pan. Add the garlic; cook about 30 seconds longer.

2. Crumble in the turkey and cook until it's still slightly pink; stir in the wine, basil, oregano, salt and pepper. Bring to a boil and cook, stirring as needed, until the liquid evaporates, about 10 minutes. Pour in the milk and add the nutmeg. Reduce the heat and simmer, stirring as needed, until the milk evaporates, about 10 minutes.

make ahead

3. Stir in the tomato paste, then add the tomatoes and their juice, breaking up the tomatoes with a spoon. Bring to a boil; reduce the heat and simmer, stirring as needed and adding ½ cup water as the sauce becomes thick (about every 30 minutes), about 1½ hours. Serve over the pasta.

Rotelle with Roasted Vegetables and Tofu

Roasting brings out the naturally sweet, rich flavor of vegetables. Experiment with different combinations of vegetables, as well as herbs—carrots, yellow squash, green bell pepper and rosemary are a tasty combination.

makes
6 servings

Per serving:
354 Calories,
8 g Total Fat,
1 g Saturated Fat,
4 mg Cholesterol,
317 mg Sodium,
55 g Total Carbohydrate,
7 g Dietary Fiber,
18 g Protein,
153 mg Calcium.

POINTS per serving: 6.

1½ cups cubed reduced-fat firm tofu

1 pound (about 5) Japanese or baby eggplants, cubed

1 small (about ½-pound) fennel bulb, sliced

½ pound mushrooms, sliced

1 red bell pepper, seeded and cut into 1" pieces

1 sweet onion, sliced

10 garlic cloves, peeled

1 tablespoon olive oil

2 teaspoons dried basil, crumbled

½ teaspoon salt

¼ teaspoon freshly ground pepper

3 cups rotelle

¼ cup + 2 tablespoons grated Parmesan cheese

1. Preheat the oven to 425° F. In a large roasting pan, combine the tofu, eggplants, fennel, mushrooms, bell pepper, onion, garlic, oil, basil, salt and pepper. Bake until the vegetables are tender, about 40 minutes, tossing every 10 minutes.

2. Meanwhile, cook the pasta according to package directions. Rinse, drain and place in a serving bowl; toss with the vegetable mixture and the cheese. Serve immediately.

vegetarian

Penne with Broccoli Rabe and Sausage

makes
4 servings

Per serving:
417 Calories,
8 g Total Fat,
1 g Saturated Fat,
20 mg Cholesterol,
530 mg Sodium,
69 g Total Carbohydrate,
8 g Dietary Fiber,
18 g Protein,
91 mg Calcium.

POINTS per serving: 7.

If you've been noticing the different cooking greens in your supermarket but haven't bought any because you don't know what to do with them, this recipe is an easy and delicious introduction. Swiss chard or kale are good substitutes for the broccoli rabe.

3 cups penne

1 red bell pepper, seeded and chopped

2 Italian-style turkey sausages, finely chopped

1 tablespoon olive oil

2 garlic cloves, minced

1 bunch broccoli rabe, cleaned and chopped

One 14½-ounce can diced tomatoes

¼ to ½ teaspoon crushed red pepper flakes

1. Cook the penne according to package directions; drain and keep warm.

2. Spray a large nonstick Dutch oven with nonstick cooking spray; heat. Sauté the bell pepper and sausages until the pepper is softened and the sausages are browned, about 5 minutes. Remove from the pan and keep warm.

3. In the Dutch oven, heat the oil. Sauté the garlic about 30 seconds. Add the broccoli rabe and cook, stirring, until wilted, adding ⅓ cup water to prevent sticking. Reduce the heat and simmer, loosely covered, until the broccoli rabe is tender, about 3 minutes. Transfer the broccoli rabe to a plate. In the Dutch oven, combine the pepper and sausages, the tomatoes, penne and pepper flakes; cook until heated through, about 2 minutes. Gently fold in the broccoli rabe.

rush hour

spicy

HINT

When choosing broccoli rabe, select firm, small stems with compact heads. The florets should be tightly closed and dark green, not yellow. To clean, rinse thoroughly in cold water and cut off the bottoms of the stalks.

CHAPTER twenty-three

SIDES

If you're like most Americans, you know you should be eating less meat, but you're probably confused about how much less and what exactly you should eat in its place. To simplify eating the right balance of complex carbohydrates and proteins, nutritionists recommend that protein take up only one-fourth of your plate—the rest of it should be filled with veggies and grains.

When your meals focus on meat, sides are often afterthoughts: boiled or baked potatoes, plain rice, steamed vegetables. Punching up your side dishes doesn't take any more time or much more preparation, especially if you happen to have a few of these gadgets and tools on hand (see pages 141–148 for more on kitchen equipment):

■ **A rice steamer:** Sure, you can cook rice in the microwave or on the stove, but with a steamer you'll get perfect results every time. Look for electric steamers that cook veggies, rice, fish, you name it. Some even have special wells for herbs and spices to infuse the food as it cooks.

■ **A tube-shaped garlic peeler:** Just drop in the cloves, roll on the counter, and presto: peeled cloves, with no garlic paper sticking to your fingers. For garlic mashed potatoes, cook the cloves with the potatoes—they'll soften—then mash in.

■ **A mandoline:** Typically made of metal and very expensive, mandolines make it easier to slice, julienne and waffle-cut without dragging out your food processor. One manufacturer has come up with a plastic-and-metal mandoline that's much less costly.

■ **A Y-shaped vegetable peeler:** Because they're shorter, these gadgets provide much more control than do the knife-shaped peelers.

■ **A pepper mill:** Once you taste the difference freshly ground pepper makes, you'll never go back to the shaker. Besides basic black peppercorns, experiment with five-pepper blends and with white, green and pink peppercorns.

Garlicky Greens

makes
4 servings

Per serving:
78 Calories,
4 g Total Fat,
I g Saturated Fat,
0 mg Cholesterol,
299 mg Sodium,
9 g Total Carbohydrate,
5 g Dietary Fiber,
3 g Protein,
107 mg Calcium.

POINTS per serving: I.

Dark-green leafy vegetables, sometimes called cooking greens, are real nutritional pow-erhouses, and they taste delicious. Next time you push your grocery cart past the display of kale, escarole, Swiss chard, collards and mustard or turnip greens, pick up a bunch to try in this recipe. In fact, try the recipe with each of them—they'll all taste different—and decide which you like best.

1 tablespoon olive oil

2–3 garlic cloves, minced

½ teaspoon salt

⅛ teaspoon hot red pepper flakes

1 large bunch cooking greens (kale, escarole, spinach, Swiss chard, or mustard, turnip or collard greens), cleaned and coarsely chopped

In a large nonstick Dutch oven, heat the oil. Sauté the garlic until fragrant and lightly browned, about 30 seconds; stir in the salt and pepper flakes. Reduce the heat and add the greens a handful or two at a time, stirring to help them wilt. Add 2–3 tablespoons water to prevent scorching; cook, covered, stirring as needed, until the greens are tender, 10 minutes. (The cooking time will depend on which green you're using.)

one pot

rush hour

HINT

Here's a way to get the leaves off the stems of greens: Hold a piece of whatever green you're using by the stem, with the stem in the air and the leaves just resting on the cutting board. With a sharp knife, cut straight down both sides of the stem. The leaves should now be separate from the stems, ready to chop.

Roasted Vegetables

Roasting caramelizes the sugar in vegetables; the sweetness imparts a richness and depth of flavor that's truly remarkable. If you have children who profess a deep and abiding hatred for any and all vegetables, this just might be the recipe that wins them over.

makes
6 servings

1¼ pounds new potatoes, scrubbed and quartered

1 tablespoon olive oil

1 teaspoon chili powder

½ teaspoon cumin

½ teaspoon salt

¼ teaspoon dried thyme, crumbled

⅛ teaspoon freshly ground pepper

3 medium zucchini, cut into large chunks

2 red bell peppers, seeded and cut into strips

1 sweet onion, sliced

Per serving:
102 Calories,
3 g Total Fat,
0 g Saturated Fat,
0 mg Cholesterol,
191 mg Sodium,
18 g Total Carbohydrate,
4 g Dietary Fiber,
3 g Protein,
26 mg Calcium.

POINTS per serving: 1.

1. Preheat the oven to 450° F. In a 13 × 9" baking pan, combine the potatoes and oil. Bake about 15 minutes.

2. Meanwhile, in a small bowl, combine the chili powder, cumin, salt, thyme and pepper. Add to the potatoes. Add the zucchini, bell peppers and onion; toss to coat. Bake until the vegetables are tender, about 25 minutes longer.

one pot

Couscous with Raisins

makes
4 servings

Per serving:
253 Calories,
1 g Total Fat,
0 g Saturated Fat,
0 mg Cholesterol,
106 mg Sodium,
56 g Total Carbohydrate,
4 g Dietary Fiber,
8 g Protein,
25 mg Calcium.

POINTS per serving: 4.

Although couscous is integral to Moroccan and North African cooking, it's actually tiny bits of pasta. Because they're so small, they don't even need to cook—just bring the cooking liquid to a boil, add the couscous and let it stand for about 5 minutes. For extra flavor, toast the couscous in a nonstick skillet for about 1 minute before you add it to the broth.

1½ cups vegetable broth	⅛ teaspoon cumin
1 red bell pepper, seeded and chopped	1 cup couscous
⅛ teaspoon salt	½ cup raisins
⅛ teaspoon freshly ground pepper	

In a medium saucepan, bring the broth, bell pepper, salt, pepper and cumin to a boil. Reduce the heat and simmer until the bell pepper is softened, about 3 minutes. Stir in the couscous and raisins. Cover the pan, remove from the heat and let stand until the broth is absorbed and the couscous is tender, about 5 minutes. Fluff lightly with a fork to separate the grains.

one pot

rush hour

Brown Rice Pilaf

To make this more of a main dish, stir in some of your favorite canned beans and some vegetables. For a slightly different flavor, experiment with the different types of rice; if you can find short-grain brown rice, try that—it has a slightly chewier texture than does the more common long-grain variety.

1 tablespoon olive oil

1 onion, finely chopped

1 cup brown rice

1 cup vegetable or chicken broth

3 tablespoons grated Parmesan cheese

⅛ teaspoon salt

⅛ teaspoon freshly ground pepper

1. In a large nonstick saucepan, heat the oil. Sauté the onion until softened, about 5 minutes. Add the rice and sauté until well-coated, about 2 minutes.

2. Slowly stir in the broth and 1½ cups water; bring to a boil. Reduce the heat and simmer, covered, until the rice is tender and all the liquid is absorbed, about 40 minutes. Remove from the heat and stir in the cheese, salt and pepper. Let stand about 5 minutes, then fluff with a fork.

makes
4 servings

Per serving:
239 Calories,
6 g Total Fat,
1 g Saturated Fat,
3 mg Cholesterol,
161 mg Sodium,
40 g Total Carbohydrate,
2 g Dietary Fiber,
6 g Protein,
70 mg Calcium.

POINTS per serving: 5.

one pot

make ahead

Creamy Garlic Mashed Potatoes

makes
4 servings

Per serving:
158 Calories,
4 g Total Fat,
0 g Saturated Fat,
0 mg Cholesterol,
83 mg Sodium,
29 g Total Carbohydrate,
2 g Dietary Fiber,
3 g Protein,
33 mg Calcium.

POINTS per serving: 3.

After you buy potatoes, take them out of the plastic bag and keep them in a cool, dark, well-ventilated area for up to 2 weeks; don't refrigerate them, because that breaks down the starch and destroys their texture.

1¼ pounds russet potatoes (about 4), peeled and chopped

5 garlic cloves, peeled

3 tablespoons nonfat sour cream

1 tablespoon olive oil

⅛ teaspoon salt

⅛ teaspoon freshly ground pepper

Place the potatoes and garlic in a large saucepan; add water to cover. Bring to a boil; reduce the heat and simmer until the potatoes are tender, 20–30 minutes. Drain, reserving ¾ cup cooking liquid. Mash the potatoes and garlic in the saucepan; stir in the sour cream, oil, salt and pepper. Gradually stir in some of the cooking liquid until the potatoes become creamy. Serve at once.

one pot

Baked Sweet Potato "Fries"

If you really want to fool the kids, invest in an inexpensive crinkle cutter to make potatoes look just like fries. For extra zip, sprinkle the potatoes with cayenne pepper or spritz with a flavored nonstick cooking spray when you remove them from the oven.

2 pounds large sweet potatoes,
    scrubbed
1 tablespoon olive oil

¼ teaspoon salt
¼ teaspoon freshly ground pepper

1. Preheat the oven to 450° F. Halve the potatoes and cut into ½" wedges. In a medium bowl, toss the potatoes with the oil, salt and pepper.

2. Arrange the potatoes in a single layer on a nonstick baking sheet; bake, turning once, until browned and crisp, about 35 minutes.

makes
4 servings

Per serving:
234 Calories,
4 g Total Fat,
0 g Saturated Fat,
0 mg Cholesterol,
153 mg Sodium,
48 g Total Carbohydrate,
6 g Dietary Fiber,
3 g Protein,
57 mg Calcium.

POINTS per serving: 4.

one pot

Steamed Vegetable Medley

makes
4 servings

Per serving:
90 Calories,
3 g Total Fat,
0 g Saturated Fat,
0 mg Cholesterol,
214 mg Sodium,
15 g Total Carbohydrate,
6 g Dietary Fiber,
5 g Protein,
69 mg Calcium.

POINTS per serving: 1.

The key to perfectly steamed vegetables is to make sure all the vegetables will take the same amount of time to cook; dense varieties, such as carrots, should be cut into smaller pieces than broccoli florets, for example. Food continues to cook after you turn off the heat, so leave the vegetables slightly undercooked and they will be just right by the time you are ready to serve. For a subtle flavor, add fresh herbs to the cooking water.

2 carrots, cut into ½" pieces

2 cups broccoli florets, cut into
    1" pieces

2 medium yellow squash, cut into
    ½" slices

2 red bell peppers, seeded and cut into
    ½" pieces

4 teaspoons reduced–calorie margarine

¼ teaspoon salt

⅛ teaspoon freshly ground pepper

Place the carrots in a steamer basket in a large pot of boiling water. Cover and steam about 5 minutes. Add the remaining vegetables to the steamer; cook until tender, about 15 minutes. Transfer to a serving bowl; toss with the margarine, salt and pepper.

one pot

rush hour

CHAPTER twenty-four

WEEKEND MAKE-AHEADS

a well-stocked freezer is a busy cook's best asset. Preparing big batches of food over the weekend and freezing or refrigerating them properly is an easy way to streamline hectic weeknights. Just remember: Freezing slows down spoilage, but it doesn't prevent it. Some tips to maximize nutrients, texture and flavor of foods you're freezing:

To cool food:

To prevent spoilage, cooked food must be cooled correctly. Although food spoils rapidly between 70° F and 120° F, bacteria grow and thrive between 40° F and 140° F. To avoid this danger zone:

■ Never put a large pot of hot food directly in the refrigerator. It will heat up the refrigerator and the surrounding food; the food at the center of the pot won't cool fast enough. In fact, even after spending all night in the fridge, the center of a pot of chili, stew or a spaghetti sauce can still be 70° F.

■ Divvy up batches of soup and sauce into small or flat containers (avoid filling large tub shapes) before refrigerating. Since texture stays best when food is frozen rapidly, refrigerate foods before freezing them (this also keeps the temperature inside the freezer from getting too high, which keeps the food already in the freezer from thawing).

■ Cool casseroles, potpies and lasagnas by partially filling a large roasting pan or the sink with ice water, then placing the dish inside.

To freeze food:

■ Wrap foods airtight in double layers of foil, in freezer bags or in tight-seal plastic containers. To get all the air out of freezer bags, squeeze out as much air as possible. If using plastic containers, leave 1 inch or so for the food to expand.

- Never freeze meats or poultry in their supermarket wrapping alone—always double wrap or put them in freezer bags.

- Remember to label! Include the type of food, the date and the amount, weight or number of portions.

- Use foods within these times for best results:

  Cooked poultry and meats: 2 months (best if packed in gravy or sauce to keep moist)

  Uncooked whole poultry: 12 months

  Uncooked poultry parts: 6 months

  Uncooked beef and lamb: 12 months

  Uncooked pork: 4 to 8 months

  Cooked beans and legumes: 3 months

  Ground meat: 3 months

  Sausage: 1 to 3 months

  Casseroles: 2 to 3 months

- Do not freeze: soft cheeses, sour cream, milk or low-fat (less than 40 percent butterfat) cream, mayonnaise, cooked egg whites, egg-white icings or baked goods frosted with such icings, custards or cooked potatoes. Remember that seasonings can change flavor as foods thaw, so add herbs, spices and other flavorings, such as lemon juice or chiles, just before serving.

To thaw food:

Allow plenty of time.

- In the refrigerator, 2 days for plastic containers; freezer bags will take less time.

- In the microwave, it will depend on the wattage. Check the instruction manual and follow the directions to the letter. Plan to cook the food immediately.

- In cold water, immerse the container or freezer bag in a bowl (make sure the bag is leak-proof). Change the water every 30 minutes, or when it becomes lukewarm.

Foods that are safe to thaw at room temperature include bread, desserts and baked goods. Thaw in the original wrappers to prevent moisture loss.

If you want to make sure the food you prepared on Sunday afternoon will last until Wednesday evening, store it in the coldest part of your refrigerator—usually on the bottom shelf, in the back, on the side opposite the handle.

Roasted Garlic and Prune-Stuffed Pork Loin

This yields lots of leftovers, and you'll have a wonderful time discovering favorite ways to use them up. Some of our favorites: Cut into thin strips for a stir-fry; sandwich between slices of fresh bakery bread spread with chutney; slice thinly and reheat in a little apple cider or juice.

makes
16 servings

Per serving:
239 Calories,
11 g Total Fat,
4 g Saturated Fat,
53 mg Cholesterol,
325 mg Sodium,
10 g Total Carbohydrate,
1 g Dietary Fiber,
25 g Protein,
34 mg Calcium.

POINTS per serving: 5.

One 4-pound boneless lean pork loin
2 teaspoons salt
½ teaspoon freshly ground pepper
½ teaspoon ground ginger
1 garlic bulb, roasted★

12 pitted prunes
1 tablespoon olive oil
1 onion, sliced
1½ cups orange juice
3 tablespoons all-purpose flour

1. If the pork loin is tied, untie it and trim any excess fat. Make a deep slice lengthwise down the center of the roast without cutting through, as though you were cutting a loaf of French bread. Spread the roast open on a cutting board.

2. In a small bowl, combine the salt, pepper and ginger. Rub half on the inside of the roast. Squeeze the roasted garlic over the seasonings and spread evenly; place the prunes down the center. Fold the roast closed and tie with twine at 2" intervals. Rub the outside of the roast with the remaining seasoning mixture.

3. In a large roasting pan with a lid or Dutch oven, heat the oil. Sauté the onion until softened, about 5 minutes. Transfer to a plate. In the roasting pan, brown the meat on all sides, including the ends. Return the onion to the pan; add 1 cup of the orange juice. Reduce the heat and simmer, covered, about 45 minutes, basting the meat occasionally with the remaining ½ cup orange juice. The roast is done when a thermometer inserted in the center, not touching the prunes, reads 170° F. Transfer the roast to a platter; let stand about 20 minutes.

one pot

4. To prepare the gravy, skim any fat from the cooking liquid. In a small bowl, combine 3 tablespoons water with the flour until smooth; stir in about ¼ cup of the cooking liquid. Stir the mixture into the roasting pan; cook over medium-high heat, stirring constantly, until the gravy thickens, 2–3 minutes. Remove the strings from the roast and slice thinly. Serve with the gravy on the side.

★*To roast the garlic: Remove the outer paper from the whole garlic bulb. Wrap in foil and bake at 350° F about 1 hour; let cool about 10 minutes, then remove the foil. Cut the top from the garlic bulb and separate the cloves.*

Roasted Garlic Chicken

makes
4 servings with leftovers

Per serving:
154 Calories,
5 g Total Fat,
1 g Saturated Fat,
72 mg Cholesterol,
282 mg Sodium,
2 g Total Carbohydrate,
0 g Dietary Fiber,
24 g Protein,
21 mg Calcium.

POINTS per serving: 3.

Who can resist roast chicken? Our secret is using a vertical roaster, which drains off a tremendous amount of fat from the skin yet keeps the bird moist.

One 3½-pound roasting chicken

½ teaspoon salt

¼ teaspoon freshly ground pepper

2 lemons

4 garlic cloves, peeled

2 sprigs fresh thyme, or ½ teaspoon dried thyme, crumbled

1. Preheat the oven to 375° F.

2. Rinse the chicken inside and out; pat dry with paper towels. Sprinkle the outside with the salt and pepper. Place on a vertical roaster in its roasting pan. Prick 1 lemon in several places with a fork; place in the cavity of the bird along with garlic on top. Carefully lift the skin from the chicken and tuck the thyme sprigs under the skin. Squeeze the juice from the remaining lemon over the chicken.

3. Roast the chicken, basting occasionally with the pan juices, until a meat thermometer inserted in the thickest part of the thigh reaches 180° F, 1–1½ hours. (Cover loosely with foil if the chicken is browning too quickly.) Remove the chicken from the roaster and let stand about 15 minutes before carving; remove the skin before eating.

one pot

Vegetable Lasagna

This tasty lasagna is a true crowd-pleaser. No-boil lasagna noodles are a wonderful innovation—their taste and texture are the same as traditional noodles, and you have one less pot to wash and no more burned fingers.

makes
6 servings

Per serving:
368 Calories,
15 g Total Fat,
7 g Saturated Fat,
107 mg Cholesterol,
1,005 mg Sodium,
37 g Total Carbohydrate,
6 g Dietary Fiber,
22 g Protein,
387 mg Calcium.

POINTS per serving: 7.

1 tablespoon olive oil

2 onions, thinly sliced

2 red bell peppers, seeded and cut into thin strips

2 cups chopped cauliflower

3 garlic cloves, minced

1 teaspoon minced thyme

½ teaspoon salt

¾ teaspoon freshly ground pepper

2 cups part-skim ricotta cheese

2 eggs, lightly beaten

¼ cup basil

2 tablespoon grated Parmesan cheese

2½ cups tomato sauce

9 no-boil lasagna noodles

¾ cup shredded part-skim mozzarella cheese

1.   In a large nonstick skillet, heat the oil. Sauté the onions until softened, about 5 minutes. Add the bell peppers; sauté until tender, 8–10 minutes. Stir in the cauliflower, garlic, thyme and salt; cook, covered, about 10 minutes. Season with ½ teaspoon of the pepper.

2.   In a small bowl, combine the ricotta, eggs, basil, Parmesan and the remaining ¼ teaspoon pepper.

3.   Preheat the oven to 400° F. In a 13 × 9" baking pan, spread ½ cup of the tomato sauce. Layer 3 lasagna noodles, half of the ricotta mixture, half of the vegetable mixture, ½ cup of the tomato sauce and ¼ cup of the mozzarella. Layer with 3 more lasagna noodles, another ½ cup of the sauce, the remaining ricotta mixture, the remaining vegetables, another ¼ cup of the mozzarella, then 3 more lasagna noodles. Spread the top with the remaining 1 cup sauce and sprinkle with the remaining ¼ cup mozzarella. Bake, covered with foil, about 30 minutes; uncover and bake until the cheese melts and the sauce is bubbling, about 15 minutes longer. Let stand about 10 minutes before cutting.

make ahead

vegetarian

Three-Bean and Pepper Chili

makes
8 servings

To make a low-fat version of tortilla "bowls," drape 6" flour tortillas over crumpled balls of foil; place them on a baking sheet and bake at 375° F for about 8 minutes. Let cool, still draped over the foil balls, about 10 minutes; fill with chili.

Per serving:
231 Calories,
4 g Total Fat,
1 g Saturated Fat,
0 mg Cholesterol,
353 mg Sodium,
39 g Total Carbohydrate,
12 g Dietary Fiber,
11 g Protein,
77 mg Calcium.

POINTS per serving: 3.

2 tablespoons vegetable oil

1 large onion, finely chopped

2 garlic cloves, finely chopped

1 yellow bell pepper, seeded and chopped

1 red bell pepper, seeded and chopped

1 green bell pepper, seeded and chopped

2 tablespoons chili powder

1 teaspoon ground cumin

One 28-ounce can crushed tomatoes

One 10-ounce box frozen corn kernels, thawed

One 19-ounce can black beans, rinsed and drained

One 19-ounce can red kidney beans, rinsed and drained

One 19-ounce can pinto beans, rinsed and drained

2 teaspoons white vinegar

Salt and freshly ground pepper, to taste

one pot

make ahead

vegetarian

spicy

In a large saucepan, heat the oil. Sauté the onion about 3 minutes; add the garlic and sauté about 1 minute. Add the peppers and sauté about 5 minutes. Add the chili powder and cumin; sauté about 1 minute. Stir in the tomatoes, corn and 1 cup water. Reduce the heat and simmer until the flavors are blended, about 30 minutes. Add the beans and vinegar; cook until the beans are heated through, about 15 minutes. Season to taste with salt and pepper.

Lentil Stew

This dish is excellent served with brown rice and a side of sliced cucumbers mixed with yogurt. Make lentil burritos with the leftovers by wrapping in a flour tortilla with a little shredded cheese; heat until warmed through.

makes
8 servings

1 tablespoon olive oil

2 celery stalks, chopped

1 onion, chopped

2 garlic cloves, minced

3 carrots, chopped

2 cups brown lentils, picked over, rinsed and drained

1 teaspoon ground cumin

One 28-ounce can crushed tomatoes

Salt and freshly ground pepper, to taste

Per serving:
202 Calories,
2 g Total Fat,
0 g Saturated Fat,
0 mg Cholesterol,
115 mg Sodium,
33 g Total Carbohydrate,
16 g Dietary Fiber,
14 g Protein,
47 mg Calcium.

POINTS per serving: 1.

In a large nonstick saucepan, heat the oil. Sauté the celery, onion and garlic, stirring constantly, until softened, about 6 minutes. Add the carrots, lentils and cumin; slowly add the tomatoes and bring to a boil. Reduce the heat and simmer, partially covered and stirring occasionally, until tender, about 45 minutes. Season to taste with salt and pepper.

CHAPTER twenty-five

NIGHTTIME NIBBLES

f you're trying to lose weight, evenings can be a lethal time—especially if you've always viewed this as the time to relax after a hectic day and eating is one way you relax. Depending on the amount of stress you've had, this eating can go from controlled to compulsive. You'll find the recipes in this chapter are sensible food solutions for handling this rough time, but you'll also need to incorporate some nonfood de-stressors and rewards.

The most important aspect of staying in control is to give the evening some structure. Allow yourself at least 30 minutes to relax and 45 minutes to an hour for dinner. Think there's no way you can snatch the time? Try these ideas:

■ To insure you don't hit the fridge the minute you walk in the door, take some time to relax before diving into dinner preparations. Meditate for 20 minutes, or lie down and listen to some relaxing music. Ask your partner and kids about their days; if the weather's nice, sit outside and watch the wind blow through the leaves. If you come home to a family clamoring for dinner, ask them to help you with meal preparations or have them leave you in peace. Stop off at the gym, a park or a nail salon to get some quiet time to yourself.

■ Next, make dinner as relaxing as possible. Set the table with candles and pretty place mats. Serve water with slices of lime or ice cubes frozen with mint. Play peaceful music. Whatever you do, *don't* watch television. Tell your kids that you're going through the effort to make dinner nice because they're special (it might improve their behavior). Anything you do to make this experience more satisfying will help you stick with your plan.

■ After dinner, do whatever you can to make tomorrow morning less stressful: Make lunches, lay out clothes, sign permission slips, pack bookbags and briefcases.

Milk Shake

makes
1 serving

Per serving:
95 Calories,
1 g Total Fat,
0 g Saturated Fat,
5 mg Cholesterol,
83 mg Sodium,
17 g Total Carbohydrate,
2 g Dietary Fiber,
6 g Protein,
199 mg Calcium.

POINTS per serving: 2.

Besides taking care of an after-dinner sweet tooth, shakes make for a speedy breakfast or a satisfying afternoon snack. Vary the fruit and frozen yogurt flavor to shake up your taste buds.

½ cup chopped fruit (try strawberries, bananas, pears, apricots, mango or papaya)

½ cup skim milk

2 tablespoons vanilla low-fat frozen yogurt

1 teaspoon wheat germ (optional)

Fresh mint sprig (optional)

In a blender, puree the fruit, milk, yogurt and wheat germ, if using, until thick and creamy. (If you prefer to use a food processor, pulse the fruit to a puree and pour in the milk with the machine running; pulse in the yogurt and wheat germ.) Pour into a tall chilled glass and garnish with the mint, if using.

Hot Chocolate Soufflé

The secret to a light and airy soufflé is to use scrupulously clean beaters and mixing bowls—when you're whipping air into the egg whites, even a trace of fat can interfere with the volume.

makes
4 servings

Per serving:
118 Calories,
5 g Total Fat,
1 g Saturated Fat,
108 mg Cholesterol,
96 mg Sodium,
14 g Total Carbohydrate,
0 g Dietary Fiber,
6 g Protein,
89 mg Calcium.

POINTS per serving: 3.

2 tablespoons unsweetened cocoa powder

2 tablespoons all-purpose flour

1 teaspoon instant coffee powder

¾ cup + 2 tablespoons low-fat (1%) milk

2 tablespoons firmly packed brown sugar

1 tablespoon reduced-calorie margarine

2 eggs, separated

½ teaspoon confectioners' sugar, for dusting

1. Preheat the oven to 375° F. Lightly spray a 2-cup soufflé dish with nonfat cooking spray. Sift the cocoa, flour and coffee powder into a large nonstick saucepan; stir in the milk, brown sugar and margarine. Bring to a boil over very low heat, whisking constantly, until the mixture is thick and smooth; simmer 30 seconds. Remove from the heat and let cool about 10 minutes. Beat in the egg yolks.

2. In a clean large bowl, beat the egg whites until stiff peaks form. With a rubber spatula, gently fold the egg whites into the chocolate sauce, using a figure-8 motion. Spoon into the soufflé dish. Bake until the soufflé rises, but the center is still wobbly, 20–25 minutes. (Don't open the oven door for the first 20 minutes of cooking.)

3. Put the confectioners' sugar in a fine-mesh sieve and, as you take the soufflé out of the oven, quickly sift over the soufflé. Serve immediately.

Apple Brown Betty

makes
6 servings

Similar to apple crisp, this old-fashioned dessert uses bread crumbs instead of a high-fat crust or streusel topping. Serve it with a scoop of vanilla frozen yogurt when you're feeling indulgent.

Per serving:
297 Calories,
6 g Total Fat,
1 g Saturated Fat,
0 mg Cholesterol,
313 mg Sodium,
61 g Total Carbohydrate,
6 g Dietary Fiber,
6 g Protein,
56 mg Calcium.

POINTS per serving: 5.

10 slices whole-grain bread, toasted and cubed

4 tablespoons reduced-calorie margarine, melted

¾ cup apple juice

¼ cup firmly packed dark brown sugar

2 tablespoons fresh lemon juice

1 teaspoon cinnamon

¼ teaspoon grated nutmeg

6 tart apples, peeled and sliced

½ cup raisins

1.   Preheat the oven to 375° F. Spray a shallow 1½-quart casserole with nonstick cooking spray. In a medium bowl, combine the bread and margarine.

2.   In a large bowl, combine the apple juice, brown sugar, lemon juice, cinnamon and nutmeg. Add the apples and raisins; toss to coat.

3.   Spoon half of the apple mixture into the baking dish; top with half of the bread-cube mixture. Repeat the layers; drizzle with any remaining apple liquid. Bake, covered with foil, about 30 minutes; uncover and increase the oven temperature to 400° F; bake until golden, about 10 minutes. Cool about 15 minutes before serving.

one pot

Chocolate Mousse

This recipe is a bit time-consuming, but the results are spectacular—the perfect indulgence for a serious chocolate craving.

makes
8 servings

1 envelope unflavored gelatin

2 egg whites

¼ cup unsweetened Dutch-processed
    cocoa

½ cup sugar

1¼ cups low-fat (1%) milk

⅔ cup semisweet chocolate chips

2 ounces low-fat cream cheese

2 tablespoons powdered egg whites

Per serving:
159 Calories,
5 g Total Fat,
3 g Saturated Fat,
5 mg Cholesterol,
92 mg Sodium,
26 g Total Carbohydrate,
0 g Dietary Fiber,
6 g Protein,
62 mg Calcium.

POINTS per serving: 4.

1. In a small bowl, sprinkle the gelatin over ¼ cup cold water. Let stand at least 5 minutes. Place a whisk and the egg whites in a small bowl near the stove.

2. In a small nonstick saucepan, combine the cocoa and ¼ cup of the sugar; stir in enough milk to form a paste. Add the remaining milk; bring to a simmer over medium heat, stirring constantly, then cook, stirring constantly, about 1½ minutes.

3. Remove from the heat and whisk ¼ cup of the hot mixture into the egg whites. Return the mixture back to the saucepan; whisk well to combine (the egg whites will get hot enough to be safe, and the mixture will thicken without further cooking). Stir in the gelatin and chocolate chips. Let stand about 1 minute; whisk again until the chocolate chips melt completely and the mixture is smooth.

4. In a small microwavable bowl, microwave the cream cheese on High until softened, 10 seconds. Stir in ¼ cup of the chocolate mixture, then whisk back into the chocolate mixture.

5. Fill the sink with ice water; the saucepan inside.

6. In a medium bowl, combine the powdered egg whites, the remaining ¼ cup sugar and ¼ cup + 2 tablespoons water; beat until stiff peaks form. With a rubber spatula, fold about one-fourth of the chocolate mixture into the egg whites. Fold this mixture back into the chocolate sauce. Pour immediately into serving dishes and refrigerate, covered, until set, at least 4 hours.

one pot

microwave

make ahead

Frozen Fruit Whip

makes
1 serving

If ½ cup of frozen yogurt isn't satisfying enough, try this healthy trick to bulk up its texture and flavor—you'll still keep your calories low, but get four times as much.

Per serving:
163 Calories,
0 g Total Fat,
0 g Saturated Fat,
5 mg Cholesterol,
140 mg Sodium,
33 g Total Carbohydrate,
3 g Dietary Fiber,
9 g Protein,
258 mg Calcium.

POINTS per serving: 3.

1 cup aspartame-sweetened vanilla nonfat yogurt

1 cup frozen peaches, strawberries or blueberries, partially defrosted

In a food processor or blender, puree the yogurt and fruit. Serve at once.

Chocolate Egg Cream

This is a great way to get a filling chocolate hit with a minimum number of calories.

makes
I serving

1 cup sugar-free chocolate-fudge soda   ½ cup skim milk

Fill a tall glass with ice cubes; pour in the soda and milk. Stir to blend.

Per serving:
45 Calories,
0 g Total Fat,
0 g Saturated Fat,
2 mg Cholesterol,
77 mg Sodium,
6 g Total Carbohydrate,
0 g Dietary Fiber,
4 g Protein,
160 mg Calcium.

POINTS per serving: I.

rush hour

Mustard Dip

This creamy dip packs just enough punch to make ordinary pretzels and veggies extraordinary.

Per serving:
165 Calories,
7 g Total Fat,
0 g Saturated Fat,
0 mg Cholesterol,
481 mg Sodium,
22 g Total Carbohydrate,
0 g Dietary Fiber,
3 g Protein,
36 mg Calcium.

POINTS per serving: 4.

3 tablespoons Dijon mustard

2 tablespoons reduced–calorie mayonnaise

1 teaspoon honey

1 cup small pretzel twists

In a small bowl, whisk the mustard, mayonnaise and honey. Refrigerate, covered, about 1 hour. Serve with the pretzels.

make ahead

Vanilla-Snap Sandwiches

Keep these on hand in the freezer for when the kids—or you—want something cold and creamy.

makes
4 servings

4 scoops (about ⅓ cup each) vanilla nonfat frozen yogurt, slightly softened

8 old-fashioned gingersnap cookies
⅓ cup wheat germ

Place 1 scoop of the yogurt onto each of 4 cookies; top each with another cookie, pressing down gently to make a sandwich. Roll the sides in wheat germ. Wrap each sandwich in plastic wrap and freeze until firm, at least 2 hours.

Per serving:
155 Calories,
2 g Total Fat,
0 g Saturated Fat,
0 mg Cholesterol,
129 mg Sodium,
28 g Total Carbohydrate,
1 g Dietary Fiber,
6 g Protein,
70 mg Calcium.

POINTS per serving: 3.

make ahead

Easy Apple-Raisin Danishes

makes
8 servings

These easy treats—and the variations we've devised—make wonderful breakfasts or after-school snacks, as well as desserts.

Per serving:
159 Calories,
3 g Total Fat,
1 g Saturated Fat,
0 mg Cholesterol,
292 mg Sodium,
31 g Total Carbohydrate,
1 g Dietary Fiber,
3 g Protein,
11 mg Calcium.

POINTS per serving: 3.

One 11-ounce can refrigerated
  breadsticks

⅓ cup unsweetened applesauce

¾ cup raisins

1 teaspoon cinnamon

1 tablespoon confectioners' sugar

1 teaspoon skim milk

1. Preheat the oven to 350° F. Spray a nonstick baking sheet with nonstick cooking spray. Place the breadsticks on the nonstick baking sheet. Spread the applesauce along the breadsticks and place the raisins on top; sprinkle with the cinnamon. Roll up the breadsticks, taking care that the applesauce does not spill out, to make a round. Bake until golden brown, about 18 minutes.

2. In a small bowl, combine the confectioners' sugar and milk to make an icing; drizzle over the danishes. Serve warm.

Variations:

Easy Strawberry Danishes

Spread each breadstick with 1 teaspoon strawberry jelly; roll up and bake as above. Mix 1 tablespoon confectioners' sugar and 1 teaspoon skim milk in a small bowl; drizzle over the danishes.

Per serving:
130 Calories,
3 g Total Fat,
1 g Saturated Fat,
0 mg Cholesterol,
293 mg Sodium,
23 g Total Carbohydrate,
1 g Dietary Fiber,
3 g Protein,
1 mg Calcium.

POINTS per serving: 3.

Mexican Hats

Spread each breadstick with 1 teaspoon salsa. Sprinkle each with 1 teaspoon shredded reduced-fat cheddar cheese. Roll up and bake as above.

Per serving:
114 Calories,
3 g Total Fat,
1 g Saturated Fat,
0 mg Cholesterol,
315 mg Sodium,
18 g Total Carbohydrate,
1 g Dietary Fiber,
4 g Protein,
17 mg Calcium.

POINTS per serving: 2.

Peanut-Butter Cup Rounds

Spread each breadstick with 1 teaspoon peanut butter. Roll up and bake as above. Drizzle 1 teaspoon reduced-fat hot fudge sauce over the peanut-butter cups.

Per serving:
119 Calories,
3 g Total Fat,
1 g Saturated Fat,
2 mg Cholesterol,
333 mg Sodium,
18 g Total Carbohydrate,
0 g Dietary Fiber,
4 g Protein,
26 mg Calcium.

POINTS per serving: 3.

one pot

Chocolate-Raisin Chewy Treats

makes
16 servings

These treats are sure to satisfy an occasional sweet tooth. For added nutrition, try kashi cereal instead of the toasted rice.

Per serving:
130 Calories,
3 g Total Fat,
1 g Saturated Fat,
0 mg Cholesterol,
151 mg Sodium,
27 g Total Carbohydrate,
1 g Dietary Fiber,
1 g Protein, 4 mg
Calcium.

POINTS per serving: 3.

¼ cup reduced-calorie margarine

One 10-ounce bag mini marsh-mallows

6 cups toasted rice cereal

½ cup semisweet chocolate-covered raisins

Spray a 13 × 9" baking pan and a rubber spatula with nonstick cooking spray. In a large nonstick saucepan over low heat, melt the margarine. Add the marshmallows, stirring until completely melted. Remove from the heat and stir in the cereal and raisins. Press into the pan with the spatula. Cool at least 30 minutes; cut into 16 squares. Store up to 1 week in an airtight container.

make ahead

Metric Conversions

If you are converting the recipes in this book to metric measurements, use the following chart as a guide.

Volume		Weight		Length		Oven Temperatures	
¼ teaspoon	1 milliliter	1 ounce	30 grams	1 inch	25 millimeters	250°F	120°C
½ teaspoon	2 milliliters	¼ pound	120 grams	1 inch	2.5 centimeters	275°F	140°C
1 teaspoon	5 milliliters	½ pound	240 grams			300°F	150°C
1 tablespoon	15 milliliters	¾ pound	360 grams			325°F	160°C
2 tablespoons	30 milliliters	1 pound	480 grams			350°F	180°C
3 tablespoons	45 milliliters					375°F	190°C
¼ cup	50 milliliters					400°F	200°C
⅓ cup	75 milliliters					425°F	220°C
½ cup	125 milliliters					450°F	230°C
⅔ cup	150 milliliters					475°F	250°C
¾ cup	175 milliliters					500°F	260°C
1 cup	250 milliliters					525°F	270°C
1 quart	1 liter						

Dry and Liquid Measurement Equivalents

Teaspoons	Tablespoons	Cups	Fluid Ounces
3 teaspoons	1 tablespoon		½ fluid ounce
6 teaspoons	2 tablespoons	⅛ cup	1 fluid ounce
8 teaspoons	2 tablespoons plus 2 teaspoons	⅙ cup	
12 teaspoons	4 tablespoons	¼ cup	2 fluid ounces
15 teaspoons	5 tablespoons	⅓ cup minus 1 teaspoon	
16 teaspoons	5 tablespoons plus 1 teaspoon	⅓ cup	
18 teaspoons	6 tablespoons	⅓ cup plus two teaspoons	3 fluid ounces
24 teaspoons	8 tablespoons	½ cup	4 fluid ounces
30 teaspoons	10 tablespoons	½ cup plus 2 tablespoons	5 fluid ounces
32 teaspoons	10 tablespoons plus 2 teaspoons	⅔ cup	
36 teaspoons	12 tablespoons	¾ cup	6 fluid ounces
42 teaspoons	14 tablespoons	1 cup plus 2 tablespoons	7 fluid ounces
45 teaspoons	15 tablespoons	1 cup minus 1 tablespoon	
48 teaspoons	16 tablespoons	1 cup	8 fluid ounces

Note: Measurement of less than ⅛ teaspoon is considered a dash or a pinch.

making progress

week I

monday

Goal for the Day: _____

_____
_____
_____

Activity: _____

_____
_____
_____

H$_2$O _____

FruitsVegs: _____

_____
_____

tuesday

Goal for the Day: _____

_____
_____
_____

Activity: _____

_____
_____
_____

H$_2$O _____

FruitsVegs: _____

_____
_____

wednesday

Goal for the Day: _____

_____
_____
_____

Activity: _____

_____
_____
_____

H$_2$O _____

FruitsVegs: _____

_____
_____

thursday

Goal for the Day: _____

_____
_____
_____

Activity: _____

_____
_____

H$_2$O _____

FruitsVegs: _____

_____
_____

friday

Goal for the Day: _____

_____
_____
_____

Activity: _____

_____
_____

H$_2$O _____

FruitsVegs: _____

_____
_____

saturday

_____
_____
_____
_____
_____

sunday

_____
_____
_____
_____
_____

week 2

monday

Goal for the Day: _____

_____

_____

_____

Activity: _____

_____

_____

_____

H_2O _____

_____

FruitsVegs: _____

_____

_____

tuesday

Goal for the Day: _____

_____

_____

_____

Activity: _____

_____

_____

_____

H_2O _____

_____

FruitsVegs: _____

_____

_____

wednesday

Goal for the Day: _____

_____

_____

_____

Activity: _____

_____

_____

_____

H_2O _____

_____

FruitsVegs: _____

_____

_____

thursday

Goal for the Day: _____

_____

_____

_____

Activity: _____

_____

_____

_____

H_2O _____

_____

FruitsVegs: _____

_____

_____

friday

Goal for the Day: _____

_____

_____

_____

Activity: _____

_____

_____

_____

H_2O _____

_____

FruitsVegs: _____

_____

_____

saturday

_____

_____

_____

_____

_____

_____

sunday

_____

_____

_____

_____

_____

_____

week 3

monday

Goal for the Day: _____

_____

_____

_____

Activity: _____

_____

_____

_____

H_2O _____

_____

FruitsVegs: _____

_____

_____

tuesday

Goal for the Day: _____

_____

_____

_____

Activity: _____

_____

_____

_____

H_2O _____

_____

FruitsVegs: _____

_____

_____

wednesday

Goal for the Day: _____

_____

_____

_____

Activity: _____

_____

_____

_____

H_2O _____

_____

FruitsVegs: _____

_____

_____

thursday

Goal for the Day: _____

_____

_____

_____

Activity: _____

_____

_____

_____

H_2O _____

_____

FruitsVegs: _____

_____

_____

friday

Goal for the Day: _____

_____

_____

_____

Activity: _____

_____

_____

_____

H_2O _____

_____

FruitsVegs: _____

_____

_____

saturday

_____

_____

_____

_____

_____

sunday

_____

_____

_____

_____

_____

week 4

monday

Goal for the Day: _____

_____
_____
_____

Activity: _____

_____
_____
_____

H_2O _____

_____

FruitsVegs: _____

_____
_____

tuesday

Goal for the Day: _____

_____
_____
_____

Activity: _____

_____
_____
_____

H_2O _____

_____

FruitsVegs: _____

_____
_____

wednesday

Goal for the Day: _____

_____
_____
_____

Activity: _____

_____
_____
_____

H_2O _____

_____

FruitsVegs: _____

_____
_____

thursday

Goal for the Day: _____

_____
_____
_____

Activity: _____

_____
_____
_____

H_2O _____

FruitsVegs: _____

_____
_____

friday

Goal for the Day: _____

_____
_____
_____

Activity: _____

_____
_____
_____

H_2O _____

FruitsVegs: _____

_____
_____

saturday

_____
_____
_____
_____
_____

sunday

_____
_____
_____
_____
_____
_____

week 5

monday

Goal for the Day: _____

_____

_____

_____

Activity: _____

_____

_____

_____

H$_2$O _____

_____

FruitsVegs: _____

_____

_____

tuesday

Goal for the Day: _____

_____

_____

_____

Activity: _____

_____

_____

_____

H$_2$O _____

_____

FruitsVegs: _____

_____

_____

wednesday

Goal for the Day: _____

_____

_____

_____

Activity: _____

_____

_____

_____

H$_2$O _____

_____

FruitsVegs: _____

_____

_____

thursday

Goal for the Day: _____

_____

_____

_____

Activity: _____

_____

_____

_____

H$_2$O _____

_____

FruitsVegs: _____

_____

_____

friday

Goal for the Day: _____

_____

_____

_____

Activity: _____

_____

_____

_____

H$_2$O _____

_____

FruitsVegs: _____

_____

_____

saturday

_____

_____

_____

_____

_____

_____

sunday

_____

_____

_____

_____

_____

week 6

monday

Goal for the Day: _____

_____
_____
_____

Activity: _____

_____
_____
_____

H_2O _____

_____

FruitsVegs: _____

_____
_____

tuesday

Goal for the Day: _____

_____
_____
_____

Activity: _____

_____
_____
_____

H_2O _____

_____

FruitsVegs: _____

_____
_____

wednesday

Goal for the Day: _____

_____
_____
_____

Activity: _____

_____
_____
_____

H_2O _____

_____

FruitsVegs: _____

_____
_____

thursday

Goal for the Day: _____

_____
_____
_____

Activity: _____

_____
_____
_____

H_2O _____

FruitsVegs: _____

_____
_____

friday

Goal for the Day: _____

_____
_____
_____

Activity: _____

_____
_____
_____

H_2O _____

FruitsVegs: _____

_____
_____

saturday

_____
_____
_____

_____
_____

sunday

_____
_____
_____
_____
_____

week 7

monday

Goal for the Day: _____

_____
_____
_____

Activity: _____

_____
_____
_____

H$_2$O _____

_____

FruitsVegs: _____

_____
_____

tuesday

Goal for the Day: _____

_____
_____
_____

Activity: _____

_____
_____
_____

H$_2$O _____

_____

FruitsVegs: _____

_____
_____

wednesday

Goal for the Day: _____

_____
_____
_____

Activity: _____

_____
_____
_____

H$_2$O _____

_____

FruitsVegs: _____

_____
_____

thursday

Goal for the Day: _____

_____
_____
_____

Activity: _____

_____
_____
_____

H$_2$O _____

_____

FruitsVegs: _____

_____
_____

friday

Goal for the Day: _____

_____
_____
_____

Activity: _____

_____
_____
_____

H$_2$O _____

_____

FruitsVegs: _____

_____
_____

saturday

_____
_____
_____
_____

sunday

_____
_____
_____
_____
_____

monday

Goal for the Day: _____

_____

_____

_____

Activity: _____

_____

_____

_____

H_2O _____

_____

FruitsVegs: _____

_____

_____

tuesday

Goal for the Day: _____

_____

_____

_____

Activity: _____

_____

_____

_____

H_2O _____

_____

FruitsVegs: _____

_____

_____

wednesday

Goal for the Day: _____

_____

_____

_____

Activity: _____

_____

_____

_____

H_2O _____

_____

FruitsVegs: _____

_____

_____

thursday

Goal for the Day: _____

_____

_____

_____

Activity: _____

_____

_____

_____

H_2O _____

_____

FruitsVegs: _____

_____

_____

friday

Goal for the Day: _____

_____

_____

_____

Activity: _____

_____

_____

_____

H_2O _____

_____

FruitsVegs: _____

_____

_____

saturday

_____

_____

_____

_____

_____

sunday

_____

_____

_____

_____

_____

_____

_____

week 9

monday

Goal for the Day: _____

_____

_____

_____

Activity: _____

_____

_____

_____

H_2O _____

_____

FruitsVegs: _____

_____

_____

tuesday

Goal for the Day: _____

_____

_____

_____

Activity: _____

_____

_____

_____

H_2O _____

_____

FruitsVegs: _____

_____

_____

wednesday

Goal for the Day: _____

_____

_____

_____

Activity: _____

_____

_____

_____

H_2O _____

_____

FruitsVegs: _____

_____

_____

thursday

Goal for the Day: _____

_____

_____

_____

Activity: _____

_____

_____

_____

H_2O _____

_____

FruitsVegs: _____

_____

_____

friday

Goal for the Day: _____

_____

_____

_____

Activity: _____

_____

_____

_____

H_2O _____

_____

FruitsVegs: _____

_____

_____

saturday

_____

_____

_____

_____

_____

sunday

_____

_____

_____

_____

_____

_____

week 10

monday

Goal for the Day: _____

_____

_____

_____

Activity: _____

_____

_____

_____

H_2O _____

_____

FruitsVegs: _____

_____

_____

tuesday

Goal for the Day: _____

_____

_____

_____

Activity: _____

_____

_____

_____

H_2O _____

_____

FruitsVegs: _____

_____

_____

wednesday

Goal for the Day: _____

_____

_____

_____

Activity: _____

_____

_____

_____

H_2O _____

_____

FruitsVegs: _____

_____

_____

thursday

Goal for the Day: _____

_____

_____

_____

Activity: _____

_____

_____

_____

H_2O _____

_____

FruitsVegs: _____

_____

_____

friday

Goal for the Day: _____

_____

_____

_____

Activity: _____

_____

_____

_____

H_2O _____

_____

FruitsVegs: _____

_____

_____

saturday

_____

_____

_____

_____

_____

sunday

_____

_____

_____

_____

_____